The Journey of Innocence

1944-1962

Veronica's Adventures – Book I

VERONICA ESAGUI

Copyright © 2024 Veronica Esagui, DC

All rights reserved. No part of this book may be reproduced or transmitted in any form or by any means, electronic or mechanical, including photocopying, recording, or by any information storage and retrieval system, without permission in writing from the copyright owner. No patent liability is assumed with respect to the use of the information contained herein. Although every precaution has been taken in the preparation of this book, the publisher and author assume no responsibility for errors or omissions. Neither is any liability assumed for damages resulting from the use of the information contained herein.

Library of Congress Control Number: 2024900049

ISBN 978-0-9826584-6-9
Third Edition

Editors: Chory Ferguson, Maria E. Chitsaz, John Fraraccio, and Rosanna Mattingly
Book Cover Design by James M. McCracken
Graphic Design by James M. McCracken

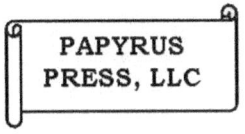

PAPYRUS PRESS, LLC

West Linn, OR 97068

To order additional copies of this book
www.veronicaesagui.com
Printed in the United States of America.

*To my parents and Aunt Heydee,
thank you for today.*

Hold on to all the experiences of growing up; someday you will need them to help you make it through life.

~Veronica Esagui

CONTENTS

Preface		1
In the Beginning		5
Chapter One	Earliest Memories	8
Chapter Two	Dandelions in the Garden	33
Chapter Three	The Learning Years	50
Chapter Four	The Enlightenment	127
Chapter Five	The Adjusting Period	151
Chapter Six	The Spanish Letters	228
Chapter Seven	Engaged to Cousin Alberto	259
Chapter Eight	The Way Out	288

PREFACE

Tigard, Oregon USA

Winter of 2004

My husband Dan is sitting across from me at the desk we both share. He is busy on the Internet, and I am using my new laptop. For the last four years, Dan has been doing research concerning dioxin emissions and other toxic chemicals to which he was exposed in Japan while serving in the U.S. Navy. The government and particularly the Veterans Administration are not offering any help, and they try to ignore his case. But Dan is very much like me. He will fight for his rights, and he is not about to give up.

We have been married approximately one and a half years. Dan is my best friend. As such, I always feel comfortable interrupting his train of thought to confide in him.

I said, "I am not sure that I should change anything I wrote over the years. I realize now that the way I felt forty or even twenty years ago is not how I feel about many things today, but I probably should leave it as it is."

He responded as if thinking out loud, "I agree with that. The only difficulty I see is for anyone to believe that you remember so much about what happened at such a young age. Most of us don't have that kind of memory."

"My goodness," I said to him. I was flabbergasted, as if I had been suddenly hit by lightning. "My past life would have been a foggy time of forgotten memories if it weren't for my mother. I can't believe it has taken me this long to realize it. While growing up, I was like a sponge when it came to catching children's diseases. It didn't matter if I got a vaccine or not. I had chicken pox, mumps, influenza, strep throat, measles, whooping cough, rubella, smallpox, and half a dozen times a year, the flu. And let's not forget tuberculosis and having my tonsils yanked out. I was bedridden quite often, and it was during those times that my mother would bring the family photo albums to my bedside. Those thick photo albums were my only source of entertainment while lying in bed and recovering from whatever ailed me. Looking at each picture over and over again, it became easy to recall the moment it was taken, including the events leading up to that particular photo and what followed. The past is gone, that's true, but the diary has kept it alive.

"I will leave this diary as it was intended from the beginning, as it happened and as I perceived it. How odd it is that I have come to this discovery, of all days to pick from, on December 5. If Mama were still alive, today would be her birthday."

The Journey of Innocence

Author's Note:

Verónica with an accent on the letter "o" is kept throughout this diary as it was originally written in Portuguese.

In the diary sequel, *Braving a New World*, my full name will change, as have the names of so many other people after immigrating to America.

The people and the stories portrayed in this book are all true as to my recollection when I began writing this diary in Portuguese, Saturday, April 26, 1986, in Howell, New Jersey. Upon translating my diary to English, I have kept it as it was written, but I have changed some names to protect the not so innocent.

IN THE BEGINNING

Lisboa, PORTUGAL

Spring of 1944

After a long and difficult night of labor, my mother finally gave birth a little after three o'clock on the morning of May 7. Verónica Leah Toledano Ezaguy Wartenberg came out "screaming her head off," as Mama described it later on. After a week in the hospital recovering from my birth, she needed a few more months at home to completely reestablish her health. It was during this time that my Grandmother Mutter (my father's mother) took over the job of caring for me. She was the one who picked my first name. Thank God for that because my mother wanted to name me Marília.

Summer of 1944

Grandmother Mutter was born in Berlin, Germany. The stories went that she would have liked to have stayed in

Portugal and continue to live with us, but the doctors in Portugal—when compared to the ones in other countries, such as England— were not considered to be the best when it came to health care. Mutter was a petite, fragile-looking lady with only one kidney, but, as my mother would describe her, Grandmother Mutter was more like a tigress when she wanted to push her point across. Everybody agreed she was better off going to England where she had two daughters, Friedel and Ilse, along with other family members who spoke German, her native language. There was really no reason for her to stay with us.

Autumn of 1944

Mama did not welcome Grandmother Mutter to live with us. She saw her mother-in-law taking reign of our home and family. My mother, who was born in Brazil, released her feelings toward Mutter by singing a very naughty Brazilian song that vented on in-laws. The song went: *Da baia me mandaram dois presentes num bau—minha sogra jaracaca, meu sogro jarucucu*, which means, *From the bay I received two presents inside a barrel—my wacko mother-in-law and my crazy out-of-his-head father-in-law*. It sounds a lot better in Portuguese!

Mutter didn't understand much Portuguese. As a matter of a fact, she got into a lot of trouble one day when she went to the farmers market to buy some fresh fish and asked in her best Portuguese/German accent for a big, fresh *puta*. Because *puta* in Portuguese means a *prostitute*, one can imagine how the women selling fish reacted to her request.

One yelled to another, "Hey, Maria Luisa, this woman wants to buy a *puta*! Do you know anyone like that?"

Laughter became contagious, roaring like thunder down the market aisles. The row of *peixeiras*, a class of working women who make a living selling fish, viciously attacked my grandmother with nasty gestures and cursing words. Mama had to rush to her rescue.

As Mama walked away with her, one of the *peixeiras* yelled out, "If you want a big *puta*, you better go downtown. That's where they hang out. My ex-husband lives with one of them."

Grandmother Mutter would not allow Mama to kiss me, unless it was on my feet. She insisted that Mama's mouth carried too many germs. Mama never forgave her for that. But Grandmother Mutter was not being mean. She was indeed very serious about her philosophy, and she wore a starched, white lab coat and white gloves whenever she held me.

Tension ran high during those days of our lives, and Mama cried a lot.

Winter of 1945

Grandmother Mutter dressed me daily in soft, white, cotton outfits and gave me daily cold baths. In the summertime, it was quite refreshing I am sure, but this went on even in the winter. Mama complained to Papa that his mother was going to kill me with pneumonia, but Grandmother Mutter felt this was going to be the only way that I would grow up to be a "tough cookie."

I am basically bald except for a few thin strands of black hair. I also have fat, round cheeks that go along with my fat, little body. I look more like a boy, but everybody praises my beauty and agrees that I look a lot like my father.

~ *Chapter One* ~

EARLIEST MEMORIES

1945-1948

Spring of 1945

It's my birthday today. I am one year old! I am wearing a white organdy dress with little pink and bluish butterflies sewn around the skirt and brand new white shoes. My shoes are one size larger than my feet, but that is good because they give me leverage to stand up. The family members and friends are gathered in our garden as they pose for pictures. A man with a black box on a stand keeps putting his head under a black cloth that covers the box. His hand goes up in the air to give us the signal to stand still and smile for the camera.

Walking is such an awesome, indescribable feeling. My toes are good to play with, and I can chew on them when I have nothing else to do, but it's a lot more fun to stand up on my feet. In the very beginning, I keep falling, but once my feet get a grip on the ground, and as long as I hold on to something, I can get to places without crawling on my knees. That is amazing!

A small *nespra* tree marks the center of our backyard. It was planted nine months before I was born. It needs no care, and in a few more months, sweet, brownish, golden-

The Journey of Innocence

yellow fruits called *nespras* will grow for our delight. The tree's thick, green leaves come in handy for grabbing on to, as I try walking around it all by myself. I am scared; no one is holding my hand. I have to rely on one of the branches close to me, within a few, but very distant, steps. Everybody is too busy talking to each other and socializing. The leaf comes off under my grasp, and I fall forward on the hard, sandy ground, bruising my knees. I cry. Mama calls me *chorona*, which means *crybaby* in Portuguese. I have not stopped crying since I left her womb, she says.

I was born with a silver spoon in my mouth, and I don't even appreciate it. I literally have it made. Papa has a very successful business, a huge delicatessen-type of German restaurant situated downtown in the chic center of Lisboa. It's a very special restaurant because it has introduced many unique items on the menu, such as sauerkraut, hot dogs, butter, corn, and some traditional German dishes. The Portuguese had never experienced sauerkraut before my father opened his restaurant, and until then, they had used corn only to feed the pigs.

Grandmother Mutter and Grandma Rica (my mother's mother) hold each other's arms as they walk together in the garden, smiling and chatting in a mutual understanding. One doesn't speak Portuguese, the other doesn't speak German, but their French is good enough to communicate. They almost look like twins with their long black dresses and hair styled in the same fashion of the day.

Mama's tummy is getting swollen, and she has not been feeling good lately.

Papa held me up in his arms. Heights are very scary to me unless I am securely held tight. I hate when someone thinks it's cute to toss me in the air and catch me midway.

Papa got busy talking to a man and his wife. I had never seen them before. The man is Papa's partner in the restaurant. His wife is shy and doesn't say much. I don't like Papa's partner, and when he picked me up I grabbed his hair and tried to pull it off. He immediately put me down on the ground.

Summer of 1945

Pictures and more pictures! I do like all the attention, but I don't like the way they always prop me up in high areas from which I can fall. A good example is what happened last week on Grandma Rica's porch. The corner of her back porch was specially set up for taking pictures. They expected me to smile, relax, and open my arms without holding on to something. They seated me on top of some very shaky cardboard boxes that had been covered with a colorful quilt. But I didn't feel safe, because it was high and slippery, and from the corner of my eyes I could see—on my left between the iron rails—the downstairs neighbor's yard like a huge hole below me. I knew I couldn't stay up in the air, and if I fell, it was going to hurt. I had fallen already several times, and I know what it feels like. They wanted me to smile with the sun hitting my eyes, but that is very hard to do because the sun makes me cry. I would rather have shade and my feet on the ground. I could tell they were very disappointed in me.

Autumn of 1945

My brother was born today, October 9. After much dispute over which one of our grandfather's names my brother was to be honored with, they came to the mutual agreement of using both their names, Max-Leão.

Winter of 1946

I got into trouble for drinking Max-Leão's milk. I love the sweet taste of his milk bottle, but I am not allowed to drink it. Mama says I am not a baby anymore.

The Journey of Innocence

Spring of 1946

I am not allowed to play with Max-Leão. I was told he is a baby boy, not a doll toy. Only Mama is allowed to hold him, and that's not fair.

Summer of 1946

Our square backyard is surrounded by a whitewashed, brick wall with a square, green, wooden door that has a wooden hinge for locking; it is no different from the other three neighbors' backyards. Everybody in our apartment complex has a piece of land just like ours, except for the two families living on the third floor who have none. A gardener tends to the gardens, and keeps the grass green and the flowers and fruit trees alive.

I like looking down from our sunroom window at the neighbor's backyard below us. They have no dirt in their yard like us. They have off-white cement walls to match the off-white cement floors. Their backyard looks like a roller-skating rink, and it's always very clean. They are special.

Autumn of 1946

Blue soap for washing clothes looks like cake in a chunk. That's what attracted me to it, but I am not allowed to eat it. I don't know why. Mama yelled at me, and the maid put the soap far up in the top drawer of the kitchen cabinet. I can't get to it. I cry.

Spring of 1947

I looked all over the house for Grandmother Mutter, but she was not anywhere to be found. I looked today and yesterday in all the rooms and behind the doors, and she is not here anymore. I wonder if she will be back later.

I am three years old today, and Uncle Augusto came over to take pictures. What a great surprise it was! I got my own playground to play, right in our backyard! Mama and Papa had someone build me a little wooden fortress under the shade of the *nespra* tree. The fortress is a large wooden barrel sawed in half with a wooden top, like a tabletop. Once inside the barrel, I get to play house with the dirt. I fill the tiny tin cans and tin cups with dirt and then throw it all around me. It is a lot of fun to see the dry dirt flying all over. When I mix it with some water, I can make little balls of clay and other things, like dogs and cats and birds and squares. Then I mash everything together and start all over again. I love the smell of dirt, and the tin cans taste very good when I lick them clean. Max-Leão is still too small to play with me.

Summer of 1947

Mama is always kissing and hugging Max-Leão. If I try to make nice to him, she will say, "Be careful, you are too rough." You better believe that I am rough. I am also bigger than him and stronger, too. I can even lift him up, and it is out of kindness that I don't drop him on his head. He is kind of cute though, always smiling even when I borrow his milk bottle. I love the taste of his sweet milk formula, and I hate the regular milk that I have to drink every day with my food. Besides, bottles—when turned over—don't spill the milk, and glasses do. My face hurts when I get hit across the face for being clumsy, but I can't help it. I am clumsy.

Autumn of 1947

I love playing with my little brother Max-Leão. After practicing how to get my leverage with him on my back, I

The Journey of Innocence

am able to carry him around the house. He doesn't mind when I drag him by the feet either. For his birthday, Mama made rice pudding. Rice pudding is not the same as cake. I refuse to eat rice with milk and sugar and a lemon peel stuck in the center of the bowl.
With a frown, I say, "I want cake!"
But Mama said, "It's not your birthday! Next year, you will get a cake if that's what you would really rather have."
I carefully sucked the sweet milky juice between my teeth and spit the rice into my hand. Little by little, I stuck it under the table and under the dessert plate. It was a lot of rice to get rid of.

I saw Maria, the maid, hiding a pretty doll and a red fire truck inside one of the closets in the room next to the bathroom. I asked her about it, and she said Santa Claus had asked her to hide some toys for Max-Leão and me. Next month, it's Christmas. I didn't want to wait so long, and I asked Mama to tell Maria to give me the doll today. I heard the conversation in the other room. We do not believe in Santa Claus; therefore, the presents are not being accepted. I cry.

Winter of 1948

Grandmother Mutter's plan of making me a tough cookie failed miserably. Mama complains that I am a weakling, always sick with something or another. She is tired of constantly having to take me to her brother, Augusto. He is a doctor. She says it's almost a waste of time to treat me for anything because, as soon as I am over one sickness, I come down with another.
 Chickenpox has not been easy with all the scratching, but I enjoy the warm purple baths in our big bathtub. The purple medicine in the water helps to stop the itching. Whooping cough was a lot tougher; it made me spit blood,

and it hurt my chest. I visit Uncle Augusto every month or so for something or another. He always smiles when he sees me because I am his favorite niece.

From the moment I was born, Uncle Augusto started taking my pictures. Every position and every facial emotion possible to a baby has been recorded by Uncle Augusto's camera. Lately things have changed a bit. Since he got married and his wife had a baby, he no longer has that kind of time to spend with me except while working in the hospital or at his office. I saw his baby once, and immediately his wife blamed me for killing her child with one of my childhood diseases. But the truth is, I had nothing to do with it. Their baby died because he had something wrong with his stomach; that was the reason he vomited every time he was fed. Aunt Heydee, my mother's older sister and definitely the wisest woman I ever met, felt that her brother's wife was the one who killed the newborn by sucking on sour candy the whole time she was pregnant and most likely giving the baby a sour stomach.

Spring of 1948

My family and I live in Lisboa, the capital city of Portugal. Our neighborhood is one of the newest and most modern areas of the city. Our building doesn't have old-fashioned tiles on the outside. It has white, pinkish marble one quarter of the way up, and above, it is painted soft green all the way up to the third floor. Across from us on the right corner of our street, there's still an empty lot of dirt where Max-Leão and I get to play once in a while with the clay. I love playing there, and I hope that no one will ever build anything on that precious ground so close to our house.

My address is *Rua Ponta Delgada*, #72, first floor, on the right. Reaching the doorbell downstairs is still impossible for me. The nursemaid has to lift me up so that I can ring the bell. Max-Leão is lucky. Because he is a baby, he gets to ring the bell a lot more often than I do. The painted green metal-and-glass entrance door is very wide, tall, and heavy. When it closes, it makes an echoing metal noise, loud enough for everyone in the building to know it closed. This is very useful, because it lets us all know when someone has entered or left the building. Inside the hall entrance, there are eight green metal mailboxes on the left wall, one for each of the eight families in our building. A very wide, whitish marble staircase has six square marble platforms on each side. The platforms display lush green plants growing from the large bluish ceramic oriental pots that adorn each side of the steps. At the top of the steps, there's a small, polished wooden landing, where a vase of fresh flowers sits on a small table covered with a dainty white lace cover. Usually we stop to take a break at that point, and then climb three more flights of shiny, always fresh-smelling, waxed, brown wooden steps covered with an Oriental rug running up the center. A matching dark wooden railing on the right side helps us to hold on. The layer of apartments below our apartment is called the *cave* or ground level. The porters' apartment is below the ground level, and their apartment doesn't have any windows. You can't go any lower than that; otherwise, you reach the center of the world. That's the way most apartment houses in Lisboa are built. I feel sorry for the neighbors on the so-called second and third floors above us; they have a lot more climbing than we do.

 My Grandma Rica also lives in the first floor of her apartment house. Like ours, her apartment also has a ground-level apartment under hers, with the porters and their family living below the ground level. But her building is a lot older than ours. Her building must be over one hundred years old, which is even older than my Grandma. They don't have potted plants, marble floors, or cork-covered walls like we do; instead, their wood is dull and the hallway up the steps is dark and smells like an old ship. At least that's the way I imagine it since I have never been on an old ship—or even a new one. You can always count on lots of steps where our cousins and uncles and friends live. Mama visits everybody, every week. Sometimes I get to go with her, so I have a lot of experience with climbing. The thick, wooden front door to our apartment is tall and green with a hole to see out of. There's a small bench inside that I climb on to see who is knocking. I have to look first before opening the door, in case they are robbers. Inside our vestibule, we have a very tall piano with dark wood and a small, antique dresser. A medium-sized, black, wooden owl hangs on the wall facing the front door as you come in. It belonged to Grandmother Mutter. I was almost three years old when she left for England to live with her daughters Ilse and Friedel. According to her and all the German people, owls bring you good luck, so she left it for us. Mama doesn't like the owl; she says it gives her the creeps, but, just in case it's true about bringing good luck, she won't take it down. I would love to remember Grandmother Mutter's face, but I don't. I feel sad that all I recall is white cotton, white lace, and the smell of mothballs.

It's my birthday tomorrow. Mama is in the hospital. The maid told Max-Leão and me that it looks like we are getting another brother or sister very soon.

My new baby brother came home today. He will be the last baby Mama will have. She has sworn to that. In order to save herself and the baby, Uncle Augusto and Cousin Roberto, also a doctor, had to cut Mama's belly open to take our little brother José out. Then they sewed it up with a needle and thread, not much different than sewing a ripped skirt or a blouse. I am glad that I am not a doctor. It must be very difficult to sew people while they are screaming with pain.

The Journey of Innocence

I got a birthday cake today, a large rag doll, boxes that fit into each other, and blocks of different sizes to make houses. Mama didn't forget my birthday. She was just too sick from having José taken out of her tummy and then having to carry him home from the hospital last month. I like my toys, but I wish I had a pretty doll like the one Maria was going to give me for Christmas instead of this big limp one made of cloth. But I am happy that my cousins came over. They had rice pudding, but I didn't have to eat it. Mama remembered her promise from last year, and I had my own little personal birthday cake with four candles.

Summer of 1948

Max-Leão and I share our bedroom. It doesn't have a window to the outside like the other rooms, but we have a narrow, horizontal window close to the ceiling. It opens from our bedroom to the Imperial Room, as Mama calls it, because it is decorated with golden furniture. We like the little window above us because it provides some form of fresh air in the summer, even if it doesn't come from the street, and we also get to listen to adults talk in the other room, which helps us fall asleep quicker.

We have two doors to our bedroom. One is our normal regular door to enter the room from the vestibule, and the other a French-style door that opens to our parents' bedroom right next to ours. When Mama or Papa comes to hit us, we use these doorways to run away from them. Around and around I run, from one room to the other, for as long as I can, from our bedroom through their bedroom and out into the vestibule. I have gotten pretty good around the curves, a few extra painless minutes of my life, but, even though I can run very fast, sooner or later I get caught when Mama or Papa extends their long arms and grabs me.

Their bedroom furniture is very pretty. The two armoires

are opulent, tall and wide, and made of golden wood with mother-of-pearl inlaid flowers around the mirrored doors and the side panels. They match the vanity fair of three mirrors. Most of our furniture came from Germany. José sleeps in our parents' bedroom because he is always sick. The other bedroom facing the street is the guest room, and Grandma Rica or one of Mama's sisters gets to use it when they stay with us overnight. When Grandma Rica is sick, she always stays with us until she is well enough to go home.

On the hallway wall between the Imperial Room and the pantry, there is a very large framed award written in gold around a silver medal with a centrally located seal of different colors. I like staring at it. The King of Spain gave this award to Mama when she wrote a musical composition just for him. This happened before she met Papa. After she got married, she gave up her career to become a devoted wife and mother. Mama is very proud of how beautiful she used to be before she met Papa and gave up her musical career for us. I like to picture her in my mind as she played the piano in the king's palace with her long, dark hair down to her shoulders and parted perfectly to the side of her face, and as she smiled with an air of pride when the handsome King of Spain kissed her hand and gave her the well-deserved silver medal.

The Imperial Room is a long and wide subdivided room that has a living room and dining room with lots of golden furnishings. It's used for special occasions only, such as for company or parties. Because Max-Leão and I are very clumsy and might break something, we are not allowed in that room; therefore, we call it *the forbidden room*.

I can remember only one time that I was allowed to have dinner with my parents and their guests, and it must have been a very special day because not only did we have the regular maids bring the food from the kitchen but we also had a man dressed in a black suit with a long-tail jacket serving us at the table. It was a very elegant experience, and I had a chance to eat with silver utensils on a silver trinket. I have dreams at night about all the possibilities that could happen there if Max-Leão and I were allowed to play in that room.

A little down the hallway, on the right side, there's a built-in wall closet where Mama keeps most of our quality linen and her antique silverware collection under lock and key. The door to this closet has four tiny holes so that air can get inside. When Mama opens it, I like to stand next to her. It is a very mysterious closet, always under lock and key.

She always says, "What are you looking at? It's nothing but linens, towels, and bed sheets."

But I know that there has to be something else inside this closet, something like a hidden treasure, way in the back. There might even be another locked door, another entrance to some strange and scary place.

A few steps down on the left side of this hallway, there is a small dingy dark room without a window. This is where the full-time maid sleeps and the groceries are stored. We are not allowed in there either, which is good because it smells of spoiled rotten groceries—like sauerkraut and other unidentified things. A few more steps down the hallway on the left side is our dining room. What I find amazing in this room is the crusted thick panels on the front and sides of the old furniture reminding me of camouflaged castle doors. The table where we eat matches the furniture with its own labyrinth of holes and spaces where I can hide any food that I don't like. Bread can be squeezed right into its niches and cracks. I really don't like bread, unless it's used as a tool to push the food onto the spoon or fork, as it keeps my fingers clean. For some reason, which I have not figured out yet, there is a real glass window from our dining room to the Imperial Room. Why would anyone put in a window that doesn't open to the street but instead opens from one room to another? It was probably built so that Max-Leão and I can look into *the forbidden room* without having to actually go inside.

We don't have to go far from our dining room to wash our hands because the bathroom is right next to it. The bathroom window is always open, for fresh air, but I always close the wooden shutters when I have to use the bathroom. I don't want any of the neighbors to see my bottom before I sit on the toilet. If I forget to open the shutters again, I get yelled at. I have a very poor memory. The bathroom window faces the neighbor's building next to us, and from my bathroom window, I can see their gardens and I can also glimpse at what they are doing if they forget to close their shutters.

Inside the bathroom, there's a deep white bathtub with metal animal paws, a white bidet, a white washing basin, and a white toilet. A small straw basket next to the toilet contains lots of small, neatly folded and cut pieces of newspaper for wiping yourself afterward. Aunt Heydee says that we are lucky to have newspapers to wipe ourselves. In Brazil, she had to use twigs or leaves from the trees, because going to the bathroom meant going outside into the woods. I wonder if ants got inside of her when she wiped herself with the tree leaves. It is a horrible thought, but a very possible one. If I were a little ant, I would not know the difference between one hole and another.

When I pull on the cord with a wooden handle coming down from the tank above our heads, the toilet gets flushed with water. The floor of white and black tiles is always cold and feels good on the feet in the summer. A long Persian carpet extends through the hallway from each bedroom, and that feels wonderful in the winter. The only heat I get on cold nights is when a hot water bottle awaits between the blankets. Sometimes it's so cold in the winter that, when I lie down, my teeth chatter for a long time and I try to hold off as long as possible from making wee in the middle of the night. Even though I have a handy ceramic pan under the bed, it is too cold to sit on it. After using it, I slip the ceramic pan right back under the bed frame as fast as I can so that I can snuggle back into the straw mattress where my body's indentation still holds its warm shape. The next morning, the maid disposes the pot's contents before she even makes the beds. Next to the bathroom is the kitchen with a smoked-glass door. If it is closed, do not enter, the cook is probably running around in circles with a knife in her hand after a headless chicken and there will be blood all over the place. Max-Leão was with me the first time we saw that happen. He fainted.

Our kitchen is huge and has a large, light gray marble platform with a dark metal stove with lots of little doors in the front. In a corner, there's a wooden cabinet, and the maid puts chunky ice blocks in its drawers. She buys the ice from the iceman in the street. Sometimes I go with her to see the ice carriage and the horse that pulls it. The iceman is always cranky and swears a lot. Not an easy job considering that he uses a long metal stick with a hook on the tip to pull the ice off the carriage and then breaks the ice into smaller pieces with an ax. Afterward he has to carry the ice chunk on his shoulder to the first floor where we live.

I can always tell when the maid is cleaning the icebox as I hear her complaining, "Taking out the melted water every so many days is a real mess, if you were to ask me, just to keep the food cold."

The kitchen has a small window that opens to the neighbors in the building next to us. This window is on the right side of the cold, pinkish-gray marble sink with a wooden storage place underneath it. The sun is always shining on the kitchen sink, even on cloudy days. From the kitchen, there are two sets of doors that open to the sunroom, a very large laundry, sewing, and ironing kind of room. The inner doors are made of hard, thick wood and painted white, and have a long wooden arm that is used to secure them at night from the inside, like the front door. Those doors stay open during the day, but the tall white French doors can be opened or closed, depending on the need to keep cool in the summer or warm in the winter.

In this room, there is an old linen cabinet, a big, gray stone basin with ridges to wash the laundry, and a pit hole in the corner of the room where the grease and undesirable leftovers are dumped. A round piece of wood covers the pit hole and on top of it sits a round tin box that previously contained sugar cookies. It is now used for keeping sewing needles, buttons, and thread of various colors. The smell that comes from the pit is really gross. Sometimes Max-Leão and I lift the lid up to confirm that the smell coming from the pit is really the worst smell we have ever experienced. Next to it is the maids' bathroom, with a small sink and barely any space to sit on the toilet. It is literally covered with mops and tools for cleaning the house. I always wonder how they can even find enough space to use the toilet, and besides, how do they take a bath? I wonder because there's no tub. I have peeked in there a few times to see if there is space for me to hide from Max-Leão when we play hide and seek, but I have never used it because there is no space to hide. No one has to tell us to stay away from the maid's bathroom.

Of all the rooms in our house, my favorite is the sunroom. I like to sit by the large glass window that opens wide like a huge smile from wall to wall to a whole outside of neighbors and their gardens. The sky is very big from this window, and straight ahead in the distance I can see a white church on top of the hill where they play the tower bells on the hour, and on Sunday mornings and festive occasions they play church tunes. The long, dark brown building next to it is a military arsenal where they keep lots and lots of gunpowder and guns. If Spain decides to attack Portugal again, as they have done so many times in the

The Journey of Innocence

past, we are ready to fight back.

From the sunroom, there's a small, green metal door that opens to a small atrium, which is shared with our next-door neighbor. Each of us has an outside wall closet with a green wooden door. It is used for storage of goods that are delivered early in the morning by the grocery boy, the milkman, and the bread man. Nobody bothers to lock it anymore. Somehow the key got lost about a year ago. The black, shiny metal staircase goes all the way up to the third floor and down to the backyard below us, where it stops at the marble patio below. Two long, marble staircases reach the neighbors below us and the porters' place below them. Passing by the porters' door on my left, there is a long, dark stone tunnel that puts me at the backdoor gate and into the busy street outside. A key is needed to get back in because the door closes automatically behind us. Even though this back exit is to be used only by the maids, delivery people, and the porters, the gypsies always find their way in to ask for bread and money.

My brothers and I always have a nursemaid during the day. Usually, she is a young girl who plays with us, takes us out for walks to the park up the street, and feeds us so that we are ready to get into bed by the time Papa is home from work. Mama spends most of her time visiting the family, shopping, or going out with Papa. The full-time maid takes care of the rooms, dusting and cleaning windows and waxing floors, and she runs errands and assists the cook in the kitchen. Her name is Maria. She was going to give me the doll for Christmas. She lives with us, and she sleeps in the smelly room with the groceries.

Mama took Max-Leão and me to the hospital for a blood test. The hospital smell makes me sick. I shake a lot when I go to the hospital; that's where people go when they want to feel pain and die. They took blood from my arm with a syringe, and I cried a lot. Max-Leão is so smart though; he fainted, and they asked Mama to come back another day with him. On the way home, we took the trolley car, but Max-Leão started to vomit. It was something about him being trolley car sick, and we had to walk the rest of the way home. Mama carried him in her arms, and I had to help by carrying her heavy pocketbook all the way up the hill from *Praça do Chile*.

I love Uncle Augusto's waiting room. In the center of the waiting room, there is a huge, dark wooden table with thick curly legs that twist into a game room. It is incredible that nobody is aware of this except Max-Leão and me. It is a puzzle to me to observe other children in the waiting room. Seated next to their parents or family members, they are obviously not aware of this playground. Even the chairs have legs that match the table. We go through an absolutely amazing maze as we crawl from one chair to another under the patients' legs! I did go into Uncle Augusto's treatment room behind closed doors willingly the first time, because I thought he was going to take my picture, but I immediately noticed a container with various needles boiling in water over a small gas burner. After he looked into my throat and gagged me with some wooden stick, he actually expected me to drop my pants so that he could stick me with one of his boiled needles. It seems to me that it has become a habit for my uncle to treat me for any ailment I might have with a shot every time we visit him. Mama, the nurse, and he don't seem to understand why I scream and hold on to the corners of the waiting room walls or the legs of the chairs with all my mighty strength. The only way I go into his office is by being dragged by my hair. Of course, I am going to scream. All they are going to do is inject me with penicillin, and that hurts.

Max-Leão and I eat a lot of carrots while seated in the

The Journey of Innocence

sunroom window. Mama told us, if we eat a lot of carrots, even though neither of us likes them, we will get pink eyes like the rabbits. It's a worthwhile sacrifice. I love pink. The sunroom is our favorite room for having fun. I like playing with buttons of different colors and feeling the different textures. Raw rice is very nice, too, for making roads on the sunroom's floor. Max-Leão likes to play with his miniature cars, and I like to build the roads for him. Together we make roads and hills and even dead ends. We have lots of fun playing together.

Mama took me to Papa's restaurant for the first time. It's in downtown Lisboa, on the *Rua do Carmo*. Women love to shop in this part of the city where everything is very beautiful and expensive. Papa greeted us at the entrance of the restaurant. He was very happy to see us. It was a surprise. He seated us at a small table overlooking the crowd having lunch below us. Our waiter brought us each a deep crystal plate filled with fresh strawberries covered with whipped cream. I felt very grown up, but I was also nervous. I was afraid that, if I dropped a strawberry on the white, linen tablecloth, Mama would never take me out again. I was praised for having good table manners.

Autumn of 1948

I am starting kindergarten! Mama wants to make sure that I know my name in full and both my parents' names. It's so much easier to say "Mama" or "Papa." It's hard to remember their names. Mama told me that she is disappointed with my poor memory. I can hum a song, but I can never remember the words. She made me stand up in front of her while she held José and Max-Leão, her two favorite children, next to her, kissing and hugging them, and she made me repeat my name and my parents' names, our telephone number, and our address over and over again.

For dinner, she prepared calf brains stewed in wine, just for me. It's supposed to help with memory problems like mine. I am scared about tomorrow.

A small school van picked me up early in the morning by our front door. I am going to a private school for rich kids. As the van went from house to house, I got a chance to see the homes of other little boys and girls along the *Avenida Almirante Gago Coutinho*. A long name for a street, but most likely it was chosen because a short name for this road would not make any sense. It is a long road to reach the airport. These homes are not apartment houses like ours; they are privately owned houses, small palaces to be described more properly, in the most expensive and newest side of town. These are the children of important people in the community who are able to afford the high monthly tuition.

I love school. There are lots of toys to play with. Inside a large box in the hallway, there was a little game that I wanted to keep, so I took it home with me. *Why leave it there overnight? Nobody can enjoy it that way*, I thought to myself as I put it in my pocket and proudly displayed it to Mama when she asked me what I had learned that day. She told me that I stole the toy! "It's called *stealing*, when you take something that doesn't belong to you," she said.

I started to cry. I'm not a robber. I cried a lot, but it didn't do me any good. I have to put the toy back where I took it from tomorrow morning. Mama says that I might be going to jail if they find out what I did. What a horrible thing to happen. I just started school, and I am already in trouble. If I get caught, I'll be going to jail forever, never to see my family again, and worst of all, I'll be forced to eat the only thing I hate, bread. I'll starve to death most likely, and without a spoon I will never be able to dig myself out of jail. I was so scared they would catch me putting the toy

The Journey of Innocence

back in the toy box. What would I say? I robbed the school yesterday, and admit to being a criminal? After lunch, when they turned the lights off so that we could all take a nap, I got up as if I were going to the bathroom. Holding tight to the labyrinth toy in the coat pocket of my white uniform, I opened the big toy box in the hallway. Then, feeling like I was going to faint as Max-Leão does so often, I dropped the toy into the box and closed it quickly. I did it! Nobody saw me.

I am learning the numbers and letters of the alphabet, and I am having lots of fun making paper toys, drawing, and even sewing little animals onto cardboard pieces with wool thread. Yesterday, I didn't go to school because the whole class was sick, something to do with a boy who brought candy to school. Mama said I was the only one who didn't get sick. She said that the boy was giving out poison candy and nothing happened to me because I was a good obedient girl.

I didn't say anything to Mama, but I think that the little boy is very nice because he shared his candy with the ones who asked for some. The only reason that I didn't eat any candy was because he had run out of it by the time I got close enough to him. I didn't tell that to Mama. I want her to think that I was being good, like she wants me to be.

Uncle Augusto has prohibited Mama from taking me to see him during office hours because of the traumatic experience that I put his patients through. It seems that witnessing my distress and hearing my screams coming from inside his treatment room is scaring the living soul out of his patients waiting patiently in the waiting room. I am just trying to warn them of what is really going on behind closed doors. At Mama's request, he gave her the needles and the penicillin so that she can give us the shots at home whenever my brothers or I get sick. I have so many lumps on my bottom now. She says it's because I move. I have to stay still so she doesn't break the needle inside my butt cheek. This should be illegal in my opinion; just because her brother is a doctor doesn't make her a medical person. Every time we get a cold or a sore throat, we get a shot. Max-Leão has a lot more lumps on his bottom than I do. He moves more than me. Lately he's been getting daily hot compresses to make the lumps soft and melt away. We both get these lumps after Mama gives us the penicillin shots. They are the cure for everything, a miracle drug, so they say.

I found out that I have pretty eyes. I was running up the school steps when two women were coming down the steps. One pointed at me and said, "Look at that little girl. Have you ever seen such beautiful green eyes?" I stopped for a moment and stared back at them. My face felt very hot as I ran into the school with an embarrassed but happy feeling. I am not going to eat so many carrots; green eyes make people say nice things to me.

I want to be a teacher when I grow up. When the teacher leaves the classroom, I like to climb on her chair and then to the top of her desk. From there, I hold up the wooden stick and point to the various letters of the alphabet that hang on the walls around us. Being in kindergarten is a lot of fun. A new teacher came into the classroom this afternoon. I had no idea what she was talking about until she asked us if we knew the name of the Father. *Well, it's about time*, I thought. *I know the name of my father really well, but no one has asked me that yet.* I raised my right hand eagerly.

"You, what's your name?" she pointed to me.

"My name is Verónica Leah Toledano Ezaguy Wartenberg," I smiled to her.

"Very well, Verónica. Tell the class the name of the Father."

The Journey of Innocence

Taking a deep breath I said, "His name is Hans!" *Oops, silly me, I should say the whole name as I had learned it.* "His name is Hans Joachim Wartenberg." And I smiled again.

"Verónica, are you making a mockery of our Father?"

"No," I said, surprised by her anger. "His name is Hans Joachim Wartenberg!"

"Come up here, right now, next to me."

When I got near her, she pulled hard on my left ear and yelled, "The name of our Father is *Jesus*. Now repeat it to the class!"

"No, it's not Jesus," I replied, very sure of myself. "You are wrong. His name is Hans, and he is not your father."

She was very mad and would not admit that she was wrong. She hit my hands with a wooden ruler until the palm of my hands and wrists were red, and then made me stand the rest of the day facing the wall. I was not allowed to go to the bathroom, and I hate getting wet. What a mess!

When I got home, I showed my bruised hands to Mama and told her about the mean teacher. I don't like school anymore, and I don't want to go back.

That night I heard Mama talking to Papa, something about religion and God and it's about time that she took me to the temple. Papa didn't agree because he doesn't like religion; he feels it's too early to put man-made, silly religious stuff into my head.

I may have all the illnesses of childhood, but my baby brother José has the kind of sickness that can kill him. He gets taken to the emergency room even in the middle of the night. A few times, he almost died from lack of air. Someone told Mama that high altitude is good for José, so they took him today on an airplane ride. I wish I had asthma, too; it's not fair that he gets to fly and I don't.

Papa rarely talks to us. Kids are not to be seen or heard. When he gets home after work, Mama tells him how bad we behaved and asks him to hit us. At first, he screams at me, and that is scary enough. I already know what follows afterward. I try to protect myself with my hands in front of my face, but it doesn't really help; his hands are big and heavy. When he hits me across the face, it stings and I feel dizzy when everything shakes inside my head. He speaks Portuguese with a very harsh German accent. I can always tell when he is angry because the words are like crushing thunder sounds except they are made with the German language. I am afraid of Papa.

I am so happy that our meals are served earlier, before Papa comes home. When we eat together on rare occasions, I have to be careful not to spill my glass of milk. If I do, I get slapped across the face for being clumsy.

In the evening, Mama will say, "Go to Papa to get your blessing, and then go to bed. It's late."

If Mama didn't ask him to punish us all the time, maybe he would not bother with us when he gets home. He must think that my brothers and I are terrible kids, and he probably hates us, too.

Our nursemaid Paula was fired a few days ago. We were alone with her at home, and she had Max-Leão and me sitting on the foyer floor in a circle format. It was kind of dark, and the lights were not on. Paula was not wearing underwear, and she put one of Max-Leão's fingers in her vagina and asked him to wiggle it around. He pulled his hand out and refused to do it, and cried when she yelled at him. She then asked me to put my finger in there and move it around. I didn't really want to do it, but I am always being hit for not being obedient, so I did it. It felt wet and gummy, and I thought she was probably itching or something because she wanted me to do it harder. I didn't know that was bad until Max-Leão told Mama that he didn't want to put his fingers inside Paula's vagina. He complained to Mama because he was not happy being

The Journey of Innocence

yelled at earlier that day. Mama fired Paula, and I was told that what I had done was disgusting.

"Why is it disgusting?" I asked, "I was doing what she told me to do."

But Mama called me a bad girl—and stupid, too, if I didn't know why it was disgusting. It seems that I'm damned if I do what adults tell me to do, and I'm damned if I don't. I should hide away and not look at anyone or talk or play with anyone. I get blamed for everything, all the time.

There was a lot of odd noise coming from the Imperial Room this evening. I heard someone crying. I took a peek between the French doors. I saw Papa sitting on his armchair with his hands covering his face, and he was crying and saying over and over again, "What am I going to do now? How am I going to feed my family? What am I going to do? We are ruined!" Mama was by his side crying, too.

"Don't worry. I can lend you some money. It's not much, but it can help," said Aunt Heydee, Mama's sister.

Wow! Papa and Mama crying! They were crying with tears coming out of their eyes just like me. They must be in pain, just like when I get spanked. No one stopped my brothers and me from entering the Imperial Room, so we went directly to the golden Viennese armoire with glass doors displaying vases and glasses made of crystals and a golden glass with a beautiful lady's face imprinted on it. We just stayed there staring at the treasures of wondrous beauty. Then the maid came in, picked José up, and ordered us to follow her into our bedrooms. I wondered what happened. Nobody would tell us why everybody was sad.

Winter of 1949

The maids are gone. I no longer can go to kindergarten school. I miss the smell of crayons and paper. I miss working with arts and crafts at school, using colorful papers and cutting them into fun pieces with plastic scissors and sewing little cards with wool thread. I miss singing French songs like *Frére Jacques* and English songs like *London Bridge Is Falling Down* while dancing along with the other children. It looks like we are on our own from now on.

~ *Chapter Two* ~

DANDELIONS IN THE GARDEN

1949-1950

Spring of 1949

When I walked in the kitchen this morning, Mama was pulling her hair and screaming as she cried out, "Now they are taking our bathtub!" Two men were carrying it out the kitchen's back door. Each day something is being sold to make ends meet. She was hugging my brothers as she cried. I stood against the kitchen door and looked at her. I didn't understand the magnitude of what was happening. I walked slowly toward her, not quite sure of what to do to console her. She called me to come closer to her, and she hugged me, too. We all held on to Mama, hoping she would stop crying. The next-door neighbor came by and said she was sorry about what she had heard. Papa lost his restaurant on account of his partner stealing from him. It had to do with his partner making bad checks and other matters that I don't understand. The fact was that Papa is in a lot of trouble. His partner ran off with his family to another country, the United States of America, and he left no address. He is nowhere to be found. He had everything well planned in advance. I hope he dies when he gets to America. There are no furnishings left in our house; most everything has been sold. Except for my parent's bedroom furniture and our beds, the house is empty. The kitchen stove is gone, too. The Imperial Room is now one long, empty room, and we can play in it. The months ahead are going to be difficult, mostly borrowing money from family members because no one will hire Papa to work. The Jewish community is no help; he is a German, and therefore a Nazi. The Portuguese will not hire him because he is a Jew. He killed Jesus Christ.

Whenever I am bedridden, Mama brings me a couple of the family albums so I don't get bored. Sometimes she tells me the stories connected with the older pictures, the family members I never met and how they came about. Looking at these pictures a couple of times a year, depending on how soon I get sick, keeps me busy until I get better. With each picture, I can hear and feel its moment drawn out of the photo album as it felt before and after each picture was taken. No words are needed. The pictures are loud and clear, twirling in the windmills of the past, connecting with the present, and still looking forward to the future, like a magic carpet promising to return each time for as long as I am sick.

Old bread is not so bad when it boils in water with garlic for a while, and by adding fresh parsley, which is free when you buy the garlic, the soup can taste like real food. Sometimes an egg is available, and dinner becomes a real treat. I also developed a taste for bread with *yummy* raw onions. Besides, I want to grow very old like my Grandma Rica so that I can have wrinkled hands like hers. Mama told me that Grandma eats a lot of onions and that's why she is still alive.

For my birthday, Mama bought me a cupcake; she knows I don't like rice pudding. She said it is very important to

The Journey of Innocence

have a cake and candles to blow out on your birthday. Right now, a cupcake is a luxury.

I don't like getting constantly beat up for things when I don't even understand the reason why. A few weeks ago, I tried to show Mama what it feels like getting hit. I followed her down the hallway and then very quickly I tapped on her backside. I wanted her to understand how it feels, and she should stop hitting me all the time. I did it very delicately, but she is too smart for me. She realized my intention right away, and she turned around and said, "You dare to hit your own mother? This is what you get!" And she hit me so hard that I went flying into the wall—resulting in a bloody nose. The whole idea of teaching her a lesson failed miserably. I am not even going to try it on Papa.

I asked Mama, "Why don't I have a penis like my two brothers? What's wrong with me?"

She put a carrot on a string and tied it around my waist, saying, "Okay, now you have one, too."

What's the matter with Mama? Can't she see that I don't want a carrot or a penis? I just want to know why I am different.

There was a crystal, bluish-tinted bottle of perfume in the top shelf of the closet in the room next to the bathroom. Max-Leão and I had our eyes on it for quite a while. We wanted to see it more up close. I got up on a chair and brought it down. We both took a sniff and agreed that it smelled really good! But my brother decided that something that smelled that good had to be very tasty too. He started to drink it. I tried to take it away from him, but he would not share it with me. He drank the whole bottle of perfume, and Mama got home just in time to rush him to the hospital where they pumped his stomach. I am the oldest; therefore, I am supposed to know from life's experience that I had given poison to my brother to drink. The punishment is always the same—a lot of screaming, and then getting hit across the face or having to pull my underwear down so that I can feel more pain when Mama puts me over her knees and hits my bottom with a wooden spoon. As if that were not enough punishment, she always adds, "Wait until your father gets home."

Max-Leão and I got into trouble today. We got caught using cockroaches for racing down the hallway. It's easy to find big ones. They are everywhere. We have been doing that since our hallway carpet was sold. We use the hardwood floor strips for racing them. We put the cockroaches side by side at the beginning of the hallway, and then we wait to see which one gets to the end of the hallway first. Because we are not allowed to play with the roaches anymore, we have to wait until Mama is out with José. Mama put cucumber skins on the ground outside the front door to our apartment and also by the back door so the roaches can't come in from either direction. Someone told her that roaches don't like cucumbers. But it doesn't look like they are using the front or back doors to come in. They must be coming in through the little holes in the walls. Mama says they are coming in from the neighbor's next door, where else could they be coming from? We keep our apartment clean, and they still come into our apartment. We don't have a way of stopping them, there's too many of them. I would love to have mice instead, like at Grandma Rica's old house. They are so adorable. Everybody screams when they see them running in and out of little tiny holes in the walls, but I find them to be very cute fuzzy little creatures.

All of our toys are gone. Mama put everything into a sack and said she was giving them away to needy children. I have a feeling that she is selling them, like everything else

The Journey of Innocence

we have I don't play with roaches anymore. I can't even think of it without getting the willies. Now that Mama said my brothers and I are too old to have a pot under the bed, we have to get up during the night to use the bathroom. I have started turning the hallway lights on this week so the roaches will run away and I won't step on one of them with my shoes. The crunching sound is just too much for me.

It all started when I got up one night barefoot in the dark and somewhere halfway down the hall I stepped on a huge roach. Thick white blood and guts came out of it. I had to wash my right foot in the bidet, because we have no tub and the washing basin is too high for me to get my foot inside.

I love going to Grandma Rica's house. We are there very often for dinner. We also go there to bathe in her chipped enamel tub, which is very large and much deeper than the one we used to have; it looks like a metal boat. Grandma Rica was born in Tangier, Morocco, where she learned to make special jams with grapes and other fruits, like apples. She also makes orange skin covered with chocolate. Everything is stored in her cool, dark pantry with other unusual delicacies. When Grandma Rica gives me a banana and bread, I eat the banana and throw away the bread. I only eat bread if there's nothing else to eat. My favorite meal is fava beans with meatballs or sweet peas with meatballs. When Aunt Heydee makes the food, there aren't many fava beans left, only meatballs. She keeps testing the fava beans as they cook. "Just making sure they don't get overdone," she says.

Aunt Heydee lives with her mother Rica, and so does Aunt Ligia, her youngest sister. I like to sit next to them and listen to their stories. Ligia is a very nervous and neurotic person. She was in a mental institution for a while. She had to have electric shock treatments to make her forget some emotional trauma she suffered a few years ago. I am going to try my very best never to go crazy like her. The idea of electric shocks is very scary. She was to be married when, one week before the wedding, her fiancée changed his mind. Aunt Ligia had a nervous breakdown. She even tried to kill herself. A few years later, she got married to someone else, but he used to beat her up and she got a divorce. Everybody feels her ex-husband was a bad man because he was not a Jew. Jews love their wives and never beat them. The whole thing was her fault. Now she is divorced and alone with two children from that marriage, she is living with Grandma, until she can afford to be on her own. She is a poetess and writes children's stories and also writes for the main newspaper in Lisboa, the *Diário de Noticias*. She started writing when she was fourteen years old; *The Sin* was never published, but her first book *Him* was published in 1942 and the year after, *Her* was published. She loves to write. At present, she is writing two other books, *Those Kisses*, a poetry book, and the novel *Bodies for Sale*. When she is not writing, which is rare, she teaches gymnastics at a high school, trying to make ends meet.

Papa found a job. He is now selling magazines and books from door to door. He climbs a lot of steps up and down apartment complexes in the city of Lisboa, and he carries in each hand one large suitcase filled with books and magazines about architecture and art. Some days he sells a few of them; sometimes he comes back with what he started with. When he gets home, he is always very tired and his chest hurts. Breathing becomes difficult when his chest hurts. Cousin Salomão, who is a cardiologist, diagnosed Papa with a heart disease that kills you when you exert yourself. Papa can die any time. He should not be straining himself climbing steps and carrying heavy books, but he is the only breadwinner in our family.

The Journey of Innocence

The German gold wine glass with the painted face of a lady is back on the shelf in one of the armoires. It never got sold. Mama picked it up from the pawnshop where she gets money for leaving it there until she has enough money to get it back.

Summer of 1949

Mama has been cooking. She creates food with what is available, which can be a horrible experience. But her cookies are very good, even if they are hard as a rock. They just have to be soaked in hot milk, or we will break our teeth. They always smell so incredibly delicious, the vanilla and orange make my mouth water every time. Last week, Max-Leão and I were throwing them at each other. One of them scratched José's head ever so slightly, but kept on going and broke the glass window in the kitchen cabinet. Both Max-Leão and I can't sit down at all.

Mama woke me up early in the morning to go to the Santa Cruz hospital with her. Supposedly, she had to see her doctor. We usually go to Uncle Augusto's office, where she takes diathermy treatments for her tummy because her tummy hurts a lot once a month. She would not tell me much about this visit to the hospital. She is always very mysterious about everything. While walking to the hospital, I hopped up and down like I do when I feel happy, and I ran up in front of her humming a few tunes. When crossing the street, I held her hand. I was happy to go out with Mama.

We entered the stagnant, smelly, hot hospital's large waiting room packed tight with sick people. There were no fun tables or chairs to run under, like in Uncle Augusto's office. There were a lot of children in the waiting room. Some were sneezing, others were coughing, and that weird acid-like smell I hate, the hospital's smell of blood and tincture of iodine and chemicals, was all around us. I have noticed that the mortuaries, with saints made of wax and candles of all sizes, are always close to the hospitals.

We didn't wait long; a woman dressed in a long, white coat with grayish hair pulled back tight, thick glasses, and a frowning face, asked me to go with her.

I looked at Mama questioningly, and she just said, "Go with the nurse. I'll be waiting here for you."

I followed the nurse as I was told, but, as soon as I entered the room behind closed doors, I knew I was in trouble. I ran for the door, but the gray-haired woman grabbed me from the back of my dress. I started to scream and called out for Mama to help me. Two men in white coats came to help her. I kicked them in the shins as hard as I could, and they got very angry and dragged me to a chair, while someone else tied my legs down. With my arms held behind my back by the nasty woman and some other nasty mean people, they asked me to open my mouth to a man with some kind of round light bulb on his forehead and a pair of pliers in his hand who also impatiently asked me to open my mouth. No way was I going to open my mouth! But then they squeezed my nose and held my head still between their hands and arms, and they pulled my hair back. I had to open my mouth in order to breathe. As they held my jaw open, one of the men in white coats started cutting the inside of my throat off with pliers. It was hard to breathe and blood was coming out and I was gagging from it. Then they let me free. I came out of the room, and Mama just took me out by the hand outside to the street. I wanted to ask Mama why this happened to me, but I couldn't talk and she was not talking to me either. She didn't even ask me what happened. Obviously, she had taken me there on purpose. What could I have done wrong to deserve such punishment?

She waited for a taxi to come by, and we got in. I held the handkerchief she gave me to my face, as blood was coming out of my mouth. When we got home, she put me in bed. She didn't hug or kiss me. I was crying, in pain and with no idea of what had just happened. Then she said, "You just had your tonsils out. Now you won't be so sick anymore." And she added, "God punished you for being happy that your mother was going to the hospital."

I wanted to talk and defend myself from such accusations that I felt were completely untrue, but I couldn't make a sound. I wanted to tell her that I hated her for lying to me. And then she offered me vanilla ice cream. I felt she was doing that on purpose, because I could not even swallow my own spit and I hated her. The only thing that I am happy about is that my bedroom is now in the front room of the house, where the sun comes in and lights it up. Mama told me that tomorrow I can try and eat ice cream because my throat will not hurt anymore.

Autumn of 1949

We have been eating our meals in the kitchen because we don't have a dining room set anymore. Mama got a table and some chairs from Grandma Rica, and someone gave us loose pieces of plywood to put over the cold tile floor in the kitchen. This way, when it gets colder in the winter, our feet won't freeze and give us a bladder virus. Mama says that's what happens if your feet get too cold. The room where we used to have our meals before we became poor is now a playroom. My two brothers and I play in there, but there are no toys to play with. The room is empty. Before locking us in the room, Mama tells us to use our imagination. We jump up and down to see who can jump the highest, and when we get tired we sit on the floor and tell each other scary stories. My brother José doesn't do much of anything but drink milk from his bottle. He is about a year and a half old and is still in diapers. He is too small for anything much but watching us. When we run out of imagination, Max-Leão and I try to bite each other's bottom by grabbing each other around the waist and going around in circles.

The neighbor downstairs has been complaining about her ceiling chandeliers shaking too much. She is afraid they are going to drop on her head. Mama says the neighbor downstairs is a troublemaker. How much can three little children shake the floor while jumping? The neighbor doesn't understand because she is childless.

I love Sunday mornings when my brothers and I are allowed to get in bed with our parents. My favorite game is putting my finger on Papa's lips, and then pulling it off before he bites my finger. But he never bites me for real, and if he does, he rolls his lips over his teeth so he doesn't hurt me. I also like to be tickled and jump up and down on their bed.

Mama tried making some artwork for sale. She made a collage out of different paper prints and glued the pieces to pottery. Papa, who is a perfectionist, felt it was very poor work and stated that no one—at least no one in their right mind—would buy it.

If Mama finds out that I have not gone to the bathroom for more than two days, I get an enema. I don't like enemas; I hate baring my bottom for the whole world to see and lying down on her lap so she can give me an enema. It's always done in the room next to the bathroom or in the kitchen, so we can get to the toilet as fast as we can. It only feels good when it all comes out. Seems like once a week, whether we like it or not, my brothers and I get enemas.

Mama is fulfilling her desire of becoming a medical doctor like her brother and cousins. Her first love was to conduct an orchestra. She had been given a scholarship to go to England to study and become a *maestro*, but her

The Journey of Innocence

parents loved her too much to lose her into the big sinful and cruel world where anything bad can happen when you are an innocent, beautiful, young girl living far away from home without adult supervision. Her parents would not allow that to happen. In those days, women left the parents' house for two reasons only—to get married or to become a nun. Being a concert pianist and getting her musical degree in Lisboa, not far from the family, was fine as long as she was home before it got dark outside. Mama's career now is being a mommy to my brothers and me, but that is not good enough for her. She is our doctor, too; after all, being a doctor is just a minor technical term having to do with some schooling and a medical degree. Her brother Augusto and cousins had done that, but as a member of the family she feels she is entitled to a certain degree of respect, which dictates she knows just about as much as they do—except for surgery, of course. It's not only Mama who acts like a doctor, as Aunt Heydee also knows a lot about drugs and dispenses them as she gets them from our medical family members when needed for colds, bellyaches, fevers, anemia, headaches, nerves, and so on. For whatever ails anyone, there's always something to take from Aunt Heydee or Mama's small pharmacy. Each owns a few shoeboxes full of medicine. Besides giving penicillin shots and enemas, Mama is also good at using the suction glasses on anyone who has a chest cold, pleurisy, or backache; this treatment also helps to clear lung congestion. Mama lights up a match and throws it into a small glass that has a little piece of cotton inside, and then turns the glass over on the area being treated. Most of the time, it's the back. Suction starts and it's fun to watch the skin lifting up like a bubble and getting red. This treatment comes from the medical doctors in China, and somehow has been passed on to the women's side of Grandma's family from generation to generation. It's that easy to learn.

Winter of 1950

Mama made me a homemade costume for *Carnaval*. We can't afford to rent one. She bought a few yards of starched cotton cloth with a pattern of colorful roses, which I wore on top of my regular warm, winter, flannel green dress. She made a red apron and a flowery scarf to match the skirt. When no one is looking, I like rubbing my nose on the vibrant colorful skirt and smelling the starched new material. I never had anything so crispy and fresh in my life except the organza white dress I used to have when I was one year old. Mama painted my face with lots of makeup, and she even drew a nice-sized black mole on my left cheek, just like she uses when she gets all dressed up to go out with Papa. As a final touch, she stuck a big plastic flower on my black fuzzy hat. I looked like a real Portuguese country girl. I really loved having Mama so close to me, combing my hair and trying to make me pretty. She promised that next year, when she wins the lottery, she would rent a real professional outfit for me to wear at *Carnaval*. She said I can be a princess, but I told her that I'd rather dress up as a pirate.

Spring of 1950

The porters and some of the neighbors are plotting to evict us from our apartment. Mama is very upset about this. It's not our fault that we are poor and don't have electricity in the house. We use candles at night for dinner, and then we go to bed. Mama keeps pointing her finger above her head as if toward some invisible power above as she says that God is good and He will protect us from our enemies and their evil ways.

It just happened that, while having lunch, Mama got a cod fish bone stuck in her throat. We were on our way to the emergency squad, which is now appropriately situated

The Journey of Innocence

at the corner of our street. Mama was running down our apartment steps, while holding her throat and gasping for air, when she saw one of the porters downstairs.

He asked her what was wrong, and Mama immediately, in an act of desperation, put her whole hand in her mouth and down her throat and removed the fish bone herself, saying right after, "Nothing is wrong, *Senhor Sousa.*"

That was a very heroic moment for Mama, who wouldn't give the porter the satisfaction of seeing her choke to death. Mama bragged to Papa that evening about her quick response to the mean and nasty porter, and Papa went on and on about how dumb the whole thing was. He had never heard of anyone choking on a fish bone, at least not so often as Mama does.

"It's all a matter of upbringing," he said in his heavy German accent. As a child, he had won an award for best manners at the table and being able to eat a fish to such perfection that only the skeleton was left on the plate with every single bone in its proper position. He was only eight years old, but that's how it is in Germany. Everyone learns at a very young age how to eat fish.

I had a horrible birthday! Someone told Mama that the dandelions growing in our yard, which is nothing but weeds, could be converted into delicious nourishing soup.

I saw her picking them and boiling them with old dark moldy bread. I would so much rather have rice pudding. The smell from the soup was a sour green spoiled smell. It was enough to make anyone puke, which I did, but that didn't stop her from making me eat it. I got hit with the wooden spoon over the head over and over again.

"If you don't eat, you are going to die from starvation," she said.

Then, as if that were not enough torture, she gave me her birthday gift. A wool dress she made out of every leftover wool piece she had collected through the years. It was too big. It was lumpy where the strings were tied with one another. It had millions of colors, and it made me itch. I didn't want to wear it. It was a warm day. But she not only made me put it on but also took me into the backyard and forced me to sit down on the old, wooden garden chair and smile as if I were happy to the camera. Her brother Augusto loaned her his camera because he was too busy to see me on my birthday.

Summer of 1950

Luisa, the little girl that lives in our building on the second floor, was playing in her yard. When she saw me leaning over her fence, she invited me to come in and play with her. We sat on the grass by the peppermint bushes, and she started to put peppermint leaves inside her vagina.
 She wanted me to do it, too, but I told her that I couldn't because I was afraid that the leaves might have gross little bugs on them, and besides, I'd rather use peppermint in tea with a lemon twist, like Grandma Rica drinks. She asked me not to tell anyone, or she would get into trouble. I have not seen her since that day when we played in her backyard. Maybe her Mama saw everything from their window and now Luisa is not allowed out anymore. It's too bad, because I would like to have a friend to play with. I am not allowed to go upstairs to find out what happened to Luisa. Mama said they moved away.
 I went to her backyard this morning and found the green door to her garden locked from the inside.

Mama was telling us a story today about the grandmother who came to live with her daughter and was given a metal cup and a metal dish to use during her meals.
 When the granddaughter saw that, she asked her mother, "Why doesn't Grandma eat from china dishes and crystal glasses, like us?"

The Journey of Innocence

"Because she is old and weak. If she uses the expensive dinnerware, she might drop it and break it."

And the little girl said, "I understand. That is a very good reason. I promise when you get to be old like Grandma, I will also give you unbreakable metal dinnerware to eat from."

Her mother realized that she was wrong, and hoping her daughter would not do that to her when she got old, she gave her mother the best of chinaware and also the most beautiful crystal glass to drink water from.

I love stories. I know this is a corny one, and Mama probably made it up, but I like when Mama talks to us.

Autumn of 1950

I am in first grade, and I don't like school; the teachers are always hitting my hands with a wooden ruler. There are other girls like me who get punished. I just hope I will never have to be punished like some girls who are forced to wear donkey ears cut out of newspapers like a hat, and then as if that's not degrading enough they have to sit in a chair outside on the veranda, facing the street so that people going by can look at them and laugh. My wrists got so sore this week from getting hit with the ruler that Mama felt sorry for me and wrapped both my wrists in bandages and sent me back the next day with a medical excuse note from Uncle Augusto, stating that my wrists are very weak and I'm not to get hit or my wrists will break. Now they hit me over the head, and my head is lumpy. I hate school.

Grandma gave us some of her old furniture, and now we have a china cabinet and a nice big table back in the empty room where we used to have our meals. I didn't mind eating in the kitchen. I thought it was fun, but in the winter it is too cold. Mama said we would return to having our meals in the kitchen when it's summertime so that we can stay cool.

Winter of 1951

Wintertime is museum time. I love museums and the mystery of ages that come with them. Times of long ago still breathing by our side, like friendly ghosts from the past. I have never seen a ghost, but just about everybody else has. The idea really scares me. I believe that dead people should be visiting only other dead people. We went to the *Monastério dos Jerónimos* this weekend. It was a family group outing with Mama, Aunt Heydee, my brothers, and Maria, the part-time maid who knows how to keep my brothers and me from running around and getting into mischief. We entered a huge, badly lit room with high stone walls and a vaulted ceiling. It was built hundreds of years ago, and the air felt stagnant and as old as the stone walls.

I heard Aunt Heydee saying, "Look. It's the tomb of the Unknown Soldier. Everybody take a look."

Not me. Why would I want to see a dead soldier? Guts coming out, eyes bugged out with the worms eating his flesh, and bony hands stretched out seeking someone's help as if screaming for help. He had to be screaming even if we heard no sound. When you no longer have a throat and all the bones are just rotting away and you have been locked up inside the coffin for centuries, only silence can be heard. But is he really silent, or just waiting? Is the coffin open or closed? And if it's closed, does he still have enough power left to open it, get out, and grab us?

My two brothers ran toward the tomb, and I ran toward the exit. Maria grabbed me by the waist, held me under her arm, and started to walk to the tomb, saying, "There is nothing to be afraid of. Now, take a look!"

I was screaming and had my eyes tightly squeezed shut.

"No," I screamed. "I don't want to look. Put me down!"

The Journey of Innocence

She stopped walking, and I could tell she was by the tomb. She put me down. I opened my eyes just a little to see where I was. Then I walked away from the stone coffin, being very careful not to look in that direction. Everybody was laughing and making fun of me, calling me *chicken*. I didn't care. I know that I am not a chicken because, if I were, I would lay eggs.

~ *Chapter Three* ~

THE LEARNING YEARS

1951-1955

Spring of 1951

A lot of commotion went on in our apartment building one evening. We were getting ready to go to bed when the maid from the third floor came down to invite my brothers and me to a special event. It was very crowded, and many other children I had never met were already seated on the sunroom's floor. The father of the birthday boy closed the curtains and turned off all the lights to make the room dark. Then he cranked the handle on the movie machine, and the light coming from the machine projected a real American movie with Cowboys and Indians on the wall. There was no sound coming from the wall, like in the movie theatre, but we knew from the actor's expressions and movements what was happening. At the end of the movie, the handsome cowboy kissed the horse's nose, and they both walked away into the sunset. It was a very emotional moment. We applauded and screamed, and we were so happy. We all asked to see the movie one more time because it was very good but only lasted a few minutes. The boy's father rewound the film in the machine and ran it one more time while we all sat quietly in complete

The Journey of Innocence

amazement. This is what I call an incredible invention. I can't believe what I saw, and it was so exciting. Movies at home!

Mama was out with José. She is always taking him to the doctors to see if they have a drug to cure him. Max-Leão and I were left alone at home. We started looking around inside the closets for something to play with. We found some jars made of transparent glass with engraved flowers and pelicans. We could tell they were very special jars because they were hidden way in the back of the closet and out of sight. We found a bottle almost half-filled with a clear liquid and a white tree branch inside of it. The label read, *Anise*. We sniffed the *anise* and it smelled real good, so we took a turn each having a mouth full of the sweet liquor inside. When we finished drinking, we went to the kitchen and got a knife to yank out the small pieces of sugar branches from inside the bottle, which tasted like the best candy we'd ever had. Just then, Mama came home and there she found us sitting on the floor holding the empty bottle. She was very upset. We had just drunk and eaten the only *anise* left in the house. The valuable jars were not damaged, so she didn't even hit us. She said, "Well, I don't have to worry about you two anymore, because the last drop of alcohol in this house is now gone."

Nothing special happens anymore on my birthday. The good old days are gone. I hinted to Mama that I wish I had a birthday cake. She got me a cupcake and put a candle in the middle of it. I acted like I was very happy about it. I didn't want to hurt her feelings over the clothes she made for me, but she could tell that I was not happy. I have to learn to hide my feelings better; otherwise, I will have to explain why I am sad, and then I feel guilty.

I have to remember that there are other kids in a worse situation than me, even though Mama keeps saying that I was born with a silver spoon in my mouth. Our last dainty German gold. glass with an engraved lady's face on it is gone again. Mama told me it is in the pawnshop. Mama has been cooking and cleaning. I have not seen Maria, the maid. Obviously Papa is not selling enough magazines to pay the rent or to buy food either. I understand what's going on without anyone telling me. We communicate in a silent language.

It was José's birthday this weekend, and Papa and Mama played with us. Papa told us he was going to take us all on a fun trip. The room where Max-Leão and I used to sleep is now empty. We both sleep in what used to be the guestroom. José continues to sleep in our parents' room in case they have to rush him to the hospital during the night because of an asthma attack.

Papa made a big secret over our mystery trip. It was going to happen inside the empty room, and only one of us could go in at a time, with Papa as the leader and Mama as his assistant. José was the first one to go in with his eyes covered by a scarf. The door closed behind them. Max-Leão and I sat on the hallway floor waiting nervously for our turn. José came out still with his eyes covered and laughing. We were no longer scared. I was next. Mama put the scarf over my eyes, and Papa held my hand and told me I was not allowed to peek. And into the room we went. It was very windy.

"Feel the wind blowing?" I heard Papa say. "It's a storm!" I wondered where the wind could be coming from. It is a room without a window.

"Yes, yes," I said. I was a bit skeptical, but very happy and excited.

"Soon, it's going to start raining," said Mama. Then she added, "Feel the rain on your face?"

"Yes, yes," I said, once again wondering how the weather elements had got inside of an empty apartment

The Journey of Innocence

room. I decided to just enjoy it and go with it. "It's wonderful," I said.

"Here is an umbrella. Hold on to it," said Papa, as he put an umbrella in my hand.

"Verónica, put it over your head. It's raining in the garden," I heard Mama say.

"The sun just came out. Give me the umbrella back," I heard Papa say. Then he added, "Hold my hand, and let's go up the steps climbing high toward the moon. Be careful. Don't trip. Wow! You have reached the moon. Now jump off, down to Earth. It's okay. I'll catch you."

I was a little scared about that, but it was all imagination, so nothing could hurt me. I could tell that Papa was holding me in the air. I moved my arms like the wings of a bird, and I had to laugh as I landed softly on the ground. What a trip! I found myself out of the room.

"Okay, now it's Max-Leão's turn," said Papa as he took off the scarf covering my eyes. "You can watch how this is done, if you promise to be very quiet," he said.

I promised to be good and not to say a word. Once again I entered the magic room. This time my eyes were wide open and looking for answers. The room was empty except for a wooden ladder in the middle of the room. Next to it was our old metal garden water can, Papa's rusty, green fan, and his big black umbrella. I had to smile. I was so happy to find that the mind can create anything with the help of sound, a touch, and the love of my parents. For a few moments, there was magic.

After dinner, I mentioned how I would love to go on an imaginary trip again. Mama said it would be a while before they had the time to do that with us again. Papa went on to tell us about his home in Berlin, Germany, and how his parents used to play games like these with him and his two sisters, Ilse and Friedel, when they were about our age. They even had a mini-theatre in one of the rooms of their house where they used to put on hand puppet shows for their parents, family, and friends. In those days as a child, Papa's voice was very weak and he could barely speak. He had been born with a defective throat, and it wasn't until he was eight years old that his parents took him to a throat specialist who knew how to fix that kind of problem. So, until he was eight years old, he was only able to play the piano, but he couldn't sing or act a part in the puppet shows. This is the reason why Papa even today won't talk on the phone. He is very conscious of his voice not having a normal pitch, and a few times he was mistaken as woman's voice on the phone. He feels very embarrassed about it. He had to struggle with this handicap all his life, and if it hadn't been for that surgeon who did the surgery, Papa would be a mute.

Papa's parents were very rich, and their house was on the same street as those of other very important people in the government. Across the street from his house lived the chancellor of Berlin. Papa still remembers the chancellor, because he always smiled and waved at him from inside his golden coach pulled by horses. On weekends, Papa's parents gave parties, and they hired famous pianists and opera singers to entertain their guests. I love hearing stories of the past because I get to know that my parents were also children some time ago, just like my brothers and me.

Summer of 1951

It has been very, very hot in the last few days. My two brothers and I are allowed to take our clothes off and bathe inside the washbasin in the sunroom. This must be the way it feels like to be in a swimming pool, cool and not scary like the ocean with big waves.

Max-Leão and I talked about having a real swimming pool built in our yard. How difficult can it be? We only need to take out the *nespra* tree and dig a square hole in the ground and fill it with water. He is going to talk to Mama and Papa and see if he can convince them this is a great idea. They should be very happy that we are willing to do all the digging; they just have to supply us with water.

We were coming back from our evening stroll to the park down the street. Mama was pushing José in his stroller when suddenly a nice lady at a window turned out to be Encarnação, a friend of Mama from the old days when they both were students at the Music Conservatory. It just happened that she lives down the street from our house. All these years and they didn't even know. Encarnação happened to be looking out at her windowsill, enjoying the fresh air, when we were going by. She doesn't wear makeup. Her hair is not colored like Mama's either; instead, it has shades of gray. She is built like a workingwoman, stocky. She is as big as Mama. I liked Encarnação because she seemed kind and smiled a lot. They reminisced for a while about their younger days in school. She is a widow and has two grown-up daughters and a sixteen-year-old son. They exchanged phone numbers.

When Papa got home a few days ago, Mama told him about Max-Leão and me fighting with each other and said that we should get punished. Papa told us both to go to our backyard and get a large, thick stick for him to hit us with.

We looked around the yard, and when I picked up a stick, Max-Leão said, "Are you crazy? He's going to kill us with a stick that size. Let's give him this little one. We'll tell him this was the biggest one we found."

Together we carried a little dried-up twig branch from our backyard, and we carried it as if it were big and heavy.

"I asked for a big wooden stick to beat you with and this is all you can find?" Papa was obviously not falling for Max-Leão's great idea.

I almost died when I heard Max-Leão saying with an

innocent look on his face, "This was the biggest stick we could find."

I nodded my head in agreement.

The fear in our eyes and the size of the stick we brought to Papa mellowed his anger.

He laughed and said, "Okay, I'll forgive you both this time, but next time you are bad I won't be so nice. You will get double the punishment."

Max-Leão and I talked about this experience, and we are going to try the same trick the next time. We are so smart!

Autumn of 1951

I miss the Sunday mornings when my brothers and I used to lie down with our parents, playing and talking about silly things that made us all laugh. They say we are too old for that now.

I got to impress both Mama and Papa this morning with the unique sounds I can make with my tongue. They were seated on the veranda, enjoying their Sunday morning, and I said, "Would you like to hear me make the sound of a horse?" And I went right on clicking my tongue against the roof of my mouth, *click, clunk, click, clunk.* They were both very impressed with my talent, and they both were laughing and feeling happy. I love seeing my parents seated together and laughing. I also showed them how I can fill my mouth with air and make funny sounds when I part my lips just a little and press my index fingers against each of my cheeks. They love me.

I got into big trouble today for no reason. Max-Leão and I were helping José, who is a lot smaller than us because he is only three years old, to climb out of the front window in our bedroom facing the street. We wanted to get him on his knees on the windowsill so that he could throw dirt on the people walking on the street. We simply wanted to have some fun with the flowerless clay pots. A long time ago, there had been six flowering plants growing, but over time the plants had died and all that was left was dried up dirt inside the clay pots. It was all going fine. Max-Leão and I were holding José by the suspenders and we were having a good time laughing. Then the neighbor across the street started screaming that José was going to fall off the windowsill. José got scared with her screams and dropped one of the clay pots, missing some people walking underneath our window. It was an accident. They called the police, and the neighbor said we were a hazard to the neighborhood and that our parents had to punish us. Max-Leão and I were accused of possibly killing José had he fallen off the window with the clay pot. I tried to explain that I was holding him by the suspenders the whole time and he was perfectly safe that way. I promised that I would never again throw dirt into the street. It didn't do any good. We got punished, and once again Max-Leão and I couldn't sit for days. José didn't get punished because he is too sickly to suffer a beating.

Mama says that I did very well in school last year and this year it will be easier. It's not true. The teachers are just as mean as the others, and I am confused about what they say and what they write on the blackboard. I still don't understand anything, and Arithmetic is the worst ever except for the multiplication tables. I memorized those out of desperation. If I don't, I will get donkey ears.

My school is on a long and steep street called *Calçada de Arroios*, only a couple of blocks down the hill from where we live. Last year, I was chaperoned to school. Now that I am older, I am allowed to go by myself as long as I don't talk to or go with any strangers. I always rush down the hill to get to school on time, and I like running across the little round park that looks like an island with three palm trees, lots of flowers, and two wooden benches for the older folks.

Calçada de Arroios is made with cobblestones just like all the streets in Lisboa, but it is very steep. I can run up with no problem, but, if I run down carelessly and without looking down for holes and bumps on the sidewalk, I will hit the tip of my shoe on something and fall.

I have bruised knees and elbows from falling several times going down the *Calçada de Arroios*. The reason the streets are so steep is because of earthquakes. When the ground moves, it produces hills filled with bodies and houses that fall and are trapped under the ground. The big one in 1755 literally destroyed Lisboa. It all happened in the middle of the day, about lunchtime. All the men working in the factories making bricks got instantly buried. That's why, when somebody dies, we always say, "They went to make bricks."

Aunt Heydee rarely falls, but she told me that she does get her high heels stuck between the cobblestones sometimes and a few times twisted her ankles, but that's it. She always wears very, very high heels because she is too short without them and men like tall women.

When school is over for the day, I love taking my time to get home. I like getting underneath the water drains coming down from the buildings and getting soaked to the skin. I love hearing the sound and the feel of my shoes squeaking as I walk. Rain is a lot of fun. I love rain because it's just like taking a shower. We still don't have a bathtub; maybe someday we will have a tub, when we are rich again.

Whatever I get in life that is good, I am very thankful for it. And I am very thankful for Encarnação, my mother's friend. She is my best friend. I go to her house every time I can. She lets me help her make cakes and chocolate cookies. Today she braided my hair and said that I was

The Journey of Innocence

pretty, and that she wished I were her daughter. When I got home, Mama saw my new hairdo and was very upset. I am not to have anybody touch my hair. If I want to look like an old lady with the hair up, she is not going to allow it. She took the pins out of my hair, combed and parted it to the side straight, the way she likes it. I am afraid Mama will stop me from going to visit Encarnação. When I come home, I will take the hairpins out of my hair before I climb the steps to our house. I don't really mind doing that because the tight hair pulled back by the pins gives me a headache. Encarnação is happy that my hair is pulled back, and I look neat and pretty when I spend the day with her. Mama is happy to see me ugly with my hair pulled down straight to the side. How easy it is to make everybody happy.

Max-Leão and I like to sit at the veranda of our parents' bedroom and watch the people and cars go by. He can always tell what brand and year a car is, even from far away, even before it reaches our street. He is very smart. To me, all the cars look the same except for different colors. Our favorite pastime game is watching the funeral processions. We count how many cars are following the black decorated carriage with heavy, chunky golden angels. If it is a long procession, that means the person who died was very popular. The carriage is usually pulled by four, sometimes six horses, which are dressed in colorful gold mountings and decorated with lots of flowers. The flowers are all over the horses and on the roof of the carriage. Two men dressed in black with matching black top hats sit on a stool and pull the reins that control the horses so they strut at a steady pace. I don't understand why they have to kill so many flowers when someone dies.

Chest X-rays are now mandatory at school. A lot of children were found to have tuberculosis, and they were not allowed to return to school. My chest X-ray shows that I have a scar in the left lung due to early tuberculosis. I am very lucky that I didn't die. I had TB when I was a lot younger, and no one even knew it. This means that I am a weakling, and I will always be sickly and can never do hard work. I will always have to bundle up in the winter, and if I don't eat more bread and soup, I will die. Mama took me to see our Cousin Salomão, who is a heart specialist, and he took another X-ray of my chest in his office to confirm that my TB is not active. I don't know why, but I don't like him or his office.

Encarnação has an adopted niece. Her name is Maria Leonor. She is my age, and I am allowed to visit and play with her at Encarnação's house. I would love to look like her with blonde hair, blue eyes, and very white, almost see-through skin. She is very pretty. She came over to our house once, but was not allowed in. It is something to do with my two brothers; one of them might like her as a future girlfriend and that can never happen, as she is of a different religion.

The last time I saw Maria Leonor was last summer. She came over to our house, and we both sat on the black metal steps in back and ate cherries from a straw basket she had brought with her. We hung the cherries on our earlobes like earrings, and we talked and laughed. Maria Leonor is very lucky. She gets to visit Encarnação a lot more than I do. I heard that Maria Leonor has been sick for the last few months. Nobody knows what's wrong.

I visit Encarnação on weekends, and I spend a lot of time in her deceased husband's study. She left everything just the way he used to have it before he died. I love looking into the African books with pictures of people with black skin and big lips stretched by dishes inside the inner lips. She told me these books are from the time when her dead

The Journey of Innocence

husband was the ambassador from Portugal to Angola and she lived in Africa with him. She actually saw wild animals in the jungle, and the people were black and walked naked because they were very poor savages. I don't blame them. It looks like it's very, very hot in Africa. Their skin is probably black from being burned in the hot sun every day. I have become a reader. I love reading books on adventure and other countries far away. *Gulliver's Travels* and *The Swiss Family Robinson* are both my favorites, and I have read them over and over again. Someday I will travel to faraway countries and write about my adventures.

Mama is always happy to send me to Encarnação's house after school. Encarnação loves me. She feeds me and keeps me warm. I love her kitchen with the big glass windows that open to her garden. The sunshine brightens the kitchen, which is always warm and cheery. The smells of a Portuguese house are alive in her house, alive with the soft scent of olive oil pouring from one of the large wooden barrels into the glass containers in the pantry next to the kitchen. The fresh batter for cakes and cookies is even tastier than when cooked. I love raw batter. I like to help by beating the eggs and peeling the almond skins after they are scalded, and then crunching them. I also like to help grind the fresh meat with the added herbs and moist bread soaked in milk. Encarnação has two maids always cooking when she is getting ready to entertain. She has a large family, but she still has room for me. She is always home, and she loves her family and all her friends.

Over the weekend, Mama had to call Uncle Augusto because I was having a stomachache and she thought I might need surgery. I was scared. Uncle Augusto couldn't come to see me because he was too busy. He told Mama over the phone to put ice on my abdomen. If it went away, it was not appendicitis. It went away, thank God!

Papa scares me when he has a temper attack. Last night Grandma Rica and Aunt Heydee came over for dinner. Aunt Heydee was telling Papa that Germans are bad people, that they are all Nazis.

Papa said that the German people are good people and they don't have anything to do with the Nazi philosophy.

But Aunt Heydee insisted that, if he was defending the Germans, he was a Nazi, too.

Papa got very angry and yelled, "I am German and proud of it." He then picked up the white tablecloth with the food and dishes, and pulled everything off the table—like you see professional magicians do—except that, when Papa pulled the tablecloth, everything went flying. The food on the dishes and serving platters and the glasses with milk and water splattered all over the floor, along with the crashed dishes. Mama and Grandma Rica were crying, and my brothers and I were sent to bed right after that.

This has happened before, when Aunt Heydee and Papa are having a dispute over world politics, and she drives him crazy with anger. Something always goes flying into the air. Mama says this whole thing has stemmed out of Papa having to wait ten years before Aunt Heydee said, "Okay, you can marry my sister."

He will never forgive her for that.

In the summer of 1933, Papa came to Portugal for the first time. His job until then was managing the production of handmade embroidery and lace in the Portuguese islands of Açores and then exporting them to Germany, where his parents had a few lace factories. He was visiting Portugal as a possible country where he might seek refuge after a German Navy admiral who was visiting the Açores confided in him that, since Hitler had been made Chancellor of Germany that year, the world was never going to be the same again. As a Jew, he should never return to Germany, and if anything, he should send word to his family to get the heck out as soon as possible and as far

The Journey of Innocence

away as they could. Papa sent the information to his family and was waiting to hear from them. While in Lisboa, he was invited to a private party, and that was where he met Mama for the first time. Papa was playing the piano when Mama and her sisters walked in. Papa saw her as the most beautiful woman he had ever seen. She was wearing a white dress and a tan that made her skin glow. Mama and her two sisters Heydee and Ligia had spent the day at the beach. Mama had dark brown hair that was naturally curly and worn down to her shoulders and a face that melted him away. She looked like a goddess, he said. She sat next to him and started playing the piano along with him. He couldn't help but fall in love with her right then and there. The problem was that he was a foreigner and without a job.

When he asked Aunt Heydee for Mama's hand in marriage, she told him, "Come back only when you have your own business, a secure, paying job here in Portugal, so that my sister doesn't have to go away like my other sister Nelly."

Ten years later, he did return, this time as co-owner of a German restaurant in downtown Lisboa, and Aunt Heydee gave my future parents her blessing.

Winter of 1952

When someone can take me to Grandma Rica's house, it's usually on weekends. When she babysits for my brothers and me, she teaches us French and Arithmetic. Her house is on the other side of the city, and we are not allowed to walk that far by ourselves. I see Encarnação a lot more often because she lives closer to our house. She has been teaching me to crochet, but Mama found out about it and told me that only old ladies do that kind of work. Besides, it's not good for the eyes to strain them with such fine needlework. I am not allowed to crochet anymore. Mama showed me how to knit instead, which in reality is a lot easier. The needles are huge, and the final product gets done faster. I am making a long wool scarf with Mama and a dainty crochet piece at Encarnação's house, but that is a secret between Encarnação and me.

Wintertime with Encarnação is always wonderful! We both sit in the living room, where she has a small round tea table with a charcoal fire underneath. This is the only heating system in the whole house. It's more than what we have, for we don't have anything to heat our house with. When her daughters are visiting, we all sit around her tea table, keeping our feet warm, and we eat roasted chestnuts and drink lots of hot milk with a dash of coffee.

Encarnacão's son Eduardo is very nice to me, and he lets me play with his toy airplanes. He told me that someday he is going to be a pilot. His two sisters are beyond their teens. They are grown-ups. Bonéca, the youngest, is going to be a flight attendant, because she is very beautiful. She looks like a model. Her sister Annette is not pretty, but she is getting married in a few months. Mama hired her to tutor me in Arithmetic. I don't like Encarnacão's daughters. Bonéca was making fun of the way I dress. I happen to agree, but that doesn't give her the right to pick me up in the air and lift my skirt to show my underwear to the maids in the kitchen. They made fun of me and laughed loudly at my colorful underwear. If Encarnação had found out, she would have punished her. I am sure of that. I will never talk to Bonéca again, and I will hate her forever. She may be very beautiful on the outside, but inside she is an ugly monster.

I have watched Mama making my underwear. She cuts two squares out of two pieces of very colorful cotton and then she cuts a V-shape at the bottom to make way for the legs, and sews it that way. After that, she inserts a drawstring at the waist to tie it up—only, when she has elastic band available, she uses that instead. Because she is

The Journey of Innocence

trying to make them last a few years, they are usually too big for me so I have to roll them around my waist, which makes me look fat and square. Someday I will have normal underwear, but right now we can't afford extra frivolous stuff.

Annette never smiles, and she treats me like a child who is bothering her. She uses a pencil for torturing me. Every time I make a mistake in Arithmetic, she hits my knuckles with it. I feel sorry for her future children if she is going to teach them Arithmetic. They will wind up with bumpy, ugly knuckles, probably to match their ugly faces, like their mother's. Encarnação's daughters are nasty. I went home and cried this afternoon. I wasn't going to cry in front of Annette no matter how much it hurt. Mama saw my red knuckles, and I'm now without an Arithmetic tutor.

I like my friends at school, but not the curriculum. I am a terrible student. I don't understand what the teacher says. It all sounds like *jibber, jibber, jibber*. I get bored, and I try very hard to stay awake in class by chewing on pencils and sticking the tip between my gums. The school building is very old and smells of ink, rotten wood, and books. The classes are very large and overcrowded.

Mama told a fib to the teacher so she would put me in the front row. Mama told the teacher that I don't see or hear very well, and unless I'm sitting up front, I will learn absolutely nothing.

Across from the little round park in front of our school, there's a tall, white church. I like to go inside once in a while just to see why everybody likes to go in. They say God lives there, but all I see are gray stone tombs, stone angels, and saints surrounded by candles. It's hard to see and breathe inside the old church. I feel much happier when I come out to the fresh air outside. I doubt that God lives inside that church. If I were God, I would not want to live in a dreary place like that. Back and forth from school, I enjoy walking into the shops and listening to the shop vendors and their customers. I like wandering in and out of their shops and looking around to see what kind of merchandise they have and what's new. Across the street from our house, the cranky lady in the cave below the first floor has no shop, just a window that opens to the street where her female clients drop off sheer silk stockings to be mended. Sometimes Mama sends me over there with a couple of her silk stockings to be fixed. It's cheaper to fix them than to buy a new pair. The stocking lady never talks to me except for giving me a scribbled receipt and saying, "You can pick them up next week." And then she closes her little window.

Around the corner, the shoemaker also has a window on the ground floor. It is level to the sidewalk, but he keeps it open. He always welcomes an exchange of small talk, and has told me his dream. Someday soon, he will be going to North America with his wife and children. He has put in all the necessary papers with our government, and now he has to wait patiently.

Down the street from him, there's a big grocery store. Senhor António is the owner, and he is always there, standing by the door of his establishment. He runs a fully packed grocery store with lots of burlap bags full of potatoes and grains and legumes and all kinds of dry goods. It's very difficult to see clearly because Senhor António never turns on the lights inside the store. It seems to me that he is trying to save electricity, or he belongs to the bat family. I don't have the courage to say anything, but I believe that I could make his grocery store a lot more attractive by having everything more neatly organized. Maybe it's so crammed full and cluttered because it's hard to see inside the shop. I don't know how he finds anything in the dark. He never smiles and doesn't seem happy. Mama buys all our dry groceries from him. She calls him

The Journey of Innocence

on the phone, and then his grocery boy delivers the groceries to our house.

The bakery on the corner only makes bread, and everything is covered with white flour, including the floors, walls, and workers. I would not want to hug a baker. It has got to be the whitest bakery I have ever seen. In the wintertime, it is the place where I take our dinner once in a while to be baked. For a couple of *escudos*, they let us use their oven, and we use it when Mama makes our favorite meal, *Empadão de carne*. I love *Empadão de carne*. It is very tasty, and I especially love the salty, oily black olives studded into the golden mashed potatoes on top of the ground meat.

The storekeeper in the gift shop is always telling me to either buy something or get out. She must be afraid that I will hear some top-secret gossip about someone in the neighborhood. This is the gossip shop. The women in the area seem to gather here to talk about everybody else. Some women are dressed in black from head to toe, which means they lost a family member. This goes on for a year, even two years, but, if one of them is dressed in black year after year, it means she lost her husband or son possibly to the sea or maybe a car accident. In Portugal, when there's a car accident, most of the time someone dies because most drivers are compelled to drive too fast and don't like to follow the laws of the road. Like frustrated bull fighters, they see the car coming toward them as the bull and themselves as the *matador*.

The manual workers' favorite places for lunch are the two taverns that are between our house and my school down the street. There are also the regulars who spend the day drinking and pass the time talking to each other and socializing. I like walking into the taverns and making believe that I'm looking for somebody. Then, as I walk out, I hit the beaded curtains on purpose with my shoulders so that they make a rattling noise as they swing into each other. I would like to know what men talk about in these dark taverns and why they drink so much. They probably like the smell of wine mixed with fish stew and olives, or maybe they tell stories of pirates and islands far away and treasures hidden inside some caves by the shore. It's even darker in these taverns than in Senhor António's grocery store, possibly because both taverns are narrow and deep, and their doorways are covered by long curtains of wooden beads that block the sun from coming in, like the beaded curtains found at the meat market's doorway. During the summer, these curtains are supposed to keep the flies from entering. I like feeling the beads on my face and body when I walk in and out, that is, if the owner of the establishment doesn't get annoyed and throw me out. I keep going around and around, under the beaded curtains until they tangle around me, then I listen to the rattling sound they make against each other as they slide back down to their original place. Most of the men inside are old and cranky, and they get annoyed with me, calling me a child and telling me to get lost. They have no humor. They were born only to drink. The walls of both taverns are covered by large, wooden wine barrels stacked one on top of the other. This makes more room for customers to walk in, but it also obstructs the light from entering the already small, narrow establishments.

I still don't like school. I am barely passing the tests. We all sit in our own designated wooden chair attached to a desk. There's a small round hole to the right of the desktop where we keep the glass inkwell along with the blotter and a long wooden fountain pen. We have to use a lot of care not to damage its delicate metal tip. We also use pencils. Writing with ink is a lot more fun, but it's a real mess when it drips on the paper if we are not careful and put too much ink in the tip of the pen—not to mention the teacher getting angry. I have gotten very good at using the blotter to go over the wet writing. I like the smell of ink. Next to my desk, there's another girl, and when she writes with her left hand the teacher yells at her and says she is possessed by the devil. She gets hit a lot over the knuckles and over her head with the wooden ruler. The teacher won't allow her to write with her left hand.

I am very lucky that I am right handed, but I have to wear wristbands to protect my weak wrists or I'll get hit with the ruler until they are red and swollen.

Spring of 1952

I like biting my fingernails as much as Max-Leão does. I stopped biting my toenails a few years ago, when my feet would no longer come up to my mouth that easily. Max-Leão and I were taken to the kitchen to be punished for our bad habit. José doesn't bite his nails. He doesn't have any bad habits. He suffers from asthma. I was scared. I thought that we were going to get beat up with some kitchen utensil. Aunt Heydee, Papa, and Mama were working together, and Aunt Heydee showed her concern by stating that only low-class, uneducated people have such a nasty habit. Mama held Max-Leão's hands and started rubbing a hot pepper on his fingernails.

"That will burn your lips every time you put your fingers to your mouth," said Josefina, the part-time maid who has a wacky look in her eyes. Ironically, she also bites her fingernails, but blames it on doing dishes and laundry.

Then the unthinkable happened. Max-Leão immediately put his fingers in his mouth and said in amazement, "Wow, this stuff is really good."

When I heard that, I requested some peppers, too.

Papa said, "This is not working out. Maybe soap is better. How about using soap for Verónica?"

But Mama didn't agree, "Verónica loves soap. She will be sucking at her fingernails even more."

Giving up on us, they told us that, every time they see us with our hands in our mouth, we are getting slapped right across the face. This is so unfair. I don't see what's wrong with biting my nails. I don't swallow them. I spit them out. Max-Leão and I decided that we would bite our nails when we are alone in our beds.

Max-Leão and I sometimes get into fights against other kids in our neighborhood. It happens mostly at the parks where we play or on the way home from the parks. A few times, we had to fight with our fists. Sometimes I go home with a bloody nose. The neighbor boys are a bunch of bullies. Mama says I am more like a tomboy than a girl, but that's not true. I am only defending myself.

I no longer go around pushing other kid's faces into the water fountain. One of the other boys thought it was funny to do it back at me, and I didn't like the way it felt when my mouth hit the metal faucet and I got a bloody lip. I have noticed that, whatever I do to someone, I get the same back, so I have to be careful not to hurt anybody anymore, unless I am defending my life and my brothers are with me.

Our garden has long been gone. The walls around it are easy to peel and inside the pitted holes are homes for the worms and the salamanders. When I am bored, I peel the chipped paint from the backyard's wall and look for the worms that, upon being touched, curl up for protection. Some people call them *pill bugs* or *sow bugs*. I call them *roly-polys*. They have very strong muscles, and it's hard to open them again, so I set them up on top of the wall, and with a flick of my fingers, I see how far I can fling them into the distance.

    The green wooden door has lost its color, and the hinges are corroded by the weather and neglect. To enter our backyard, the door has to be lifted and then dropped.

The Journey of Innocence

Otherwise, it will stay up in the air. Our garden is just an arid area of dirt with a few stalks of artichokes, which I eagerly await to grow so that Mama can cut off the thick and delicious stems and cook them with meatballs. Our most cherished possession is the *nespra* tree, still alive and providing us with its sweet fruit. Our neighbors look down at us because we are poor and can't afford a gardener anymore. Besides the *nespra* tree, we also have a gum tree. It was planted about three years ago, and we have been using the sticky gum to starch Papa's shirts.

I can't wait for the summer so the neighbor's sweet peas can grow, climb over the cement wall, and fall on our side of the yard. Then I can sit next to the wall and read my books while breathing in the summer smell of sweet peas. I also love climbing the *nespra* tree, which is my personal island. From the very top, I can see the neighbors' gardens, their chicken coops, and their pet dogs and cats. Farther in the distance, I can see other trees and houses and mountains and valleys. While I sit in the middle of the desert, in my oasis surrounded by *nespras* and their lush, green leaves, I dream of flying away to faraway lands and traveling like Gulliver and Marco Polo.

I have a serious problem in Arithmetic class, where we all sit on long benches next to each other because the class is so overcrowded. The girl who sits next to me keeps trying to slip her hand under my skirt. It's my fault because, if I were sitting up front, she wouldn't dare do that. But, if I sit up front, the teacher will ask me questions, so I sit in the last row hoping not to be seen. I hate school. I hate Arithmetic. I don't know who to talk to about this girl in school. When I move away from her, she moves in my direction. I know that, if I say something to Mama, I will be in trouble for not sitting in the front row. The schoolteacher is not nice either, as she was making fun of Mariana, a girl who used to be pretty before her parents punished her for misbehaving. They punished her by cutting all her long curly red hair very, very short. Now the teacher calls her unsightly, and she is no longer her favorite student. I feel sorry for Mariana.

When I tried to go back into class after lunch today, there was a big commotion about the tall, heavy, wooden bookcase in the hallway. It had fallen on top of a student. Some of the girls said another girl had gotten killed. I also heard she was taken to the hospital half alive. Nobody knows for sure, and nobody knows who it was. I wonder if it was the girl that used to sit next to me. I hope she didn't die, but I do wish for her to be gone forever.

We celebrated four birthdays over the weekend. Papa is not only selling magazines, but he also sells butter door to door. He must be doing very well, or they borrowed the money from Aunt Heydee to buy movie tickets for the whole family. Papa's birthday was April 30, mine was May 7, Aunt Heydee's is May 9, and José's will be at the end of this month. We all went to the movie theatre to see the Disney movie *Snow White*. I loved it! It was very good, but the best part was being with my parents, my brothers, and Aunt Heydee next to me. What a wonderful day it was. To top it off, at the movie theatre Papa bought the Disney book of stamps for my brothers and me, and we can now spend days sticking the stamps of the movie characters in the Disney book.

Summer of 1952

Max-Leão and I heard some very alarming news while sitting on the park bench very close to where Encarnação lives. Yes, we were eavesdropping. We both wanted to know what old people talk about. Or maybe I just wanted to

The Journey of Innocence

know it myself, because I gave the idea to Max-Leão.

"Let's sit next to those two old ladies and see what they talk about," I said.

One old lady said to the other, "It's just appalling that birthdays have to be celebrated. They should do away with birthdays. We are as young as we feel."

And the other one said, "Oh my dear, but that is exactly what's going to happen. Birthdays are just going to be a thing of the past within a few more years. No one will celebrate their birthday. After all, it's just a number."

When I got home, I told the story to Mama and asked her opinion. She said, "Don't worry, when you get to be that old, you get senile and don't know what you are saying." Obviously those two ladies were very old. What a relief!

There's an old woman who lives in the building next to our house. I watch her a lot as she sits for hours on one of the benches in her backyard. She is dressed all in black from head to toe. She stares into space and talks to invisible people. Mama says that the old lady is talking to herself, because that's what happens when you get to be so old. You lose your mind. But I wonder if she is seeing something that we are not able to see.

Autumn of 1952

When I got to school today, there was a line of kids having vaccines given by some doctors in white jackets. These doctors looked like the ones who took out my tonsils in the hospital a few years back. I hid behind a door and saw some kids crying as they were getting shots in their arms. I sneaked out of school, and when I got home, the only place I could think to hide away was under the kitchen sink. I closed the wooden doors behind me and stayed curled up until about lunchtime, when I heard Mama and Aunt

Heydee calling my name. The more they yelled, the more I was scared. I tried to stay very still hoping for a miracle. It was going to be painful once they found me. I figured that Mama was going to beat me over the head, and then later in the day I would get the same dosage from Papa. I decided that, if necessary, I would spend the rest of my life under the kitchen sink.

Then I heard Mama saying, "We know that you ran away from school because of the shots. I don't blame you! It's okay to come out from wherever you are hiding. I promise you don't have to have the vaccine if you don't really want it."

I came out, and after a few yells, they were all laughing about my fear of needles and I didn't get hit. I was surprised that they were actually relieved and happy to see me.

Uncle Augusto made a special trip to Grandma's house just to give me the much-hated vaccine shot. It's either that or I cannot go back to school. At Mama's request, he gave me the shot on my bottom instead of my arm.

"It's bad enough that she was born with an ugly beauty mark on her abdomen," Mama said to her brother, who was insisting that the shot is normally done on the arm. She wasn't going to give up that easily. She made the argument that she was afraid that the shot might leave a scar on my arm, and men only marry women with perfect skin.

He told her he had never heard anything so dumb in his life, but had no time to quarrel with her because he was already running late.

Celeste, our part-time maid, came to pick me up from school today. She told me that Mama and Papa wanted me home immediately. Lisboa was burning to the ground because of a huge fire in one of the arsenals. My brothers were already home from school. The neighbors and all of

The Journey of Innocence

us climbed up to the very top of the black metal stairs behind our house to see the spectacular fire that was causing all kinds of fireworks. We all took turns using Papa's binoculars to see if the church next to the arsenal was in danger of getting burned. It was a beautiful sight of fiery red and yellow flames in the distance. The church bells were ringing, alerting everyone to get away from the fire. This is the way Rome most likely burned to the ground when the Emperor needed inspiration to play his lyre. We kept taking turns with the binoculars so that we could enjoy the colors of the flames up close. Lisboa didn't burn, nobody got burned, and the church only got lots of smoke inside, so everyone agreed it was a true miracle by the grace of Saint Mary, Mother of Jesus.

Last week, the teacher made a hat from the daily newspaper *Diário das Noticias*, and after shaping it with donkey ears, she put it on my head and forced me to sit on the classroom veranda facing the street so that the people passing by could laugh at me. I thought I was going to die of shame from being seen as a donkey. It was while seated at the veranda that I developed a crying technique. I let the tears build in my eyes until they were covered and I couldn't see anything.

Max-Leão has it a lot rougher than I do. I learned multiplication last year, but he is having problems remembering the 7's and 8's tables, and Mama is teaching him. The way she teaches is by making him repeat the multiplication tables while she sits on top of him and hits him over the head with her hands. I am surprised that he doesn't faint. I consider myself very lucky. I'd rather use a donkey hat and have people laughing at me than get beat to a pulp.

My friend, Maria Leonor, has a brain tumor. She needs brain surgery, or she will die. Mama always tells me that I am a weakling and that I have weak lungs, but what Maria Leonor has sounds a lot worse. They say she might not survive the surgery, which means she might die. Dying means you can't breathe anymore and you can't see or feel anything around you. You stop existing. You turn into dust, and people walk on top of it not even realizing that they are stepping on someone's dust. I don't want to die, and I hope and pray that Maria Leonor will live. I am scared of death.

Mama likes to tell us the joke about dirt and death: Once upon a time, there was a woman who didn't like cleaning her house and refused to dust. It got to a point that the dust became really thick. When a friend of hers came over to her house and realized that she wasn't home, she left a message on the dusty table, "Dear Maria, how many people have died in your house? There's dust everywhere!"

I used to think that was funny, but not anymore. It is a stupid story.

Aunt Morena, my mother's other sister, just came back from Funchal on the island of Madeira to live in Portugal. She left her overweight, abusive husband who liked to drink beer and fool around with other women. According to Morena, her husband remarked upon seeing his newborn baby girl, "Too bad she is my daughter. She sure is going to be a beautiful girl."

Aunt Morena is waiting to be legally divorced from her monster husband who is also a Catholic. That explains why he is not a good husband, as he is not a Jew. She now lives in Grandma Rica's house with her fifteen-year-old beautiful daughter, Esther, and her seventeen-year-old, ugly, tall, skinny, pimple-faced son, Leão.

I don't like Leão. He asked me to sit on his lap, and he slipped his hand up my skirt and tried to touch me between my legs. I immediately got up, and I have been successful at staying away from him. I can't tell Mama. I'm afraid to get into trouble. I know that I would be blamed for it

The Journey of Innocence

somehow. When he comes near me, I spit at him, and I know that he knows why.

Winter of 1953

I just can't believe this is happening. Mama made Cousin Leão my private Arithmetic teacher at home. And because of him, I got into serious trouble at school on Monday. Over the weekend, Leão came over to our house and Max-Leão and I showed him our new blackboard hanging on the wall of our bedroom. We have white and colored chalk! We use the blackboard to write Arithmetic problems, and Portuguese and French grammar. If we make a mistake, we just wipe it off with a soft flat brush, but the dust makes us cough a little when we breathe it in. José's asthma really gets messed up when he is in the room with us. The three of us like collecting as much powder as possible on the bottom shelf of the board and playing with it. It's fun to make the dust fly and see it hit by the sunlight coming through the bedroom window shutters. Cousin Leão was very impressed with our huge blackboard, but, instead of teaching us Arithmetic, he showed us how to draw a naked woman. All it took was six lines and a bunch of dots in the right place for the pubic hair. It was truly amazing. I can't even draw a jar in school. It always comes out crooked on one side. This was too great of an art skill not to show it off. So, on Monday when I was between classes, I gathered a few of my classmates, and trying to impress them, I drew six lines and a few dots with my black ink pen and there it was, a naked woman's body. Someone must have run out of class and snitched on me to the principal, because, before I knew it, I was standing in front of the class with a teacher yelling at me for producing an obscene drawing to a bunch of innocent fellow classmates. Mama was called in, and I was suspended from school for a week.

That was a very good thing to happen, because, when

Mama found out that I had gotten the *art* lesson from Cousin Leão, she stopped his private tutoring with me. I couldn't tell her that Leão always found a way of putting his hand palm up on the seat just before I sat to study Arithmetic with him, and it was very annoying and hard for me to concentrate on the problems when I was trying to crush his hand with my weight. He is a lousy teacher, and I hate him.

We no longer have a piano at home, but I get to hear Mama play the piano at Grandma Rica's house. It is wonderful, because children are allowed to be in the room and I can sit and hear my Aunt Heydee sing opera like Madame Butterfly and other very high-pitched singers. She makes some of the older women in the room cry because they feel sad when she sings about love and losing the one you love. I like being with everybody, but I don't care for opera with its high-pitched dramatic sound.

I love when Mama plays popular songs very fast and loud on the piano, and everybody sings along. That is a lot of fun. I get to sit on Grandma Rica's lap, and I get kisses and hugs. Grandma Rica lost her husband Leão, my Grandpa, many years ago, even before Mama got married. Grandpa was born in the south of Portugal. One night he had a dream about a girl who lived across the water and he would be marrying someday. So, he took the boat across the Gibraltar waters and went to Tangier to look for the girl of his dreams. While in Tangier, he was invited to a party, which happened to be at the house owned by the parents of my future grandma. As was customary in those times, young girls looking to be married would come into the living room and dance or sing for their parents' guests. Rica and her sisters came into the room one at a time to meet Leão, my future grandpa. When he saw my Grandma, he immediately fell in love with her. She must have felt the same way, because they were soon married and went to

The Journey of Innocence

Brazil to raise their family. After their first child died, they successfully had five girls, Heydee, Simy (my Mama), Nelly, Morena, Ligia, and two boys, Augusto and Abraham. They all lived in a very small village called Ticaticuaria by the Amazon River, a long, long ride by horse-pulled carriage from the city of Manaus.

Grandpa Leão had a grocery store and a rubber plantation. He was very successful. Grandpa Leão was very kind and very smart. His name Leão, or Lion, fit him perfectly because he was very strong. When a carriage pulled by a horse fell over a man crossing the street on a rainy evening, he saved the man's life by lifting the heavy carriage with his bare hands. When a giant snake attacked a mother giving milk to her baby, he ran into the cottage after hearing her screams and pulled the snake off her and the child. He broke the snake's neck with his bare hands.

Mama remembers everything that happened in the days when they lived in the jungles of Brazil. One of the grossest stories I heard was that, once in a while, the kids were constipated and Grandpa had to slip one of his fingers into their anus and carefully pull the poop out—kind of like unclogging the sink when it's stuck with junk.

Living by the Amazon River in those days, one had to be very careful not to fall into the hands of the Indians who shrunk heads as a prize, or cross the river when the piranha were swimming close by. Children are like candy to a hungry piranha. A horse and even a cow is a lot bigger than a child, but still they have no chance for survival if they happen to be crossing the piranha-infested river.

An interesting story happened one day when Grandma Rica was taking care of their grocery store. She cut her finger while peeling potatoes with a very sharp knife. She was alone, and not knowing what to do to stop the bleeding, she stuck her bleeding hand into the nearest open white wine barrel. It was one of those instant reactions a person has without even thinking about it. Just then, someone came in and noticed the pink wine. "Mrs. Ezaguy, you got pink liquor now. That is incredible. Please give me two full bottles of it."

She was too embarrassed to tell him what had happened. That day, she sold the whole barrel of wine because everyone wanted to try the pink wine. She never again put her blood into wine. It was just an accident that turned out good.

As the years went by, the ships stopped coming to Ticaticuaria, and when that happened, they were impoverished and had to return to Portugal. Grandpa Leão died from a stroke when Mama was still very young. How young, nobody will ever know. That's Mama's secret. She doesn't want anyone to know her present age, and if anyone dares to ask her such a question, she will say, "A woman is ageless and should never be asked such an offensive question."

Aunt Heydee, the eldest daughter, took over the financial burden and full responsibility of helping with the household and raising her siblings. Grandma Rica taught French, Latin, and Arithmetic at home, but her health was not the best. Aunt Heydee taught French and gave piano lessons privately in people's homes, and with that money she helped her family with the apartment's rent and monthly bills.

Mama has names for all our neighbors in the building. They go by what they do. The woman above us is called *drip woman* because Mama can hear the water running when she uses the bidet several times during the night. This annoys Mama because it wakes her up. The drip woman's real name is Rosa. The neighbor Sofia above Rosa, on the third floor, is the *woman in black*, and her two daughters are the *girls of the woman in black*. Sofia is a widow, and black is the only color she has worn since her husband died twenty years ago.

The Journey of Innocence

The neighbor below us is the *kept woman*, and she is called that because she doesn't work. Her lover, who is married and with children, pays for all her living expenses. Her name is Maria Elena.
Next to us is the *next-door woman*, because she is next door. Above her are the *foreign woman* and her *foreign family*. We rarely see or know who lives there, as they are always out traveling. On the floor directly above them, nobody knows who lives there. The *renters* are the ones below the *next-door woman*. There's always someone new moving in, and as soon as we learn their name, they move out.

I have gotten into trouble again. I'm going to lose my best friend Encarnação. What am I going to do? But I didn't lie. I was spending the afternoon at Encarnação's home with her niece Laura. We were both sitting at Encarnação's tea table with the hot coal below our feet. Laura was reading a book, while I was studying my grammar. Then a man came in. It was Laura's boyfriend, because he called her *honey* and they kissed on the lips. While they were seated on the couch, he kept trying to put his hands into her blouse, but I made believe that I wasn't seeing anything. He said they were going to the kitchen to make me tea. They left the room, and later they brought me tea and cookies.
While I was seated at the table, they both sat on the floor. He tried to put his hands under her skirt. She kept asking him to stop and pushing his hands away, looking at me embarrassed.
Finally, I said, "Stop that. Don't you see that she doesn't want you to touch her that way?"
He got angry and told me to shut up and keep studying. She asked him to leave, and he did.
When I got home, I told Mama what happened, and she must have told Encarnação. The result was that both of them said I had exaggerated what I had seen. As such, I

was damaging her niece Laura's reputation and conduct. I am so embarrassed over this. I didn't mean to hurt anyone. I just thought if Mama spoke to Encarnação then she could protect Laura from that man. I have to learn not to react to other people's problems and, most of all, not to tell Mama anything.

For a couple of months, a ghost has been knocking at Grandma Rica's door. That is the only explanation according to neighbors, friends, and family, because every time they open the door there's nobody there. This is very, very, very scary. The knock can happen in the middle of the night or any time during the day. A policeman was hired to stand behind the closed door and wait for the knock, and the neighbors were on the lookout, but no luck. It all started after Christmas. It looks like it is a ghost because, while the policeman was there, the knocks stopped, but then started again when he left. After months of sleepless nights, Grandma Rica and others in the house are becoming nervous wrecks.

What a relief! The ghost was the neighbor downstairs! They were trying to scare Grandma into moving out so that their daughter, who is getting married in April, could move into the apartment above them. Aunt Heydee was the one who discovered the plot. Without telling anyone, she drilled a hole from inside the closet wall facing the steps to Grandma's front door. With a flashlight in hand, she spent a few nights awake, looking through the hole to the outside. Sure enough, she saw the neighbor's husband running up the stairs. After knocking at the door, he would run up to the next flight of steps so that he would not get caught. Aunt Heydee saw it all and called the police. His wife cried for mercy, and Grandma felt sorry for the "ghost's wife," so he was told to stop and was not arrested. From all the embarrassment, there's talk that the "ghost family" will be

The Journey of Innocence

moving out soon.

I like reading the comic books at Sofia's house, our neighbor on the third floor. I can only read them when I am visiting her. She won't allow me to take them with me to read at home. But that's okay. I have learned to enjoy the smell of her apartment. It is furniture wax mixed with garlic, vinegar, and cleaning fluid. She doesn't talk too much. She looks sad in her black dress, black apron, black socks, and black shoes. She stays busy cleaning the house, and she leaves me alone to read the comics in her sunroom.

My favorite comic book is about the old prairie man who lived in the desert of Arizona in North America. He was very old, about a hundred and five years old, so he no longer could kill buffaloes. One day, he got sick from old age. Everyone was outside his tent while waiting to see if he was going to live or die. Of course, everyone knew that he was going to die very soon, because nobody lives past a hundred and five. Then, as everyone came into his tent, surrounded his bed, and looked anxiously at him, he sat up and said, "Present!" He took a deep breath, and falling peacefully on his back, he was dead. He had gone to God without suffering. I hope I drop dead too when I have to die.

Grandma Rica has new neighbors. The other neighbors are in an uproar. They are complaining because their neighborhood is becoming low class and they can't do anything about it. The apartment where the "ghost family" used to live has been rented out to very beautiful older girls, barely covered with colorful silk robes and busy opening their front door to strange men. When that happens, while I am going up the steps to visit Grandma, I am to turn my head the other way. I'm not allowed to look in that direction, but I peek to the left side and they always say hello to me and smile. I heard that these girls play with men's penises to give them pleasure, and they get paid very well for it. A lot of the men visiting them are married men, and they go there because their wives are not perverted and refuse to give their husbands perverted sex. This is the only way they can get it, when they pay for it. According to Mama, her sisters, and her girlfriends, only single men should be allowed to visit these girls, and if anything, the whole whorehouse should be in another part of town and not right under Grandma's apartment.

I was playing yesterday on the lower steps of Grandma Rica's house with my two younger cousins Sonia and Elsinha, when a fat, ugly, old man with moles on his face walked into the hallway. As he walked up the steps, he pinched Sonia's buttocks very hard. She was crying after that, and the man just laughed as he knocked at the "girls" door and a pretty girl in a pink silk robe let him in. We all ran upstairs to Grandma, who was very upset over what happened, but nothing could be done about it.

I like being helpful, but I get into trouble when I try to be nice. I am clumsy. I am defective, and I have known that for a long time. Something is wrong with me. I don't know exactly what, yet. I can tell that I am different from everybody else. I can also tell that everyone else is a lot smarter than I am.
    I was visiting Sofia, as I always do when I have nothing else to do. I like sitting in her guestroom and reading the comic books she has kept through the years from when her children were younger. She doesn't throw anything away. I also like to follow her around the rooms as she dusts and shines her silver platters and silverware. Her apartment is very clean and organized. Her two daughters are all grown up and don't visit her as often as she would like them to. Her husband died a long time ago. She lives alone, and she doesn't mind when I come over. I have never seen her bake

any cakes or sweets. Her kitchen never smells of vanilla or toasted almonds or melting chocolate, as Encarnação's kitchen does. Sofia doesn't like sunshine, and her wooden shutters are always closed. When she is in the kitchen, she is always busy grinding meat in the metal grinder or soaking rabbits in vinegar or boiling snails with garlic and olive oil. Sofia always puts a few snails in a plate for me to eat. I love snails. I use one of her safety pins to pull the little creatures out—very tasty, indeed. She never offers me other food, just snails. Thank God, because I would not eat rabbit, that's for sure. I have never seen a skinned cat, but I bet you couldn't tell the difference if they were skinned side by side with a rabbit. So, there I was watching her cut some meat and put it through the meat grinder, when suddenly she couldn't turn the handle. The wheel inside the grinder was stuck with all the meat and gristle inside of it and would not roll over. She was cursing the grinder and life because she had to pull the whole grinding machine apart, so I decided to give her some of my expert advice. I asked her why she did not use a knife to pull the meat out, like my mother does. Just stick it inside like *this*—and I showed her how. I twisted the knife inside the roller blades and broke the knife inside the grinder. She yelled at me and told me never to come back to her house again.

A whole week has gone by, and Sofia sent a message downstairs that I should come and visit her. She had made me something very special. I was relieved to find out that she was still my friend. She had prepared my favorite dish, a batch of snails. But she had bought giant snails with long antennas, and I simply could not put one in my mouth. I would have to be a cannibal to eat something that big. She kept saying, "C'mon, try it. I got the big ones this time, just for you. Don't you like them?"

They were gross and plain disgusting. How can anyone eat those creatures when they are huge and have long antennas? I didn't want to hurt Sofia's feelings, so I made believe that I was eating them by putting them in my mouth, but then carefully stuffing them to the sides of my mouth. When she left the room, I ran out the back door and spat a mouthful of snails into the downstairs neighbor's yard.

Mama got a call from Encarnação. Maria Leonor's surgery to remove the brain tumor was a success, and she is back from the hospital, alive—but blind. I was invited to stop by and say hello to Maria Leonor. Luisa, our part-time maid, went with me.

As we entered Encarnação's home, we both backed away when we saw Maria Leonor. What had happened to my once-beautiful play friend? Her long blonde hair had been shaved off, and there was a big nasty scar in her skull. She was standing there looking into space, emaciated and surrounded by darkness. Luisa grabbed my arm as she backed away, horrified. I didn't recognize Maria Leonor except for her eyes, which were still blue, and her smile, still soft and without anger as she said, "Is that you, Verónica?"

My stomach twisted inside out, and I thought that I was going to throw up. Then I picked up my courage and went up to her and hugged her even though I was scared that what she had was contagious. She was horrible to look at, as if she were dead. I didn't cry until I left their house. I am better off being plain, even dumb. I don't care anymore if I am really nothing special to look at, but I can see. My hair is dark brown and my eyes are green, thank you God for that. I feel fine the way I am, any color. It doesn't matter, and I promise that I will never be jealous of anyone, ever again.

Later today, Mama told me that Encarnação had called to tell her that she was very impressed with me because I had hugged Maria Leonor, and the maid had backed away.

The Journey of Innocence

That meant that I had a good heart. I didn't tell Mama that I don't have a good heart and that I didn't hug Maria Leonor because I am good. I did it because I thought that, if it were me, it would be nice to have a hug from a friend. I was really afraid to catch her blindness, but I didn't want her to know how horrible she looked. I didn't want to hurt her feelings. If I didn't hug her, she would also know that she looked totally disgusting, and I couldn't do that. I am sad and ashamed to feel this way about my best and only friend. I don't feel good about my feelings this morning. I am selfish.

I told Mama what happened the other day when I visited Sofia. Now I am not allowed to visit Sofia anymore. I shouldn't have told Mama about it, but my feelings were hurt. What happened is that Sofia was having a friend over for tea. I was seated on the floor and reading some magazines when Sofia said to her friend, "Do you smell something—like a smelly fart?"

"Now that you mention it, yes, I guess so."

"Verónica, come here," said Sophia. As I approached her, she added, "Are you being a disgusting little girl by passing gas in our presence?" And before I could even reply that it wasn't me, she grabbed me and pulled my skirt up and took a sniff at my underwear. She said, "Yep, it's you alright. Get out of here and go home."

I left, crying of course. I knew I didn't smell bad, and I knew I had no gas either. It had to be her or her friend, but it wasn't me. I had to tell Mama about it, because I don't like to be called a liar unless it's true.

I brought home three of my girlfriends from school to play with me. I could only play with them in our backyard. Mama is ashamed of our house, empty of furniture with decaying walls and closets. One of the girls asked me if she could use our bathroom. I went running in and asked Mama if Joana could use our bathroom.

Mama's response was, "Tell her to go home and use her own bathroom. This is not a public bathroom."

I was so embarrassed that Joana was not allowed to come in to use our bathroom. She said she would never make it all the way home, and she made poop in one of the corners of our yard while we all looked the other way. Later that day, Mama made me go in the yard and remove the poop with some newspapers. I don't like Mama anymore. She is mean.

Spring of 1953

Last Sunday, Luisa took me to visit her family. They live in Alfama, the poorest borough of Lisboa. The house was very old and small, but very clean and smelled of green vegetable soup, my favorite. With each spoonful, I like to take my time and suck the mashed potatoes between my teeth. That way, I am able to maintain the finely chopped collard greens in between my lips and front teeth. I do that because I like the taste of chewing the collard greens at the end.

Then Julio, her spastic nephew who is six years old, so they said, came in the room and decided to look under my skirt. He didn't even tell me. He just lifted my skirt and stuck his head under it. So, I pulled him out, made a fist, and knocked him out.

When I got home, I heard nothing but abuse because I took advantage of a little boy. I should have been more understanding. Give me a break! Any boy, small or big, who pulls my skirt up to look up at my private parts is going to be knocked out cold.

Summer of 1953

I get to spend a lot of Sundays with Grandma Rica. She

The Journey of Innocence

helps me with Arithmetic and French, my two worst subjects in school. I don't like either. They are both boring. Spending the day with Grandma is like being in school, no time to play or simply have fun. I love hugging her and playing with her wrinkled hands, which I wish I had, but I don't want to spend my free time learning school stuff. She put me in her bedroom, closed the door, and told me that I could not play with my brothers until I studied more. My goodness, it's summertime, and I need some time off from using my brain. I am on vacation, and this means I should be playing and having fun. I cried because I was angry, frustrated, and jealous that Max-Leão and José were playing in her kitchen. Studying French is like learning Arithmetic, a brain torture. I wished that Grandma Rica would die, and then I could be free to go out and play.

I like sunshine, but I don't get along with too much heat, as I found out when I spent the day yesterday with Aunt Heydee at Estoril, her favorite beach. As always, Aunt Heydee knows how to find a free lounge chair available to sit on under one of the large umbrellas by the water at the esplanade, where everyone who has money sits and sips ultra-expensive cold drinks. I didn't play in the water or take a walk on the rocky cliffs. I just sat there next to her all afternoon. It's always fun watching the people go by and listening to Aunt Heydee's interesting conversations with whoever sits next to her. It was a hot, slightly hazy, lazy day, and the sun never really came out from behind the clouds.

When I come home, my room can be anywhere in the house. Mama is always changing the furniture from one room to another. This morning I got up and went to the bathroom next to my bedroom. I sat on the toilet and passed out. I came back to the world with my face burning from being slapped, and I was lying in bed shivering.

Uncle Augusto told Mama that I had a heat stroke from

being at the beach yesterday. From now on, I have to use a hat in the sun, and if it's too hot, I am to stay inside the coolest place around. I am a weakling, a good-for-nothing. I would never make it if I had to cross the desert or got shipwrecked and found myself on a deserted island without the shade of palm trees. The city is too hot in the summertime. Our only relief is to go to the beach at least once a week and cool off in the ocean. It's healthy to be near the ocean and breathe in the salty air. Everybody says the salty ocean water kills all illnesses. We can only afford the train ticket to the smelly beach of Oeiras, not too far from Lisboa. As soon as you exit the train, you can't miss the strong whiff of raw sewage. The small village of Oeiras must be dumping their sewage directly into the ocean and onto their beach. The Oeiras population must be very poor, because nobody cares to fix the problem. My brothers and I like to play in the sand. We build sand castles, but we are not allowed in the water because it's too polluted, which makes no difference because we can't swim anyway. Our only fun is catching the small purple ocean creatures that wash ashore and squeezing their purple ink out. We have contests to see who squeezes the most ink out of each one.

Aunt Heydee has taken me a few times to Cascais and Estoril. These are the only two beaches she will visit, because she likes to mingle with the rich and more intellectual people. There are no foul smells at these beaches. The air smells of salty seawater, seaweed, American tobacco, tanning lotions, and the perfumes that rich foreigners bring in from their countries.

My favorite park used to be the *Cesário Verde Parque* by Encarnação's house, but it has turned into a park for adults only. I used to like it a lot because it was small, and not too far from home so I was allowed to go there and play by myself or with my two brothers. I especially liked to roll on the grass from the top of the center mound and down the little hill until I hit the ground below. Then one day, the new gardener removed the smooth grassy hill and covered it with spiky plants, flowers, and bushes. None of us kids can use the hill to roll down. Our playground has been destroyed. A bunch of wooden benches have been added for people who need to sit. Nothing lasts forever.

I spend many afternoons at the *Parque Estefania*, a few blocks from our house. I sit there for hours and read the books they have in their outside library. For the most part, nobody bothers me. Then one afternoon, I noticed some girls and boys my age improvising on stories, like Cinderella and Little Red Riding Hood. One of them came up to me and asked me if I would play with them. I said "yes." But soon I found that we needed a director, and because I was the only one volunteering, I did it gladly. We have been gathering every Wednesday and Friday after lunch to perform for ourselves. It has been my passion this summer. Following the pattern of the story, and with imagination as our friend, we make fantasies become a reality.

Autumn of 1953

When Grandma Rica was young, she belonged to the Masons. Mama told me that her mother belonged to this group of secret people who helped others less fortunate. If it weren't for her, they would have died. Grandma Rica had been a spy for France during World War I. She was one of the very rare women who were accepted as a member of this secret society because of her education. Besides being proficient in many languages such as Hebrew, Arabic, Spanish, Portuguese, English, and French, she was a wizard at Arithmetic. She used to travel with her father as his secretary and bookkeeper, and it was while she was in France that she was inducted into the Masons and become an active member. When she married Grandpa Leão, she burned all the secret papers and buried what was left in her backyard. She could not divulge the names of the people she had worked with.

Aunt Heydee became the breadwinner at a young age. After her father's death and with her mother being sick, Aunt Heydee felt that, as the eldest, it was her obligation to see to it that her family was cared for. With a family to care for, she could only pay for the education of one of her two brothers. She had to choose between Abraham and Augusto. Because Augusto was smarter than Abraham, she took Augusto under her wing and paid for his tuition through medical school while my mother and her sister Ligia continued their studies at the Conservatory of Music.

Aunt Heydee's nickname is *Napoleão,* because, if she had been born a man, she would have conquered the world. She has never been married, and she will not settle for anything less than what she deserves; therefore, no one is perfect enough for her. He has to be religious, rich, handsome, young, intelligent, sensitive, yet strong and—most of all—has to like opera. She is not only the breadwinner of the house, but she is also the oldest of all the brothers and sisters, and she takes this position very seriously. Everybody respects her because she knows everything. On their wedding night, Aunt Ligia and her husband were having problems consummating their marriage because she was a virgin, whatever that means, so they called Aunt Heydee on the phone and asked her for advice. She told Ligia and her new husband to use a pillow under her bottom and to relax while having sex on the hard floor instead of the soft bed. After that, Ligia got pregnant. I learn a lot from sitting next to adults and listening to their conversations.

Grandma Rica fell down the other day. I heard that she is bleeding inside and might die. She is very old, and they say nothing can be done about it. I went to see her. She was lying down on her right side, facing the wall. I kissed her face, and she didn't even move. I am scared. I do not want her to die. Please God, I didn't mean for her to die. I just wanted to have time off to play. I say stupid things all the time because I was born stupid. I hate myself.

Grandma Rica died. I cried as hard as I could today. The more my eyes were burning from the tears, the better I felt. I was hoping that I could go blind like Maria Leonor. Never again will I see my Grandma's smile and kind look, as she would give me bread with bananas or homemade orange-peel jam. No longer can I play with her wrinkled hands. She will never hold me close again. I want to die, too.

Mama asked Papa to take me in his *lambretta*, a small motorcycle that he bought used. It's very cheap on gasoline. The ride will dry my tears away, she told him. Going for the ride and holding onto Papa made me feel better.

He said that from now on he would take me with him on business trips around Portugal because I am his oldest child and I liked riding the motorcycle with him. He is going to teach me how to read maps.

I heard Mama and Aunt Heydee talking about their brother, Uncle Augusto. He gave Grandma Rica a special injection so that she could die in peace. She was in too much pain, and nothing could be done to save her. He is a very kind doctor, and he also loved his mother a lot and couldn't bear to see her suffer when nothing could be done medically to save her. I hope I get to be old like my Grandma someday, but I don't want to suffer for many days before I die either. Mama likes to tell everybody how she was blessed because she held her mother in her arms as Grandma Rica took her last breath.

Winter of 1954

Sometimes after school is over, some of my school friends take me along to the church across the street. The church is a tall simple white building, with lots of white marble steps leading to a dark wooden double door. The inside is dark, and it takes a while to get your eyes used to the only available light coming from the smelly candles and narrow dusty rays of sunlight squeezing through two small stained-glass windows, as if daring to take no for an answer. It is always dark and smelly inside this church, and the stone walls inside are covered with saints made of wood and marble, dressed in gold, and adorned with precious stones.

It is a community church, and it doesn't have the splendor of the big churches made for large amounts of people like the one Encarnação took me to during last Easter's festivities when I got to kiss Jesus's feet. That church was so big that we both stayed in line all morning before we finally made it to the altar. Even though Jesus was made of wood, Mama had a fit when she found out. Mama blamed me for going to church with Encarnação. I should have refused to go. I was grounded for one month, and I was not allowed to visit Encarnação. This is not fair. Encarnação just wanted me to see her God, and she was sharing him with me. I will always love Encarnação.

Every year, probably to welcome spring, about a dozen poor couples are married at the community church, all at the same time. They get lots of gifts including expensive housewares paid for by local business people. This not only promotes their business as being run by good and kind people but also helps keep these girls in line for marriage and with good morals, which is what all Catholic girls are encouraged to do before they get old and become spinsters like my Aunt Heydee.

My friends at school are Catholic, and they are going to

The Journey of Innocence

Heaven. They want me to go to Heaven, too, when I die. They have told me over and over again that, if I repent and become a Catholic instead of being Jewish, Jesus would forgive me for having killed him. I have told them time and time again that I had nothing to do with it.

My two best friends Maria José and Josefina say that, if I go to church with them after school, I have a better chance of going to Heaven. I want them to be my friends, so I go to church with them at least twice a week. I don't want to offend them, but this church is very depressing with lots of dead people in stone coffins above ground and under the church floor. You have to step over them in order to walk inside the church—very creepy, indeed.

The people who lived a long time ago are now saints made of stone. Sinners now pray for forgiveness on their knees. They pray to these statues and ask for miracles. There are also lots of dark paintings with scenes of Jesus, a man who was crucified on the cross, and his mother, other saints suffering with him, and fat little angels all around.

The old and pale priest dressed in black walks inside the church rolling a necklace of beads between his fingers. He never smiles and speaks a foreign language called *Latin*. I don't know what he says when he does his sermon while we sit on the hard benches. The smell of candles and incense gives me a headache, just like when my friend Encarnação fixes my hair back into a bun on top of my head. Confession is very important, my girlfriends told me. You must confess every week to the priest behind the curtain.

I asked them, "What if you don't have anything to confess?"

They told me they have to make it up. Otherwise, they will be going to Hell. I don't want to be a Catholic if I have to lie for God to love me.

When Mama has company she always tries to impress her

guests. My brothers and I come into the living room, and then she asks the big question, "Tell everyone, where do babies come from?"

All three of us say in a chorus effect, "From big huge sunflowers!"

Mama and her guests giggle and go, "Ah, they sure are innocent!"

I have known that this is not true for quite some time. I am a good listener at Mama's gatherings with her sisters, and I collect a lot of information about life in general, including a lot of our family history. But because it makes Mama happy, I don't have the courage to tell her that I feel like a retard every time I have to act ignorant. What I don't know is how the baby got inside the belly in the first place.

I have been looking for God, but I have not been able to find Him. Mama took me to the temple a few months ago, but I didn't see God there either.

This is the only Jewish temple in Lisboa, and it's hidden behind a large metal door. Even the neighbors next to it don't know there's a temple next to them. Mama told me the reason it is this way is because of prejudice. If it's not seen, people with other religious beliefs can't destroy it. They think only their God is good. They are called *fanatics*. So, our temple is not like a church where everybody going by can make the cross across his or her chest. Also, our temple doesn't have saints on the walls or buried dead people inside tombs. Our temple is very simple inside except for the really nice, dark mahogany chairs. The temple was built for praying only. The men pray downstairs, and the women sit upstairs so there are no distractions while praying to God. It does have a medium-sized niche with doors, almost like an altar to God, but, when they open the doors, there are no stone saints nailed to crosses like in a church. Inside are the rolled manuscripts with words from God. I believe it's the Bible, but it's

The Journey of Innocence

written in Hebrew, so I don't know what they are saying when they read it out loud. I have been keeping my eyes and ears open at the temple. When I first saw a ray of sunshine coming through one of the small windows, I was hoping that was going to be it, but I don't believe that was God.

I admire the people praying inside. They must know something I don't. God must be invisible, just like Mama and Papa have told me so many times. Being invisible has to be a good thing. I would love to be invisible. Then I could go into a candy store and eat all the candy and chocolate I wish. I was at the temple last week and got bored listening to the rabbi (he has the same type of job as the priest in the Catholic Church) and the men below us praying in Hebrew, a very strange language. I have no idea what they were saying. It sounds a lot like German. They move their bodies back and forth as if they are dancing to the sound of their voices, and they never look up to see the women.

They are very religious. I don't understand why God doesn't understand Portuguese and can only be spoken to in foreign languages like Hebrew or Latin.

I made a big mistake! I told Mama about my visits to church with my friends from school. She gave me a big lecture about us being Jews and that it is a sin for us to enter a Catholic church. We have endured a lot of suffering and prosecution through the ages and during World War II.

Our ancestors would have wasted their lives in misery and abuse for nothing if I were to become a Catholic. I am not to date a Catholic, and when I get married, it will be to a Jew so that my children will be Jewish. Otherwise, my children will also marry Catholics and our religion will be lost forever.

Mama hung a picture of my two cousins from Germany on

my bedroom wall. They were very pretty girls, dressed in white organza dresses with big matching white bows properly set up on their long brown curly hair. One is seated by her piano, while the other stands holding a flute. They are both smiling at the photographer. They look like angels should look. They are only a few years older than I am. They were eleven and twelve years old when they were taken to a concentration camp. They were the only two daughters of my father's youngest sister, Ilse. The story goes that upon the rising of Hitler to power, her husband ran away. He abandoned her and the children in Germany. She arranged to save her children first by sending them to a school in Holland, thinking they would be safe there. She didn't expect the Nazis to invade Holland and take away all the children from that school into a concentration camp. All these years, Ilse has been writing to the Russian government to find out if their soldiers took her daughters to Russia when they attacked Germany. Until today, her letters have never been answered.

Mama gave us an anatomy book, where all the parts of the body just pop out from the page. When I looked at Max-Leão, who had been standing next to me as I flipped the pages, he was flat on the floor. He fainted when he saw the inside of a pregnant woman's belly with a baby inside of her.

Mama informed us that it's called a *fetus*. Mama must have realized that it was time for us to learn where babies come from. I already knew that, but, when I asked her how the baby got inside the belly, she said I was too young to know.

Spring of 1954

Mama brought home a clay pot with red and white carnations, Grandma Rica's favorite flowers, and she put

The Journey of Innocence

the container under the *nespra* tree. I see Mama watering the carnations just about every day with a tin can, and she cries. She really misses her mother. I miss my grandma, too.

Sofia, our upstairs neighbor on the third floor, died from a stroke. She went into a coma for about two weeks. The whole neighborhood was praying for her recovery. I wanted to go upstairs to see her. She was my snail connection and my silent friend—except for when she falsely accused me of making farts. But I already forgave her for that. It wasn't that important anyway. Mama would not allow me to see Sofia, but said that she was dying and that was no place for children. I was very sad after Sofia died. I will never see her again.

After they took Sofia's body away, I went to visit her oldest daughter, who was living in Sofia's apartment. Angela spoke of her mother with tenderness while washing her own personal underwear in the bathroom sink. It was made of silk and of different colors, not black. She told me that it was okay to have colorful underwear, as long as she wore black dresses to cover it in respect for her mother's death. Besides, it was just underwear, and that didn't represent how she felt in her heart. I told Mama how beautiful Angela's colorful underwear was. Mama said it was terrible that Angela wore colorful underwear. After all, her mother had died not even a month ago. Not wearing black was disrespectful.

I don't agree. I think that colorful underwear should be optional.

We were having lunch when Mama got a codfish bone stuck inside her throat once again. We all ran out of the apartment on the way to the first aid squad when the neighbors below us and the porters, living below them, upon hearing all the commotion, came out.

"What's wrong, Mrs. Wartenberg?"

Out of embarrassment, Mama put her fingers down her throat and, in desperation, pulled the fish bone out. She responded as rapidly as possible, "Nothing is wrong. I was just checking. I thought I heard the doorbell ring."

She ran back up the steps and into the apartment, and said, "I wasn't going to let them rejoice at seeing me choke to death."

Papa would never choke on a fishbone because he is an expert German fish eater. I have choked a couple of times on the very thin bones, but I coughed really hard until they came out. I hope Papa never chokes on a fish bone. He would be so humiliated.

The porters have made a list of offensive acts on our part, such as not taking care of our yard, making too much noise when my brothers and I play, not closing the door downstairs when we come into the building, or closing the door downstairs too hard—all petty stuff. The landlord is trying to throw us out so that he can rent our apartment for more money, but the law protects us as long as we pay the rent—even if it's at the last moment.

I won't be going to high school very soon. I have finished the four grades needed to enter high school, but our parents cannot afford to send Max-Leão and me to school at the same time. I would have to go to a private girls school, and they can't afford the expense. Mama doesn't want to take any chances that I might meet and marry a *goy* (a non-Jew). Max-Leão is not only smarter than me but also going to be a man. He will have to have an education so that he can work and take care of his family. Mama said I would be getting married to my Cousin Alberto from North America, so I don't need to be educated. My husband will take care of me. Besides, if I go to public high school, I will most likely fall in love with a *goy*, and if that were to happen, it would be the end of our religion from my side.

The Journey of Innocence

Max-Leão will go to an all-boys school, but only for a couple of years. Then, at fifteen years old, he will be sent to England where our cousins will make sure he goes to college and becomes an architect, which is what seems to be his inclination. When he gets married, he has to work and be able to provide for his own family. Our family in England has the finances to help him toward a good career.

"Our parents have set up our future," I told Max-Leão just before we dozed off to sleep last night. We like to talk about many wonderful things before falling asleep. Our favorite subject is fantasizing about an earthquake and we both get stuck under the entire rubble of a building for a week. Of course, we would like to be inside a candy store or a bakery when an earthquake hits Lisboa someday.

Summer of 1954

We are spending two months in Costa da Caparica, a huge beach across the River Tejo. We all got here on the back of a small pick-up truck. My brothers and I were sandwiched between the pots and pans, mattresses, some furniture, and boxes of clothing. It was a very bumpy and windy trip, and a few times I thought one of us was going to be part of the asphalt road. But we need everything we brought along, because the place where we are staying doesn't have anything except four walls, a door, and a wood stove.

This is not a beach for sissies like Cascais and Estoril, which are beaches for tourists and city people who don't really want to travel far. This beach is for the people of Portugal: clean, sparkly sand for hundreds of miles. I already tried to walk to the end and gave up after hours and hours of walking. Most likely, it keeps going until it reaches the Algarve way down in the south of Portugal. It was from the Algarve that the great Portuguese navigators made history when they left to conquer the world. Mama found our little cement shack for absolutely peanuts to rent.

The days are always the same. We get up, make the bed, get into our bathing suits, have a tall glass of coffee and milk in equal parts, and a *papo seco* (a small bread very close to French bread), and run to the beach to play. We carry the lunch bag, a bottle of water, a towel, a small tin bucket and a spatula for building our castles, and *the nail*, my favorite sand game.

We have our own white cloth tent that we rent for the whole time we are on vacation. Everybody has one, even the people who are here just for one day. It's used to store everything we have with us when we leave to play in the water. When the sun is too hot, we seek shade inside the tent we call *cabana*. Our *cabana* makes a great place to nap after lunch, even though it can get very hard to breathe without any fresh air inside. I usually lie down on the outside, on the side of shade where a breeze somehow passes by me. All the *cabanas* are made with four wood poles that stick into the sand. They are covered on all sides, including the top, with a white thick clothlike material. When you want to leave your valuables inside and go swimming, the front gets dropped and tied to the sides with rope.

Our valuables are food, towels, and water. Our lunch usually consists of fried fish and rice, or codfish cakes—which are potatoes and codfish, minced garlic, eggs, and parsley mashed together and molded into small cakes and then fried and served with fresh lemon. I don't like eating fried food because I always get nauseous afterward. I would rather have salad or fruit, whatever is in season, but we can't afford these luxuries. We are lucky to have codfish and potatoes every day.

During the week, Papa stays in Lisboa to work. He only comes over to visit us on Saturday afternoon and then leaves Sunday evening, back to the city. He has to work very hard in order to pay for our food, our stay at the beach for the summer, and all the daily things we need. I feel that

The Journey of Innocence

Mama should be working with Papa by his side instead of staying at the beach with us. I feel she is selfish, but I am not saying anything. I admire Papa for not giving up on all of us and working so hard, but that doesn't change the fact that I am afraid of talking or being near him. He never shows me any affection, and Mama never hugs me either. My brothers are her favorite children. José is the youngest and always sick, so he is definitely her favorite. Max-Leão ranks second in her heart. I am not loved by anyone. But, on the other hand, my parents no longer hit me as often as they used to, and for the most part they leave me alone to do whatever I like, which is mostly reading. I intend to read every book I can get my hands on this summer.

Last night, we went to bed without dinner. One of the soap boxes kept on a shelf above the stove fell into the open soup pot. No matter how much Mama tried to scoop out the soap bubbles, it just wasn't eatable, so we all went to bed hungry. Even though there isn't enough space for all of us in this house, I don't mind sleeping in the kitchen with my two brothers.

Mama feels very embarrassed to be staying in this place and hopes that no one she knows will see us living here. I am very glad to be here, and I don't care where I sleep as long as we have something to eat every day.

I believe that Mama has gained a certain kind of wisdom that has grown out of her personal experiences in life. She no longer gets upset about losing material things.
    Her favorite statement for everything that goes wrong is, "Better to lose the diamond rings than your fingers."
    I agree with that, but why lose anything at all?

Last night Max-Leão and I spent the evening peeling off the skin from under each other's feet. Not a good idea. We had to stay home today. We can't walk because the soles of our feet are very painful to walk on, so we read some books and then spent the rest of the day peeling the skin off our backs.

Mama believes that if she stands in front of the ocean waves when they crash for as long as she can bear them hitting her, they will beat the fat out of her body and she will lose weight. I don't think that's going to happen unless she stops eating. She is always pointing to other women who look bigger than her, but to me she doesn't look any smaller than them. I think it has to do with her eating so many raw eggs with sugar. I don't blame her though. It is the best dessert I can think of. She beats the raw yellow of the egg with sugar, and keeps adding sugar until it changes into a paste of just the right consistency. Then she adds pieces of bread to it, mashes it down with a spoon, and eats it like a cake. I believe this is a Spanish delicacy, because every time Uncle Augusto travels to Spain, he brings me a little wood barrel filled with egg and sugar. Last time he went to Spain, he brought me a silver bracelet, which was very nice of him. I do like it a lot, but I miss the little barrel of sugar and egg. Mama said the reason he brought me a bracelet instead is because I am a grown girl, not a baby anymore. What does a little barrel of egg with sugar have to do with me being grown up? I still like it.

We can't afford treats, but Mama found someone who was selling rennet apples by the box, and we now have enough apples for the whole month as long as we have only one each day. The apples are kept on the floor under my bed, where the stone kitchen floor keeps them fresh. I love the aroma coming from under my bed. I feel like I am sleeping on top of an apple orchard.

The days are very relaxing at the beach. Playing with my

The Journey of Innocence

brothers, we make holes in the sand and cover them with newspapers, and then, with just enough sand to hide the newspapers. We wait for a victim. While we hide inside our *cabana*, we laugh our heads off and hope that someone will fall into the hole. We have not had any luck so far, and this is a bit disappointing. We make sand castles and other artistic shapes like people and boats out of sand. We dig huge holes and take turns burying each other up to our heads in the sand, just like in Arabia when the warriors would ride their horses and, with a quick sweep of their swords, cut their enemies' heads off. When you are buried in the hot sunny desert of Arabia with just your head sticking out, you know your luck just ran out.

We spend endless hours just trying to outdo each other with stories and games, particularly the nail game. The purpose of the nail game is to get the nail to land straight and upright in the sand after some ingenious moves, as with sliding it off our elbows and other creative moves like interlacing it between the fingers. After we have our lunch of fried codfish cakes and bread, we have the midday nap inside our *cabana*.

We have started to relax on the water. Because we are less afraid, we now are able to float on our backs as long as the ocean is calm and there are no waves to run over us. We even ride the small waves on our tummies, but none of us is swimming far into the ocean like other people do. Then Mama had the great idea of paying a beach boy to take my brothers and me into the ocean. Why? Because it's good for us! The nasty bastard took José, who was smaller, under one of his arms, and Max-Leão and I followed him innocently, with no idea what was about to happen. He was supposed to be teaching us to swim. When he got to an area where the water was to his waist, he threw José into the water and pushed him under. Max-Leão took off as fast as a bullet. I tried to do the same, but the beach boy grabbed me by the hair and pushed me under, also. Gasping for air, I swallowed lots of water and thought I was going to drown. Somehow I slipped out of his hands, and between swimming and running, and by a miracle of God, I got to the shore where I cried and cried as I lay on the sand. I was screaming at the top of my lungs, cursing him, Mama, and the whole world of stupid, nasty people around me.

I no longer make holes in the sand and wait for people to fall into one of them. Whatever I do to someone, it will sooner or later happen to me. I fell into a hole in the sand. Some stupid kids were playing the same prank we were. My ankle got twisted as I fell into it, and they laughed as if it were a big joke. No, it's not a joke. I didn't laugh. It's so embarrassing to fall in front of strangers. I told my brothers about it, and they thought it was funny. I am staying away from them when they are digging. I will not be part of it anymore. Besides, it is absolutely childish.

It's almost time to go back to Lisboa. We have to be back to the city by the end of this month. Mama spends a lot of time in the sun, and we don't see each other unless it's lunchtime or dinner.

I was very sick a few days ago with fever and a stomachache. I was lying down in bed. Mama came to me and put her hand on my head, and said, "Verónica, you are going to be fine."

I started to cry with happiness. Her hand on my head was like being in Heaven, but I didn't say anything. I just closed my eyes. I didn't want her to think that I was a weakling begging for her love. The pain was gone, and I fell asleep.

Autumn of 1954

According to Mama, I have so far had every illness known

The Journey of Innocence

to children. Nope, it doesn't matter if I got vaccinated or not, and right now everybody at home has the mumps. I gave it to them. Even Mama and Papa are sick with it. We all have big chins, except Max-Leão. He says he refuses to catch it, and that's it. Mama is worried about him, because, according to her brother Augusto, it's better to have the mumps while you are young, in particular for men, because they can become sterile if they catch this disease while adults. This means that Papa is now sterile, too, which makes no sense because men don't have babies anyway. But whatever that means, he no longer can be a father again. Mama is on a mission to make Max-Leão catch the mumps. She kisses him in the mouth every day, and that is what I call disgusting. She even had him sleep with her so that she would breathe on him all night long, but he kept saying, "No, I won't catch it!"

I admire my brother. When he puts his mind to it, he really sticks with it. I wish I were like him. He is so smart.

Uncle Augusto has diagnosed me with juvenile rheumatoid arthritis. That's why I get horrible pain in my legs. I was born this way. Sometimes it hurts very sharp like knives sticking into my bones. Uncle Augusto is always giving me medicine, but it doesn't help at all. Mama makes me sit in the backyard with my legs in the sun. She says the heat is good for it, but that doesn't help either. The only thing that helps just a little is rubbing my legs, but they have to be rubbed really hard so that it hurts more than the bone pain. I cry a lot when it hurts. Thank God it doesn't hurt every day, just some days for no reason.

This morning I went to the *Parque da Estefanea*. I was looking for my friends the actors, but they were gone except for two girls I recognized. They were now mostly strangers, and they had another director. She was very bossy, and I could no longer be a director. I could only be an actress. I didn't care for that, so I returned to reading books at another park because I had already read the ones left there or were boring.

Papa has kept his promise. Whenever he has a trip out of town, he takes me with him on his *lambretta*. He is like a teacher, always correcting everything I do or say, and he has been teaching me how to read a map. He will pull his *lambretta* to the side of the road and say in his very heavy German accent, "Okay, Verónica, look at the map and tell me where to go from this point."

I am always scared that, if I mess up in the directions, he will never take me with him again, so I am very careful when I answer, "I believe that this map might be a little off. It looks like we should be going the other way."

"Yes," he responds. "Of course, because most Portuguese maps are either outdated or they are incorrectly printed. In Germany, maps are very specific and voyagers can depend on their precise and accurate maps. Germans are perfectionists, not like the Portuguese who could learn a lot from the Germans and how to make maps that are reliable and precise."

He is always bragging about Germans being of a superior race, at least much more superior than the uneducated Portuguese. I don't like the way he comes down on my fellow Portuguese since I am Portuguese and proud of it.

What I like about these trips is that I am with Papa and not only get to see the countryside but also get to hug him while I hold on to dear life when we travel over bumps and holes and between cars and up hills and down valleys. He stops at different towns and goes inside business buildings while carrying two large cases of magazines, one in each hand. My job is to keep an eye on his *lambretta*.

On the last trip to Sacavém, a little town not too far from Lisboa, I was waiting for Papa. I was standing with my

The Journey of Innocence

back against the building wall and trying to stay cool in the shade, when two old men came walking along the sidewalk. One stopped, looked at me, and said to the other, "Isn't she a lovely little girl?"

He walked over to me and squeezed my nose, and twisted it between his two fat fingers. He didn't count on my nose not being ready to be squeezed. I had been wiping it on my sleeves to blow off all the road dust from my nostrils, and now here was somebody's fingers. I was smiling when he found his fingers covered with snots from my runny nose. He will never again think it's cute to squeeze kids' noses.

I wish I could come up with a natural way of stopping Mama from doing something that is just as bad as the old man squeezing my nose. Just before we enter my cousin or aunt or some family or friend's house, she has the bad habit of slapping me on both cheeks to give me a rosy healthy look. Then, to top it off, she spits on her fingers and smooths down my eyebrows.

"Look everybody. Doesn't Verónica look so healthy! And such healthy pink cheeks!"

Well, how about mentioning the smelly lipstick spit on my eyebrows!

Max-Leão is going to marry a blonde girl someday. Every time he puts his mind to something, he does just that, and that's how I know. We were sitting at the community center and watching a children's show on stage. There was a blonde girl sitting in front of us. He kept staring at her.

"Verónica, look. Isn't she beautiful with blonde hair? Someday I will marry a blonde girl!"

He said it very sure of himself, and that's how I know it's going to happen.

Mama likes for me to massage her feet, but I don't like to because they smell funny, and besides, feet are dirty and gross to touch unless they are my own. She has an ugly scar that goes around the bottom of her right foot. When she was about five years old, she climbed on top of a cabinet in the back storage room of her family's grocery store. She lost her balance when she was reaching for a large glass container full of cookies. When she fell, the bottom of her foot got cut on the broken glass. The whole bottom of her foot was sliced off and laying on the floor when her father—hearing her screaming—came to her rescue. There were no hospitals where they lived in Brazil, but her father was a very smart man. He immediately got some honey and used it to glue the bottom of her foot back on, and he bandaged it together with a strip of burlap material. A few days later, it had healed, but it had left a scar. Mama is very proud of her father's ingenuity and how it saved her foot. I can't even imagine Mama being a naughty kid.

Winter of 1955

Cousin Esther has been caught drinking vinegar. Someone told her that drinking vinegar helps to lose weight, and she wants to maintain her slim waist. Vinegar has been banned from Aunt Heydee's apartment, but no one can stop Esther from buying it at the grocery store and drinking a bottle before she even reaches home. It sure works. She is beautiful. She has a slim little waist and big boobs, which show well when they stick out from her low-cut blouses. She looks like the movie star Marilyn Monroe. Men go crazy when they see Esther walking in the streets. Every time we go out, we get a flock of half a dozen of them following us like lost dogs.

    I had a lot of dogs following me home when we stayed at Costa da Caparica this summer. Every time I saw a stray dog, I kind of conned him into following me by whistling at him. Then another one would appear at a street corner, and then another. Sometimes I would get home with about three or four dogs. I bragged to the family about the dogs following me as if I had some kind of magic power, but I stopped when Max-Leão made fun of me and said I probably smelled like a dog and that's why I was being followed.

For *Carnaval*, Mama got me a cowboy costume. A blue cowboy hat to match the silky blue pants and jacket rented from a real costume shop. We all went to Grandma's house for pictures. Grandma Rica no longer lives there, but Aunt Heydee, Aunt Ligia, and Aunt Morena do, and somehow Grandma Rica is still there in spirit.

Papa says that when you are loved you don't really die; you continue to live in the hearts of the beloved ones.

I don't agree with him, for living is feeling and Grandma Rica doesn't feel anymore. I know that, because I have seen her stone in the cemetery. Maybe what Papa means to say is that she lives as a memory, like pictures are memories, and sometimes they can live longer than people.

Uncle Augusto had fun taking our picture. When he asked me to create a pose, I pointed my cowboy gun at Cousin Leão, whom I hate.

I really like Cousin Esther, because she is fun to be with and we get to talk about all kinds of stuff. She talks to me as if I were her own age. The only thing that bothers me is what happened last Sunday. We were lying down in her bed while talking and trying to stay warm under the blankets. In the wintertime, it's almost as cold inside as it is outside. Just because there's no rain or cold wind blowing through the house, it's still very cold unless someone has a fire going, like Encarnação does in her living room, or like Papa who uses a small kerosene heater when he brings paperwork to do at home over the weekend. Nobody is allowed to use Papa's heater except Papa. He is the only one who knows how to light it properly. It gets nice and warm in the room he works in, but I stay away from it because sometimes he farts really badly. He asks me to sit in one of the chairs and study. I don't want to sit in a heated room warmed up by farts and heat. I can't breathe. I'd rather walk outside and freeze to death in the cold.

So, Cousin Esther and I were lying down under the blankets and talking about stuff in general, and then she told me about our Cousin Marcus, the lawyer. She is in love with him, and he really knows how to kiss her. He takes her on trips to the country in his car, and he touches her "down there" and makes her feel good. She hopes that someday he will marry her even though all the family is against the idea. He is fifty-eight years old, and she is only eighteen.

Then she told me to put a finger in my vagina and play with it, like she was doing to herself. She would not talk to me while she was doing that. She was busy moaning instead. I didn't have the courage to tell her that I was confused about the situation. I didn't want to hurt her feelings and decided to imitate her moaning sounds. I was wondering what was next. Then she suddenly stopped and said, "Wasn't it wonderful? Did you enjoy it, too?"

I said, "Yes, of course." And I looked away, afraid that she could tell that I was lying.

"This is our little secret," she said. "You are not to tell anyone."

I agreed wholeheartedly.

Max-Leão is so lucky. He had dinner with the porters downstairs. I have always wondered what the porters' house looks like on the inside. When they talk to me or anyone else, they always stand with the door half closed behind them so you really can't look inside. Because they are very short, I imagine they have very small rooms with very small furniture like the small people in *Gulliver's Travels*.

The Journey of Innocence

Max-Leão told us that their place is nicer than ours. He also said that the husband porter made a lot of noise while slurping the hot soup from his spoon, and so did his wife and their son. I couldn't believe it! But I guess that's the way it is when you are not well educated in the manners of social life. If Encarnação had not shown me how to eat properly a few years ago when I was having lunch with her, I would be slurping, too, and also chewing food with my mouth open.

Max-Leão and I have a lot of fun sticking bubble gum into doorbells and running away. We always ring the bell to the top floor, because they can't catch us this way. It takes a while to get down the steps, and that gives us time to run away. The people have to come downstairs and pull the gum out if they want the bell to stop ringing.

Spring of 1955

I have been placed into a semi-private class for Arithmetic and Portuguese grammar at the home of two old retired teachers. We are about eight kids of all ages, and we sit at a long wide table and get tested every day. I don't know anyone, so I don't talk to anybody. I try to do my work, and that's all. One of the teachers gets really bothered by my hairstyle and keeps coming up to me and pulling the hair off my face. She doesn't believe that I can see anything that way. She doesn't know that I cover my face purposely so that I can feel invisible. Mama thinks that I am trying to look like Veronica Lake, the American movie star, but I am not. Besides, she is an adult and I am still a kid. I just like hiding from everybody, so that I don't really exist. I enjoy being in my own miserable and lonely world. I don't talk to anybody, and I walk alone. Mama doesn't let me have friends, and I don't need them either.

As I left the tutoring house, one of the teachers was rubbing Vaseline on her hands. She was explaining to one of the mothers picking up her daughter that Vaseline kept her hands soft and young. I wonder why she doesn't use the Vaseline all over.

Summer of 1955

Cousin Esther was handcuffed and taken to jail this weekend. Two policemen were scouting the beach of Estoril and took her in for indecent exposure. I was there when it happened. She was wearing a two-piece bathing suit that only showed a little bit of her midriff, and even the leg length was longer than my shorts. When Cousin Esther puts on a bathing suit, it becomes indecent automatically because she is very sexy. If she lived in America, she would be a sexy movie star.

It has become a summer tradition since last year for Papa to give us thirty *escudos*. Max-Leão and I run all the way to the ice cream factory just one block away from the *Cesário Verde Parque*. When we get there, we hand them our small tin cooking pot. They fill it up with strawberry ice cream. José doesn't come with us, because he can't run. Max-Leão and I take turns holding the pot, filled to the brim with strawberry ice cream, as we run back as fast as we can so it doesn't melt too much. When we get home, Mama divides the ice cream among all of us. Mama and Papa get larger amounts because they are bigger than us, and we kids get a large tablespoon each. This is the most delicious ice cream in the world, even better than the sorbet they sell in the streets. I eat it really slowly, and I let it melt in my mouth little by little so I can taste it longer. Besides, if I put a big spoonful in my mouth, it's going to be gone in one gulp and my teeth will hurt from the cold.

I don't like water with ice either. I tried it the other day

The Journey of Innocence

at a coffee shop. I asked for a glass of water, and they put ice cubes in the water. I had never had ice in water before. The water was too cold. It froze my tongue and throat and hurt my teeth, and I could not taste the water. I threw the ice out, and then drank the water. I was really thirsty. I don't like icy water, but I do like ice by itself to chew on because it's like chewing on crunchy glass, except it's safe. I like to feel it as it melts in my mouth, going back and forth from one cheek to the other.

This summer we are not staying at the mud hut in Costa da Caparica. We are going to spend the two summer months on the second floor of a modern building in Eiriceira, which is a very small fishing village north of Lisboa. It has a shower in the bathroom! The other place only had a washbasin, and we had to shower at the beach. Living here is almost like being in Lisboa in our apartment, and it even came furnished. We have to walk a bit to get to the beach, but I like it because I am allowed to play with other kids my own age. It's easy to make friends because there are so many kids and the beach is very small. Everybody knows everybody. Every day I play volleyball and soccer and hang out with another girl my age. Her name is Madalena, and she has beautiful small feet. Her toes are short and stubby, not long like mine, which causes a problem finding my shoe size. I have a lot of calluses from wearing shoes because they are always too stiff and tight. I told Madalena all about Grandma Rica, but I was too ashamed to tell her that I had killed Grandma with a death wish.

My favorite time of the day is during low tide when the ocean offers ponds of water within itself. I get to splash from pond to pond, but I have to be careful. Without much warning, the high tide comes in, and it's a long way back to the shore. I almost drowned a few days ago. I was saved by Madalena's father, who happened to be by the shoreline and literally pulled me out by the hair. He is an arithmetic teacher, and Mama hired him to tutor my brothers and me at home when we get back to Lisboa. Mama is now wearing a whistle around her neck, and she enjoys being called the *crazy mother*. She uses the whistle to find us. She tells everyone that José is her heart, Max-Leão is her soul, and I am her blood. What a dramatic statement. Everything is a drama with Mama. Papa says it's because she was born in Brazil.

Mama has been sewing a bathing suit for Manuel, a friend of my brothers. She says Manuel's family can't afford to buy him a bathing suit. They are even poorer than us.

I don't like Manuel because he told me that he had seen me naked the other day when I was changing into my bathing suit inside the *cabana*. Consequently, I should be his girlfriend because he already saw me nude.

That has to be a lie because I always pull the *cabana*'s front cover strings nice and tight so that no one can see me while I change my clothes; therefore, he had to be spying. I don't like him. He rubs me the wrong way by making a fib. He acts like he has one over on me, and he follows me around. I told him to get lost. I feel embarrassed when he looks at me. Maybe he did see me naked. What a horrible thought. I hate him. I told Mama about Manuel, but she defended him by saying he is just a kid and most likely he said that because he likes me. But I don't like him, and he had better like someone else instead of me.

This morning was one of the most embarrassing days in my life. My beach friends and I were sitting and talking up on one of the sandy hills behind the *cabanas* when Mama found us. She was laughing and being friendly with all of them, and then she proceeded to teach them the Brazilian game of kissing. My own mother, whom I cannot recall ever playing with us, suddenly turned into the best buddy anyone can wish for. My friends were impressed with her when she had a boy and a girl sitting back to back. Each

The Journey of Innocence

would turn their head sideways, and if they turned it to the same side, they would have to kiss each other. I was horrified. The idea of kissing a boy that I don't like, like Manuel, is plain disgusting to me. I think Mama is crazy. Some of the kids got all excited about the game, and they were willing to try it. I left when it came close to my turn to sit back to back with some icky, pimple-faced boy.

While I was treasure hunting for seashells, I fell down on some green rocks by the ocean. The green was slippery slime, I found out. I cried from the back pain and my legs felt paralyzed afterward. It was very scary, and it took a while before I could get up and walk again.

Autumn of 1955

Max-Leão and I were walking home from playing at the park, and he found a couple of odd-looking balloons on the street corner down from our house. Why people throw away perfectly good balloons is beyond us. He gave me one balloon. We filled them up with water as best we could, and took turns spraying each other. We also like to blow them up to see how far they can stretch. Max-Leão is greedy. He has more than one balloon, but he doesn't want to share them with me. I have to go out to find my own. Max-Leão is very lucky, indeed. He even finds coins around park benches. It never fails. Every time we go out, he will find at least one *centavo*. I have no luck. I have never found any money, and now I got into trouble because Mama found a used balloon in my skirt pocket. Mama was very upset and said, if she ever finds out that we are picking up balloons from the street like gypsy beggars, we will be beaten so bad that they will have to take us to the hospital.

I told her that they were perfectly good balloons and they didn't even have holes. She told us that they are not real balloons. They are rubber balloons used for spitting by street drunks with disgusting contagious lung diseases. Max-Leão and I were totally grossed out by what she told us, and we will never again pick up rubber balloons from the streets, that's for sure.

Papa is still working hard at selling magazines and butter door to door, but we are doing okay with what we have. Max-Leão has become lazy and is not doing well in school. José is always sick, and Mama's health is also bad. Papa says that I am his miracle because I am the only one who is healthy and without problems. I guess he doesn't know that my bones hurt a lot every once in a while.

Aunt Heydee comes over to help me with household chores, which is great. I have to do the washing in the large stone basin where I used to bathe with my brothers when we were kids. After washing and beating the clothes onto the stone ridges, and then twisting the water out, I have to hang the bed sheets and all the other clothing on the ropes outside our sunroom window. After the wash is dried I have to stretch everything and sprinkle it with water to get some moisture back before I iron the towels and bed sheets. Papa's shirts have to be ironed with starch, and the pants have to be cleaned and brushed with soap and water and aligned just right to get the crease in the right place. I feel like Cinderella. We both have a lot in common when it comes to working like an animal all day. It takes hours to iron the bed sheets and towels, and the worst is the starching of Papa's shirts. I burned my left wrist yesterday while ironing one of his shirts because the light is not strong enough in the kitchen. Once it's dark outside, the room is gloomy, too. The iron is an old clunker that has to be heated up first until the coal is burning just right. It is a very heavy iron.

    I hate waxing the floors once a month and, oh yes, dusting. That is what I hate the most: dusting.

The Journey of Innocence

I am sick again. I caught a very bad cold. Mama told Papa that I got sick because I have weak lungs and doing this kind of housework can actually kill me. A part-time maid was hired again. Cooking over the stove is still something that they don't expect me to do. The little stove we cook on is not safe for me to handle because I am a child. Mama asked me to make a lettuce salad, and when I brought it to the table, she reprimanded me for not cutting the leaves into smaller, bite-sized pieces.

"What are we, rabbits?" she asked me.

"No, we are not rabbits," I responded. Trying to control my tears, I said, "But this is my very first salad and no one showed me how small the leaves are to be cut."

Without any sympathy, she said, "Now you know! Take the salad back to the kitchen and cut the pieces smaller."

When I am not working like a slave, I read. During naptime, I always wander into the park to read their library books or visit Encarnação to read her oversized African books. Thank God for books, and thank God for my friend Encarnação most of all!

How I love Aunt Heydee's cooking! She cooks the best food in the world. When she comes over to visit us, she rarely eats our food. She lives on what she makes from teaching French and giving piano lessons. She pays her bills and rent, and is totally independent from everyone. She keeps her personal groceries in one of our kitchen drawers. She has a lot of pride and does everything not to be a burden on anyone. She considers having a room in our house, free to use whenever she comes over, a very special treat from my parents.

Aunt Heydee's meals are simple and tasty. My favorite is eggs and tomato. She fries minced fresh garlic in olive oil, and then she puts fresh sliced tomatoes in and lets it all cook until it turns into a brown paste. After that, she adds two beaten eggs and mixes it up with a wooden spoon until it has the right consistency. Served with a sliced boiled potato on the side, and a sprig of fresh parsley on the side, it sure is an incredibly tasty meal. Grandma's old apartment is her house, and she shares it with her sister Ligia and her son Haim. I like visiting Aunt Heydee because her house always smells of fresh parsley, thyme, basil, and flowers. She always has a bouquet of fresh flowers in the dining room next to her sewing machine.

At Uncle Augusto's request, Mama took me to the eye doctor. They had me read some letters from a wall chart, and the eye doctor said loudly to one of his colleagues as he threw his arms in the air, "That girl is blind as a bat." Then he came over to Mama and reinforced his opinion once again. Giving her a piece of paper, he said, "You better get this prescription filled as soon as you can. Your daughter is basically blind."
 He was nasty and crude like all doctors are. I hate all doctors except Uncle Augusto. He would never say something like that in front of me. He would have taken Mama to the side and then told her privately, "Verónica is blind as a bat." I don't believe that I am blind, because I can see everybody around me. This thing about being blind is complete news to me. This has got to be payback, I already know. I used to tease some of the kids around our neighborhood. I called them "four-eyes" because they wore glasses, and now it's my turn to be made fun of. The eyeglasses will be ready at the end of the month. I don't intend to use them. I can see perfectly without them.

I like it when I am sick. Mama always treats me kindly when I am not well. She went to a lunch party and brought me a little piece of turkey. "This was all I could hide in the paper napkin inside my pocketbook," she said as she handed me the tasty morsel. I had never had turkey before. It was a little drier than chicken, but tasty. Mama was thinking about me. She must love me after all. The truth is that I don't know if she really loves me, but at moments like this, when she carries a piece of turkey all the way home just for me, it makes me believe that she does love me, somehow. She is not as affectionate toward me as she is toward my brothers. I wish that she would kiss and hug me like she does my brothers. Maybe she brought the turkey piece out of pity for her sick, dying child.

Wow! I am blind! I can't believe how much better I can see with glasses. Everything is brighter, and I can see so much better from far away. Across the street, I can see people's faces, if they are smiling or just going on with their own business. I love it! It's like having binoculars. But Mama hates it! I am not to use glasses when we go out together. As a matter of a fact, glasses make me so ugly that I'm not to use them when visiting family with her. It must embarrass her that I am almost blind. I'm allowed to use them only when I really need them, like when I am alone or when I go back to school someday.

Winter of 1956

José and I were alone at home and lying in our parents' bed. They have the softest and thickest blankets. It was cold and we decided to get under the blankets to keep warm. Naturally, trying to stay warm under the covers, we cuddled up to each other really close. It felt good being so close to him, but it scared me because he is my brother and not my boyfriend. I immediately got up and said that I was warm enough. I can never tell this to anyone. I don't believe that José was aware of what happened to me. I would die if he did.

Mama hired a rabbi to come to our house to teach Max-Leão and me to read Hebrew. Papa refuses to go to the temple. He doesn't believe in religion. He says it's all manmade, a way to control the ignorant masses. There aren't many Jews left in Portugal. "Everybody is getting old," Mama says, "and dying, and the younger ones are either getting married to *goyim* (non-Jews) or leaving to other countries where there's a chance to have a future and a better life."

Max-Leão will be having his *bar mitzvah* when he turns thirteen years old. He has to learn Hebrew whether he likes it or not. To me, the Hebrew language is as hard to understand as Arithmetic! The rabbi wants us to learn the alphabet like parrots, but first I need to know what each letter means. This is like learning Greek or Chinese. It makes no sense to me.

He wants us to memorize it first, but I can't. I can't even memorize a poem. I can't even remember the words to a tune. I was born with a lousy memory. And to make it worse, the rabbi falls asleep while he is teaching us. This can only prove that he is as bored as we are, since he is seated and not lying down. I can never sleep sitting up. I need a pillow and a bed. Max-Leão was trying to kick me under the table and hit the rabbi's shin instead. The rabbi woke up angry, rubbing his injured knee. The rabbi wanted to know who did it. Max-Leão pointed to me, and the rabbi believed him! So, when the rabbi started to doze off again, I kicked as hard as I could under the table, trying to get Max-Leão back, but once again the rabbi's leg was in the way. He was furious and complained to Mama, and now I don't have to learn Hebrew. Only Max-Leão has to do it. It serves him right for getting me into trouble that he started!

A few days ago, Mama sent me out to the corner store on an errand. I was closing the front door to the street when the grocery boy who had just delivered our groceries was also coming out of the building from the servant's door. It was raining hard, and he asked me if I wanted to walk with

The Journey of Innocence

him under his umbrella. We were both going in the same direction. I saw nothing wrong with the idea and accepted the offer. He was about my height and was very friendly in a brotherly way toward me. We talked about the rain and rubber boots, and when we got to the street corner, I said goodbye and crossed the road to the bakery and he went on to the grocery store a little down the street.

This morning I got up with a fever and a cold. And then, as if being sick was not enough, I heard Mama telling everybody that I am sick because I am in love with the grocery boy. She saw me walking down the street under his umbrella. This really makes me mad because it's not true. I am not in love with him or anyone else. This is totally stupid, and I could scream with anger at these false accusations.

I was lying down on the old, falling-apart, green couch, and I began picking the lose strings that were just begging to be pulled off. I know this makes Mama very upset, but what the heck. I was bored, and the fever kept me lying there without anything to do but stare at the ceiling. So, I picked one string carefully. The idea was to pull one string and see if I could outdo it with the next one, longer than the first. The problem came as to where to hide them. As I pulled each string, I rolled it with my fingers into a little ball and put it in my ears, and then my nose, and finally running out of holes, into my vagina. It seemed to me to be a good hiding place to put the strings. My plan was to get rid of the evidence when no one was looking. But Mama must have been watching me from the half-closed door, because she came in all upset—not because I was pulling the couch's strings, but because I was putting them in my vagina.

She said I was a nasty girl and that I was playing with myself.

I kept telling her that I was bored and there was nothing

else to do but pull the couch's strings. I showed her the strings coming out of my ears and my nose so that she would not be mad at me, but she would not believe me.

She said that I was probably thinking about the grocery boy. What the heck is she talking about? I have no idea.

Mama is more messed up in the head than I thought to be possible. She took me into the bathroom this morning asked me to sit down on a chair and open my legs because she was making an inspection of my vagina.

I cried and cried and begged her not to do that to me, but she would not listen and forced me to sit there like a nincompoop with my legs opened while she kept saying, "Keep your head up and stop trying to see what I am doing." Then she presented to me, pinched by her own personal eyebrow tweezers, a caterpillar worm. "Here," she said, acting as if she had just found the worm inside of me, "you have worms growing in your vagina because of playing with yourself yesterday." I started laughing. "Mama, I was only storing the strings," I said. "This is crazy. I know it's not true what you are saying. You got those creatures from our backyard!"

"Are you calling me a liar?" she asked.

"No," I said, giving up. "You are right. I was playing with my vagina. That's why I have worms growing inside of me." And I started to cry. I was afraid that she might beat me up if I didn't go along. It takes so little to please people, just lie and go along with whatever they want. It's the only way they will leave you alone.

Mama always has something to say that makes me feel guilty. Papa rarely talks to us, for he is too busy working to show any interest in our lives. He works and gives all his money to Mama. Papa never says anything to make me feel bad. For that reason, I tend to appreciate him more than Mama. She knelt next to my bed last night and asked me,

The Journey of Innocence

"Verónica, who do you love more, your father or me?" With my fingers crossed, I answered, "You, of course." But she got angry. "You are lying," she said. "You love your father more than me." And she left the bedroom. I wondered how she knew. I cried myself to sleep.

I lost my front tooth! Max-Leão, José, and I were playing in my bedroom veranda facing the street. They decided to play the game "squeezing oil," which is a boy's game, a real stupid game. The idea is for everybody to grab one person and squeeze that person against the wall, as hard as you can. They ganged up on me, squeezing me against the wall, and then I got a good turn at squeezing Max-Leão with José helping me. But Max-Leão squeezed himself out, and I fell forward and hit my mouth on the corner of the brick wall. My front tooth came out, root and all. We were all screaming, seeing blood all over. Mama came running, and after washing my face, there I was, crying, toothless.

After I finish chewing "Chiclets," my favorite gum, I stick it between my two front teeth. Even though I no longer smile, at least I know that there's no empty space when I talk. Mama took me with her to visit Encarnação a few days ago and I sat next to her, keeping my mouth closed, trying to nod at everything. Eduardo, Encarnação's son, came in and asked what was wrong with me.

Mama said, "Oh, she is shy because she lost one of her baby teeth, but it will grow back soon."

Everybody was surprised about her comment, including Eduardo, who immediately asked, "She is still losing baby teeth at almost twelve years old? Isn't that kind of late?"

Mama was ready with an answer. "Yes, but this is the last one. If you look up close you will see that there's a little white piece starting to stick out, her new tooth—just about breaking through."

So, there I was with my mouth wide open so that

Eduardo, Encarnação, and her Cousin Carlos, the accountant, who was also visiting, could take turns at admiring the tip of my new tooth. Mama knows very well that the white is just an imaginary thing, since they were all staring at my gum and nothing else. How Mama gets away with her stories is beyond me.

"How long will it take for the tooth to grow completely out?" they asked.

"Hmm," Mama said as she took a few moments to come up with another fib. "Hmm, according to her dentist, who is a specialist, about two more months."

Two months, I was thinking to myself. *This is definitely going to be a miracle. The tooth and the root are in the garbage, gone into the "La de da Tooth Land of No Return."*

I was very lucky that I didn't cut my face open or cut my lip with a huge gap, or worse. I could have been scarred for life, said Mama on the way home. Yeah, and how about punishing my two stupid brothers for pushing me into the wall? No, it's always my fault!

It's all over the radio and the news. North America has a new sound, and it's called *rock and roll*. The singer who can make everybody move is Elvis Presley, "The Pelvis." When he sings, nobody can stand still. Even old people in wheelchairs get up to dance to his music.

~ *Chapter Four* ~

THE ENLIGHTENMENT

1956

Spring of 1956

I like sitting and listening to Mama and her sisters talking. I learn a lot that way, and I am so quiet that I believe that for the most part they don't even know that I am there. I have learned that *goyim* have different penises than Jews. *Goyim* have a skin hanging out on the tip of it, and a lot of them are not very clean and give infections to their wives. I don't dare ask how that happens, but I heard Aunt Heydee tell Mama that one of her piano students likes that her husband has extra skin hanging out, because it gives longer pleasure while having sex. I'm starting to realize that sex must have something to do with rubbing the penis against the vagina and also putting it inside, but, at the same time, I can't even imagine such a thing. It must hurt like hell.

I can smile again. Aunt Heydee took me to her dentist. He likes her a lot, and because of that, he gave her a special discount price to take a mold of my teeth and build me a tooth on a little pink transparent plastic plate. It sticks to the roof of my mouth with a touch of dental cement. At night before I go to sleep, I scrub the tooth and the plate attached to it with a toothbrush and soap, and soak it overnight in a glass with water. This gives me time to recover, because the roof of my mouth is very sore and red. I am allergic to the plastic.

I am never going to get used to Mama's cooking. I was getting yelled at for not eating dinner, which consisted of boiled spaghetti mixed with boiled chunks of meat, and I was trying not to breathe in the dreadful smell coming from my dish. It reminded me of a dog, and I mean a dirty street-dog smell. I was praying for a miracle, anything that would get me out of eating the food in front of me, when we heard the screeching of brakes from the street accompanied by a lot of screaming. We ran to the window, and what happened was a car hit a dog. He was lying on the ground, dead. The dog owner had grabbed the motorist and was trying to choke him for killing her dog. When we got back to the table, I wanted to throw up even more from the smell of the food. Mama was very understanding when I told her that I could not finish dinner, as I had just seen a dog die. Max-Leão offered to eat my food because he loves spaghetti. Thank God!

Cousin Esther finally got her way and married Cousin Marcus, "the old goat," as everybody refers to him. He told the family that he is going to keep Esther pregnant and barefoot, and in less than five years she will look as fat and old as him. Not a pretty picture.

José is so lucky! Just because he has asthma, he gets special meals, like steak and fried potatoes, while Max-Leão and I get fried liver. José gets sandwiches made with finely sliced deli meat, like ham and cheese. Max-Leão and I get bread with butter. Whenever Mama gives me money to run to the grocery store and get some meat and cheese for José's sandwiches, I always steal a slice of the delicious salty

The Journey of Innocence

ham. I feel guilty that I am stealing food from my sick brother, and sometimes I only take half of a slice. I am afraid to get caught.

I have been practicing at making asthmatic sounds by breathing hard. Max-Leão put his ear to my chest and said it sounds real. I have become very good at it. Mama might fall for it. Max-Leão told me that, if it works, he would do the same.

My lungs sound terrible when I take a deep breath. The wheezing can't be missed, and Mama believes that I have asthma.

My plan didn't work. Mama took me to our cousin who specializes in sick children. He was too smart for me because he asked me to clear my throat and cough before using the stethoscope on my chest. Once I coughed, I had nothing in my throat to play with. I was given a clean bill of health.

Summer of 1956

Something very strange and wonderful happened to me today. When everybody at home was taking a nap after lunch, as is customary, I decided instead to take a walk up to the *Fonte Luminosa*, just a few blocks from our house.

Now that I am twelve years old, I am allowed to walk in the city by myself as long as I am not too far away from home. The *Fonte Luminosa* is an inviting fountain for cooling off, and I like to stare at the bigger-than-life marble statues of beautiful naked women and men on horses. From the top of the fountain, a cascade of waterfalls fills the pool below with cool water. If I am lucky to be in the way of a breeze, the waterfall turns into a misty shower around me. I like taking my sandals off and sitting on the fountain's edge and dangling my feet in the water. It feels refreshing.

Sleeping in the middle of the day is impossible for me,

and this time of the day it's more like torture since I can always hear the snoring coming from my parents' bedroom. It is an irritating, annoying sound. Papa sounds like a rolling train with brake trouble, and Mama whistles. Everything closes down at this time of the day, and for two hours the city sleeps. This was going to be the perfect time for me to escape.

I never reached the fountain. It was hotter than I thought. As always happens when it gets too hot, I got a pounding headache. The sun was unmerciful, heating the top of my head so it felt like a bursting volcano. I could barely see except through the slits of my eyes as I squinted through the unbearable sunlight, trying to see the street pavement below my feet. The farther I walked, the more my hands got puffy and stiff, and I could hardly close them. There was no shade, just long stretches of cobblestone streets. I kept thinking that I should turn around and go back home, but, as Mama says, I am hardheaded and once I put my mind to something there's no turning back. The heat from a broken-down brick wall showed me how hot it was when I barely rested my back against it. Nothing was living around me except a tiny salamander running up the wall.

Beyond the tall wall and through the cracks and holes, I tried to see what was on the other side. Except for some spots of burned-out weeds and dried-up grass, the soil was just a huge canvas of desert ground. After a few more steps, I looked again beyond an old, rusty metal door with a lock and metal chain around it, which meant that it was off limits to enter. In the distance, I could see a huge home that, by its neglect, must have been abandoned many years ago. It looked desolate, as if crying in the loneliness of its surroundings. I wondered, what had happened to the owners. Was the ground salted so that nothing could grow there, like they used to do a few years back to the enemies of the state? Perhaps a girl my age and her family had been killed for political reasons. It would not be the first time. Everybody knows that our president Salazar is a dictator, and as such, he is merciless against his enemies. I looked around. Not a soul walking or a car going by. There was only silence and the sun burning my skin and my vision. I was thirsty and tired of walking, when I smelled roses. Not just the smell of roses, but the smell of tiny little baby roses. There it was, one wild, little, pink button rose escaping from the dead garden and squeezing itself through the cracked wall and peeking out into the world outside. A few steps down where part of the wall had fallen, the same rosebush was sprouting all over, covering the ugly wall and screaming how beautiful life is. I stayed there next to it, taking one deep breath after another and immersing myself I stayed there next to it, taking one deep breath after another and immersing myself in the scent. There was a complete sense of being, the sense of what it feels like to have God all around. I laughed and screamed from outside inwards. The sound of silence was loud and clear within me, and the feeling was joy to my soul, running through my skin and inwards again, from my eyes and from my mouth and lungs. I was breathing in life. I am not telling anyone about this. No one would believe me, and they would think that I am a sissy. This is my secret, my very intimate secret. I no longer have to look for God in a temple, a church, or any specific place, because God is everywhere. I will never be alone again.

We are back for the summer at Costa da Caparica, but I don't really care for this beach anymore. It's too big and lonely. I would rather be in Eiriceira with my friend Madalena.

Mama gave me a big speech about walking around the house in my bathing suit when Papa is home for the weekend. She said that a bathing suit is not the proper attire to use at home. It is indecent to walk around half-naked. Just because Papa is my father, he is still a man.

I get hurt when she says things like that. She makes me feel ashamed of my body and being a girl. I wish I were a boy like my brothers, and then perhaps I could be closer to my parents, without all these bizarre innuendos.

Summertime can be very boring. It's been very, very hot and muggy, and it's hard to do anything but be immersed in the ocean for hours. The shade is no help. I was sitting on the sidewalk with my brothers and a few of his friends. We were passing the time talking, and they gave me a cigarette to try. All Americans and British smoke, because they are fashionable and educated. We see that in foreign movies, too. It's very "cool" and chic to smoke. I was dying to try it. I took a puff and choked on the smoke. I didn't like it, but I didn't want to say anything. I didn't want to offend the kids I was hanging out with, so I held the cigarette in my hand and pretended that I was puffing away. I would have felt more appropriate if I had a chimney on top of my head. When I tried to breathe in and out to make little circles of smoke like they did, the smoke went in the wrong pipe and I couldn't breathe, very much like drowning in smoke instead of water. I didn't like it at all, and then, to make it more embarrassing, an old man went by and criticized me with a disgusted look in his eyes. "It's disgraceful to see a pretty young girl smoking like a man."

Everybody made fun of the old man going by, calling him "old fart." I threw my cigarette away.

Maria, our part-time maid became friendly with a fisherman who owns one of the giant half-moon shaped fishing rowboats, and she offered to take my brothers and me on a trip to the sea this morning. We all sat at the tip of the boat, the highest spot. I was very excited about my fishing adventure, but I didn't expect the tall waves that

The Journey of Innocence

made the boat feel like it was going to turn over. It went up and down like a roller coaster. I screamed and screamed. I told them I was going to throw up and I wanted to go back to the shore. When I threw up all over, they turned the boat back to shore and, after calling me names, left me there. They were yelling at me, as if it were my fault that I have a weak stomach. I was shaking, and it took a while before I felt normal again.

Papa is still selling butter door to door. The gold glass with the lady's face engraved on it is always in and out of the pawnshop along with the diamond moon-shaped pin with thirty-five diamonds that Grandpa Leão bought for Grandma Rica when they were still rich. It belonged to the last queen of Portugal. These two items have saved us various times when we are having a drop in finances. Papa has been selling a lot more books and magazines to architects and foreigners, and that is why we can afford to come here for the summer. Still, we only see Papa on weekends. He still drives his *lambretta*, and last week he told me that one day, when he can afford a new one, he will show me how to drive it and will give it to me. I didn't tell him that I am afraid of driving a motorcycle. I have never even ridden a bike. He always thinks that I am able to do anything, but he is wrong. I am a *medricas*, which means that I am a "scaredy-cat" when it comes to possibly getting hurt.

I hang out with Max-Leão and José all day like Mama wants me to, but I have not told her that we play with *goyim* and I use my glasses so that I can see better. We are all buddies and take long walks through the woods. We have been trying to find a nude beach that's supposed to be only a few miles south of us, but we never seem to find it no matter how much we walk.

These last few days have been very, very hot, and I have

stopped going out with them. I get sick with a pounding headache from the sun. If the boys want to do that, they can go by themselves. I feel funny being the only girl in the group anyway, and besides, I don't need to look at naked people. I already know that women have a vagina and two breasts, men have a penis and no breasts, and everybody has a butt, some bigger than others. What's the big deal?

I had to fight for my honor today! Max-Leão told me that one of the boys in our group was passing the word around that I had kissed him and that I was his girl. I went out looking for him. Costa da Caparica is not that big. The beach is enormous, but the town is less than an hour to tour. There he was, the scoundrel, the liar, sitting on a bar stool at the local tavern, most likely telling the bartender about me. I walked up to him and made a closed fist. Then without a single word, I punched him in the face with all my mighty force. He didn't even know what hit him. It was that quick, and he was on the ground on his back with a bloody lip and holding his face as I walked out, proud of myself.

I saw him a few times in town, and he always walks away from me. There have been a lot of mixed opinions. Some said he got what he deserved. Others said I was not very ladylike, and I should have talked to him instead. I am too shy to do that, and I can't deal with confrontations. In the back of my mind, I wonder if the whole thing was a lie. Maybe he was innocent, and I punched the wrong person.

Aunt Heydee said that, if I accuse an innocent person of a crime, I am guilty of that sin myself. I must be very careful before I point the finger, or God will punish me for it. From now on, I promise never to jump to conclusions until I know for sure that what someone tells me about someone else is true.

We spend a lot of our time at the coffee house in the main

The Journey of Innocence

street in Costa da Caparica. Mama likes to sit there with company like aunts Heydee, Morena, or Ligia. When they come over on weekends, we sit in the shade under the large umbrella outside, each sipping a cup of coffee that lasts all afternoon. I usually have mine with lots of milk added to it because coffee makes me jittery and my hands shake like those of an old lady. We sit and watch all the tourists going by, and there's always some kind of gossip going on. Sometimes I can't believe my own ears.

"Did you see the way our young Cousin Carlos was holding Alexandra by the waist while teaching her to roller skate?"

And the other would say, "She is married, but I bet you that on the way back to Lisboa while on the bus they really got closer to each other."

"Well, can you blame her? He is very handsome. I bet they went straight from the bus into his bed."

Gossip is very entertaining, and it helps to pass the idle time while we hang out at the coffee shops during the long and hot afternoons.

Television is a new household item. It is so new that no one can afford it except coffee shops and tavern owners who use it to entice customers to shop and spend long hours in their establishments. The only person I know who has a television at home is Encarnação, but she is not very rich, just well-to-do with her monthly pension. She also lends money to Mama every once in a while when Papa is not making enough to pay the rent, buy food, and so on.

Our favorite coffee shop is situated in the center of Costa da Caparica. The owner will always have more customers than the other coffee house down the street because he has a television for the customers to look at. This is the place to catch all the news from the outside world. For a couple of months now, Papa has been trying to sell colored filters to television owners. Basically, the filter is nothing but a colored plastic sheet, a see-through plastic film with three basic colors. The bottom is green, the middle is brownish red, and the top is blue for the sky. That is supposed to make the black-and-white television look like color television. The film is also supposed to stick to the television screen, but most of the time it slides off. It is the latest in technology from Germany. Papa gave the coffee shop owner a colored filter in hopes that it will serve as an advertisement and someone will want to buy one for their black-and-white television. But no one at Costa da Caparica has inquired about buying a filter from Papa. I really don't believe that Papa is going to do well with these colored television filters. People here are very poor and don't have a television. That's why they come to the coffee shop to see the news. Papa is also selling German perfume, a special perfume that is supposed to take headaches away when rubbed gently on the temples. I tried it, but the smell gave me a headache.

I am in love! Of course, he doesn't know that I love him. I would rather die than let him know it. His name is João and he is one of Max-Leão's friends. He is slim, taller than me, and has dark hair and beautiful almond-shaped brown eyes. He is one year older than I am. We all go out together during the day, but we rarely say anything. We just stare at each other because we are both shy. Saturday night, I was in my bed and reading a murder mystery when a small stone hit my bedroom window. It was João and two other friends asking if both my brothers and I would like to go out with them. My heart almost jumped out of my chest.

    I only see João during the day. I am not allowed to go out at night. So, Max-Leão and José went out with the boys and I stayed home. I tried to read my book, but I couldn't concentrate. I wanted to go out, too, and have some fun with our friends. I feel so sad. I feel so lonely and sad.

The Journey of Innocence

João commented on my white blouse this afternoon because it has seashells all around the top. This is my favorite shirt, and I wear it every day with my green shorts. I know that this shirt makes me look the best I can look. Mama made it for me, and of all the clothes she made, this is a masterpiece of design. It's not too big or too tight. It's my size and it's made of white cotton. It goes well with anything I want to wear. Anyway, João was smiling at me and said, "You have nice seashells."

I didn't know what to say. I just smiled back. I know he likes me, too. He might even love me.

We are going back to Lisboa in two weeks. It's the end of the summer, and most likely we will never see each other again. After all, he is a *goy*. Love is so painful. I wish him the best. I will think of him every day from now on and imagine being in his arms as he holds me tenderly and kisses me passionately, just like in the American movies.

Summer is almost over. It's already getting cooler at night. Running around in the water, walking on the sand as far as my feet can take me, lying in the sun all day, playing the nail game with my brothers, going for long walks in the afternoon, reading, and listening to Mama and my aunts gossiping at the café will be old history soon.

"Did you see what happened to that young couple on their honeymoon? They had to leave after a week of too much sex, swimming, and staying up all night, not necessarily in that order." They were laughing heartily.

"Yes," one of my aunts agreed. "Poor girl. She got really sick, probably anemia, and he had some kind of a virus. Who knows what they both wound up with? A honeymoon can make you seriously ill, even kill you if you are not careful." I can't believe this nonsense, as if getting married and being happy can actually hurt you. I didn't say anything. The couple was probably sickly to begin with.

Autumn of 1956

We had a fire in the ground-level apartment directly underneath our apartment in Lisboa. Heavy dark smoke was coming out through the windows below us. The firemen were yelling for everyone to evacuate the building immediately. Max-Leão, José, and I followed Mama as she ran to her bedroom to grab her lottery ticket for the week. Then we all ran out of the house. A fireman had to break the window of the apartment below us, where the *kept woman* lives. They were yelling at Maria Elena to open the front door, but she had locked herself in and couldn't find the key. It was horrible to hear her screaming from inside the apartment. Finally, one of the firemen climbed up a ladder to her window, broke it with a hammer, and went in to get her. He carried Maria Elena out in his arms as we all clapped our hands in admiration of his courage and successful mission. Everybody noticed and commented that the fireman who carried Maria Elena out had a big smile on his face. She was wearing a sexy blue, dainty, lacy nightgown covered by a matching silk robe.

She was taken in an ambulance because the bottoms of her feet had been severely torched by the burning wooden floors. The firemen did a great job controlling the fire from spreading up to our floor or down farther into the porters' apartment. Later, when Maria Elena returned from the hospital, we found out that she had the key to the front door in one of the pockets in her robe the whole time that she was screaming while burning her feet. She had panicked and forgotten where she had the key. Everybody felt that the *kept woman* deserved whatever bad happened to her because she is living off a married man and destroying his family.

I don't agree. There is no good reason for anyone, including a kept woman, to get burned alive. How about the married man? How come he is looked upon as the innocent

The Journey of Innocence

victim of her spell? Besides, Mama is the one who always says, "It takes two to Tango."

I was walking home from Encarnação's house when I almost got killed. Two blocks from our house, three auto mechanics were taking a break standing outside by the entrance to the service bay. When they saw me, they began whistling at me and one of them said, "Come here, little girl. I have a doll for you." They were laughing.

"What's the matter," yelled the man next to him. "Don't you believe us? Come here, you cute thing!"

I started to run. Scared, I ran all the way home. I realize now how lucky I am that I was walking on the other side of the street instead of the sidewalk next to the garage. They could have grabbed me.

A few weeks ago, Papa explained to me what strangers do to girls my age when they offer dolls, candy, or any kind of presents.

We were having dinner all together, and Mama said something about me looking older for my age. The way that I am blooming, she probably meant my breasts. I have also noticed that my body has been changing lately. I keep wondering if my breasts will grow as big as Cousin Esther's.

"Soon men will start wanting to use you."

What was she trying to tell me? I looked at her perplexed.

"What do you mean, use me?" I asked. Mama never says anything directly. I'm supposed to know automatically what she is referring to.

I guess that from the look on my face, Papa could tell that I really wanted to know what she was talking about. He said, "Have you noticed the way I lovingly and very tenderly hug and kiss your mother? Well, these strangers have no loving feelings toward you. They don't love you. They will grab you for the fun of it and then squeeze you like a lemon until there's no juice left." And Papa squeezed the half-lemon next to his plate all over his boiled codfish.

That was enough for me. I promised myself that I would never again squeeze purple sea creatures at the beach, and most of all, I will always stay away from strangers.

Papa's sister and her second husband Curt came from England to visit us for three days. Curt lost all of his family, including his wife and children, in the concentration camp. He met Ilse for the first time when they were both hiding in London, England. They are very loving toward each other. They hold hands when they walk the streets and when they sit next to each other. They are even more loving than Mama and Papa are with each other. This surprises me, because I always thought that the English and the Germans were a cold stiff kind of people who never show feelings or emotion.

Ilse asked Mama if she could take me to England with her, but Mama would never let that happen.

Aunt Ilse and Curt took me out for ice cream, and then she gave me the bad news. The last time she had been in Israel to play the violin in a concert, she was reading the engraved names of the children killed during the war upon a stone wall, and that's when she came across her own two girls' names along with the list of other children who were with them and had been gassed in the concentration camp. There was no mistake. Her children's names had been taken from the books the Nazis kept. When it came to keeping track of whom they had killed, how, and when, their records were well organized. I can't even imagine what she must have felt after so many years of hoping that maybe, just maybe, her daughters had been taken to Russia by the Russian soldiers who had taken a lot of the camp survivors with them when the war was over.

She cried and cried as she spoke, and then, as she wiped her tears with a little white lace kerchief, she said, "I still love Germany, my country. I have a lot to do yet, playing the violin and bringing happiness to the less fortunate in Germany."

After they left, I heard my parents talking about her. Basically, she was to blame for having sent the two girls away to school in Holland when the war was going on. She should have stayed with them instead.

It's always easy to figure out a better way of doing things after it's done, and I am sure that Ilse feels the same way. She cannot change the past. She lives with it, and every note that she plays on her violin cries like her soul is being ripped open. I don't like the sound of the violin anymore.

I was sitting in the kitchen and watching Aunt Heydee fry tomatoes with eggs for lunch. I was hoping she would share some with me, as she always does, when Mama came in with two pictures of my cousins from North America.

She asked me, "Which one do you like the best?"

I thought she was just asking my opinion, and I chose Alberto who seemed to be younger and had a nice smile. Gabriel looked older and too serious for me.

She agreed with me. "Alberto is definitely the best looking of the two brothers. He is twelve years older than you, but that's okay. A woman should be a lot younger than the husband. That way, he can't ever get bored with his young wife." And she added, "How would you like to marry him?"

"Are you kidding? Do you mean Aunt Nelly's son, my cousin?" I was shocked.

She picked up the pictures from the table, and walking away, she said, "Yes, him. And you better hope and pray for it, because, if that happens, you will be going to North America, and you will be the luckiest woman in the world."

I didn't say anything. I didn't know what to think of all of this. I believe she is just fantasizing like she does with so many things.

Our building is starting to show its age. The landlord is still collecting the same rent he charged in 1943. Nobody is moving out, and by law, the rent can't go up with the original owners or new family members living here. When the eldest dies, the younger takes over the rights to the apartment. It goes from father to son, and from son to grandson, and so on, but the rent remains the same. The problem is that the cost of living keeps going up, and the landlord is getting the same rent he did some thirteen years ago. Everybody feels that all landlords are rich and too cheap to fix the buildings when they start needing a paint job and repairs. The carpet on the wooden steps has long been gone, worn out by the up-and-down traffic of the tenants. The wooden steps are still kept clean and are waxed once a month by the wife porter. The old couple continues to get a free apartment to live in, in exchange for cleaning the building. The plants died a few years back, and there's only one cracked ceramic pot left on the right side of the steps with a plant stalk that has no leaves. Our building is starting to look more and more like Grandma's apartment house. Our bathroom is literally decaying. The cracked mirror above the chipped sink reminds me of a Picasso painting as I see myself with two half noses. Aunt Heydee gladly painted some colorful flowers with oil paints to cover the ugly cracks and made it very artistic. It looks kind of French. She is an artist. We need a new mirror, but we can't afford a new one. Besides, the landlord is the one who should replace it with all the money he gets from our rent. If I prop myself between the cracks, there are flowers on my hair; otherwise, they are on my face. The toilet water tank has brown water spots from leaking, and the rope has to be wiggled in a certain way or it won't flush. The floor tiles are damaged, and some of the stones have lifted up. The rooms need a coat of paint real bad, because the walls

The Journey of Innocence

have been peeling for some time. The old curtains in the living room that is part of the dining room have faded to a light shade of something that used to be.

I am not allowed to bring anyone home. I stopped asking a long time ago. A girlfriend can mean that one of my brothers falling in love with her, and then I would have to carry that on my conscience. Mama and Papa's grandchildren would be Catholic! I don't have any friends, and I don't need any friends anyway. As long as I have books, I don't care if I never talk to anyone either.

The wooden kitchen cabinets have started to rot on the inside, but they came in very handy a few days ago. I came home with a huge bleeding gash along my right leg from getting cut on my neighbor's metal bike. I wanted to try riding it. The cut was from below the knee to the ankle. I was bleeding a lot, but Josefina, our part-time maid, knew what to do. She scraped the rotten wood from the kitchen cabinets and applied it to the open bleeding wound. It worked like a cork on an open faucet. It stopped the bleeding. Mama came in at that moment and was appalled by the treatment. But Josefina swore on Mother Mary and Jesus her son that my leg would heal without a scar.

I have the worst cold of my life. It's been three miserable days of dripping nose, coughing, and having a fever. I am not allowed to leave my room, except to go to the bathroom right next to my bedroom. Nobody will come near me. They are all afraid of getting infected.

I am so bored. I already went through the usual ritual of looking at all the family picture albums, and I've read all the books next to my bed. The movie star magazines have been read over and over again. After taking a good look around my bedroom, I realized how drab it looks. There's no window, no street noises, no sunshine. The only sound I hear is when someone is flushing the toilet next to my bedroom, letting me know that there's life out there. Mama believes that by changing the rooms around, the house always has a new look, but I don't agree with that. It's just junky furniture moving around from one room to another.

I have decided to be a little creative with my time today and brighten up my bedroom. I'm the only one who sleeps here, except for Aunt Heydee when she is visiting us. She gets to stay overnight, and she sleeps in my bed with me. Wintertime is my favorite time for sleeping next to Aunt Heydee. I get to curl up to her and stay warm all night.

I am going to decorate my bedroom today.

I spent the morning cutting all the pictures of movie stars from the magazines I have collected over the last few years. I worked hard all afternoon with a bottle of glue and the movie star "cut outs." I glued them to the beat-up bookcase and to the old armoire. I glued them to the walls. I glued them to the small side table next to my bed. I worked at it all day long. The start of a new life in decorating was opening up in front of my eyes. I carefully closed my bedroom door every time I went to the bathroom because I didn't want anyone to see my work of art until I was finished.

American movie stars are the most elegant and beautiful in the world. The French, English, and German movie stars are okay, but nothing like the American movie stars. My favorite is Audrey Hepburn, even though she is from Belgium. I would like to look like her, but my bones are a lot larger than hers, and even if I starved to death, I could never be as thin as she is. There's Paul Newman and Susan Hayward (my favorites), Marlon Brando, Elizabeth Taylor, Marilyn Monroe, Burt Lancaster (Mama likes his muscles), Rock Hudson, Doris Day, Steve McQueen, Shirley Temple, William Holden, and Ava Gardner (Papa likes her, he says she has a beautiful neck, like a swan). I glued my favorite pictures so that anyone walking into the bedroom could not

The Journey of Innocence

miss them. They would be greeted at first glance. The ugly ones, or the ones who are movie stars because they are probably good actors or they know someone who got them to play in the movies, like Katharine Hepburn, Charlie Chaplin, Ingrid Bergman, Fred Astaire, Joan Crawford, Edward G. Robinson, Charlton Heston, Humphrey Bogart, and Betty Davis, I put them up as fill-ins.

It was six in the evening when I heard Mama closing the front door as she came into the house. Our front door makes a very distinct sound that cannot be mistaken by any other door opening or closing. I was literally exhausted from all the work I had done. My bedroom door opened about ten minutes later. She would have hit me if I hadn't looked so sick. She was livid with anger. I was to get a scrub and a bucket of water and remove every single glued picture, right then and there. According to her, it was the most tasteless thing she had ever seen.

I cried and begged, but her decision was final. I spent the rest of the evening peeling and scrubbing the pictures off the walls and the furniture. No matter how much I coughed, Mama didn't feel sorry for me.

Once in a while Mama can be nice, but most of the time she is a witch. She hates me. Half the time, I don't even remember why she hits me. A few years back, in order to protect myself from amnesia, I purposely stayed awake most of the night engraving into my memory the beating I had suffered that day. I swore to myself that I would always remember that beating, even if I already forgot why she beat me that day. I engraved it into my memory, like a woodpecker does to a tree. I swore that I would remember that day for the rest of my life so that I would never feel bad for not loving her. It will always be easy to recall that day, because she hit me over the head without stopping all the way from my bedroom to the bathroom, which in those days was at the end of the house on the farthest side. I bled from my nose all over the floors and the sink where she finally grabbed me by the hair and pushed my head into the cold water. When I become a mother, my children can decorate their bedroom the way they like. I will listen, and I will be understanding. I will never ever hit them.

The *kept woman*'s lover not only had her apartment fixed up like new, but for Christmas he surprised her with a brand new red sports car parked right outside the front door. Everybody realized that, even with her burned feet, he is never going to leave Maria Elena because he truly loves her.

Winter of 1957

I get a lot of bloody noses even when I am not getting hit across the face. Mama has taken me twice now to a doctor who has burned the inside of my nose. They call it *cauterization*, and it's supposed to help. I hate it! I think it's making my nose even more sensitive. In my opinion, my nose got damaged from getting hit all of the time across my face, and now getting it burned is making it worse. I feel like a boxer after being in the ring a few times.

This afternoon I got electrocuted. I found out that my brother Max-Leão is not only lazy but also a coward. I went into the dining room in the dark. I was trying to find the socket on the wall to plug in a lamp so that I could read in Papa's favorite armchair. While I was feeling the wall, my two right fingers went into the socket holes. The cover had fallen off like most of the other sockets in the house. I learned what electricity feels like when it's running through the body instead of wires. I was shaking and could hardly stand up. There was nobody else at home as I ran toward Max-Leão when he came to see what I was screaming about. When he saw me, he ran into his bedroom and closed the door behind him. I went after him, opened his

The Journey of Innocence

door, and walked toward him so that I could hold on to him. He grabbed a book from his desk and threw it at me while screaming, "Stay away from me."

One book hit me really hard on the head, and I had to leave his room and go into my room. I was cursing him for being so mean to his beloved sister and friend.

Thank God for roasted chestnuts in the winter. As long as there's a chestnut vendor on the street, I can always buy a few and hold them in my hands to stay warm. When they get cold, I eat them.

Mama is right. Just like Papa, I'm hardheaded. I am like a stone, unmovable. I am getting better and better at hiding my feelings, and it's working magnificently. Over the weekend, I was in a musical play at the Jewish Youth Center. When I went outside onto the back porch to pick up a pin to hold my headpiece that kept falling off, I reached into a basket with needles and pins, and stuck a pin in my right thumb. I was there trying to find something to put a stop to the bleeding when Uncle Augusto appeared on the veranda and asked if I was ready to get on stage. Of course, he also asked me to pose for a picture. I held my hand tight behind my back, and he didn't even know what happened. I felt too stupid and ashamed to tell him that I had hurt my hand. I am such a klutz.

A new family moved in to our apartment complex about six months ago. They have a son about my age, and he is really cute, with dark hair and dark eyes. They are renting the apartment below our next-door neighbor. He likes me, I can tell, because he looks and smiles at me when we see each other on the stairway. Then, to make my wishes come true, he sent me a love letter yesterday. He gave the letter to Teresa, our maid, to give to me. Teresa gave the letter to Mama. But, of course, I only heard about it when Mama spoke to his mother and told her to keep Jorge, her brat son, away from me. I went to bed thinking about him and then, out of nowhere, I had this flushing feeling of pleasure coming up and filling me with happiness. Wow!! That's all I can say, because this is a real discovery about my body. My goodness, this must be what everybody is talking about. Sex!

Papa's oldest sister Friedel came from England this week to spend a few days with us. She asked me to be her guide around Lisboa, and I noticed that she was the opposite of Ilse, her sister. When I suggested having some ice cream, she said, "Not in between meals. If you start eating in between meals, you will lose your appetite and that is a waste of food."

She was very proper, a blend of German and British manners. Her German attitude was very much like Papa's personality about everything. She made a few observations concerning the Portuguese being so melodramatic and how unnecessary it was to get up from their seat to leave the bus or trolley when it had not yet stopped completely. I'd never noticed that until she mentioned it. She also suggested that Mama should lower the gas on the stove once the food starts to boil, because it's a waste of energy and not cost-effective. Mama was upset about Friedel's meddling, because that meant she was criticizing Mama's housewife knowledge, but I thought Friedel's idea of setting the gas lower was a good idea. It does save on gas once the food starts to boil.

After Friedel returned to England, Papa said he admired his sister's intelligence and went on to state that the difference between his sisters was very obvious: one was definitely smarter than the other. For example, when Ilse has company, she spends days cooking and making food and preparing a feast; when Friedel has a gathering, she goes to work and makes arrangements to have a caterer bring in the food all done. Consequently, Friedel has the most common sense in efficiency, and she is the wiser of the two sisters because she doesn't waste precious time. How German can one be!

I heard that Jorge's family is moving very soon, and he is sick with a cold.

"I want to see him," I pleaded with Teresa, our maid. "You have to help me. If you are my friend, you will help me. I didn't even have a chance to read my first love letter because Mama threw it away."

Teresa said, "I feel bad that I showed the letter to your mom, so, okay. Just don't get me into trouble by telling her anything, and I will help you."

She closed the sunroom door behind her, and holding my hand, she whispered, "I have an idea. Just stay close to me and don't say anything."

We went downstairs through the back of the house and into the basement, where she knocked at his family's door. "Excuse me," said Teresa with the face of a real actress as she smiled at their maid. "We are locked out of our house. I don't have the key to get back in unless we use the front door. Do you mind if we go through your house? By the way, how is Jorge? I heard that he isn't feeling too good."

The maid let us in, saying, "Oh, he is just a pain. His mother is trying right now to give him some medicine for the cough, but he is very difficult to handle. Well, you know how kids are."

My eyes were wide open, not wanting to miss anything around me. I wanted to see the man of my dreams, even if just a glimpse. I followed Teresa, taking my time with small steps behind her.

Then I heard a crying voice, "No, no. I don't want it. It tastes terrible."

I looked, and there he was, Jorge dressed in blue flannel pajamas with little white bears. He was crying while his mother was trying to hold him down to make him swallow the spoonful of medicine. What in the world was I seeing? He was a crybaby! A weakling! I imagined him strong, courageous, and ready to fight the world with me.

I thanked Teresa for her kindness in jeopardizing her job for me. I didn't tell her how disappointed I was. *The romance is over!*

I spent the afternoon with Cousin Esther. She invited me to her house, and she made tea and gave me ginger cookies. We did lie down on her bed, but this time she didn't play with herself. She told me how happy she was being married, and that she was very jealous of her husband. She said she was always giving him demonstrations of how she felt so that he knew how much she loved him. She asked me to stay until he got home, and she put on an act of jealousy for my benefit so that I could see how it was done. She yelled and cried and accused him of not being at work but cheating on her instead, and then she winked one of her eyes at me.

The whole thing was truly theatrical, as Aunt Friedel would say, *melodramatic*. I felt sorry for Cousin Marcus. I will never do that to my husband.

~ Chapter Five ~

THE ADJUSTING PERIOD

1957-1959

Spring of 1957

Max-Leão came home yesterday and told Mama that he had seen a trolley accident where a man crossing the street got run over and was decapitated. The man's head got cut clean off from his body. It had rolled over the pavement and stopped at Max-Leão's feet. He acted very upset about it, and Mama forced him to take some of her medicine drops that help to calm the nerves. Mama takes a lot of medicine, which she gets for free from her brother and cousins.

The problem with Max-Leão's story is that today's newspaper mentions that a man had been hit by a trolley at *Praça de Chile*, but the man had suffered only minor bruises to his legs. Max-Leão had lied.

Mama said, "No, he has not lied. He has a vivid imagination, and he should be praised for his creativity."

Later in the day, I heard her tell Papa that she was worried about Max-Leão and wondered if he was suffering from hallucinations. Personally, I think he wants attention and he got it.

A family from Africa has moved into our building, into the downstairs empty apartment where Jorge and his family used to live. Teresa told me that she has seen them and that their skin color is black like coal. I have never seen a black person except in the big books at Encarnação's house. I was curious, so I went in the backyard and made believe that I was playing. I was hoping to see at least one of them. I saw the mother and two of her five daughters. They were not naked like in the pictures I had seen at Encarnação's house. Amelia, the mother's youngest daughter, is my age. We started talking, and I asked her if I could touch her skin. She smiled and let me touch her arms and hands. Her skin was soft like mine.

Amelia likes to talk to me about Angola, where she was born, and I love listening to her African stories. We are the best of friends. I am welcome to her house, and today I helped Amelia's mom prepare for a party this weekend. They let me beat the eggs for a while, until they noticed that I beat them like a left-handed person, in reverse of what's normal. I lost the job right after that. They said, if the eggs get beaten in the wrong direction, then the cake won't rise.

Mama doesn't mind that Amelia and I are friends. I always heard that, if you are walking in the street and see a black person, you should throw them a kiss. That day, you can wish for anything and it will come true because black people bring good luck. I don't believe in that. To me, they are black people, not lucky charms.

For a few months now, Mama has been cutting up our old bath towels and some other thick fabric she bought, and making little square towels of one foot by one foot. It's a big secret. I have asked her twice what they are for, and she said, "In due time, you will find out."

The Journey of Innocence

I was invited to Amelia's party downstairs. Amelia's family likes to wear perfume, and they are always having parties where they serve champagne with fresh fruit inside tall glasses. The music is loud and lively, people dance, and everybody smiles and is friendly.

I asked Mama why we don't bathe with perfume and have parties like that. It's so much fun.

She said that black people sweat a lot, and that's why they have to use perfume. We don't have that problem to worry about. And their music is always too loud because they are loud people and have no responsibilities.

I don't agree, but I didn't say anything. I am afraid she will stop me from visiting them.

Amelia tells me everything. Her mom and sisters all work. They all have regular jobs. It's only on weekends that they like to be happy and celebrate life with their friends. Amelia also confided in me about the boy who lives on the second floor of our building. She and one of her sisters were invited to a small gathering at their apartment. Claudio, the *white boy,* as she called him, took her into his bedroom, where they kissed each other on the lips. She confides in me. We tell each other everything. We have become sisters. We made a little pinhole on each other's finger, and we held our fingers together so that our blood could run from one into the other. We are blood sisters and friends forever.

Down the street from Grandma's house, there is a bakery that sells fun candy. They are very expensive, probably because they have liquor inside. These candies must be made for children because they are very cute, in the form of a little baby wrapped in a blanket. They are made of hard sugar and come in pink, blue, yellow, or green. I always buy two of them, a boy and a girl. It was a great surprise when I bit into one for the first time and delicious sweet liquor came out. I can only buy them once in a blue moon because I also love potato chips and chocolates. Chocolates are my very favorite and also a lot of fun to buy. They are sold at cigarette and magazine shops that offer the chocolate game board. This is a large punchboard. The way it works is that you push one of the many dots on the punchboard with a pin, and the other side tells you which chocolate bar you get. I hope I get the grand prize someday, which is a box of chocolates. Most of the time, I get small or medium-sized chocolate bars, and once in a while, very rarely, I get the super-sized chocolate bar. It's all luck.

Aunt Heydee is a very independent person, but she is soft like butter when it comes to the arts. She is very sensitive. Two weeks ago she came home crying as she described a young boy singing opera on a street corner. He didn't sing like everybody else, according to Aunt Heydee. He sang like Caruso. Then she reconsidered her words, "No, he sang like an angel. I have to do something to help him. He needs someone to look out for his interests. He will never make it alone. He will be lost in this city. I can't allow that to happen; it would be a crime!"

And she left to go looking for him, hoping to find him so she could take care of him or even adopt him if necessary. She came back a few hours later, crying. This time she was hysterical because she couldn't find him anywhere.

She has been looking for the young singer daily, asking people in the street if they have seen him. Everybody has forgotten the little boy with the golden voice, and he is nowhere to be found. Most likely, he went back to his hometown and back to sowing the fields, disillusioned and heartbroken. There is no future for him in a big city like Lisboa, even if he sang better than Caruso.

I don't like beer. Mama says beer will put some meat on

The Journey of Innocence

my bones, and best of all, it will make me less constipated. I tried and tried to drink it, but it makes me throw up every time. Finally, she gave up making me drink beer with my meals because I throw up the meal with the beer. Beer is gross, and wine makes me sick. Liquor is the only thing I like, and my favorite is still anise.

Mama has a hard time finding a good maid. She tries to pick someone nice when they answer the newspaper ad, but she always gets the wrong person. One after another, either they have syphilis, are pregnant, or steal everything they can while we are sleeping. Sometimes they get fired because they can't cook or they don't present the food in an appetizing manner. Mama is very picky about presentation. She says food should appeal first by the way it looks and smells, and burning it is not acceptable. I was sorry when Teresa left us to go back home, but her family needed her.

Once in a while, we get a maid who decides that she is going to flirt with Papa. She uses very sexy smiles, or wears low-cut blouses displaying the breasts and brushes against him while serving dinner at the table, or says naughty things like, "Mr. Wartenberg, would you like some more of my delicious noodles with your fish?" Mama catches on very quickly when that happens. Matter of fact, Mama no longer hires anyone who is young or good-looking. They have to be over fifty years old, and if they have a mustache, that's a good requisite to getting hired. I notice things like that.

Over the years, Mama has become an expert in hiring and firing maids. For example, if they wear black stockings, she makes them take the stockings off and looks at their legs for syphilis sores. We sent one maid to Uncle Augusto because her belly was getting bigger every day. She told Mama that it was the result of eating too many fava beans. Mama's suspicions were correct, and the new maid was fired. Then there was the one who would not take the garbage out by five in the morning. Mama told her that, if she didn't take the garbage out, then she could not work for us anymore. That night Mama woke up hearing the maid opening the back door about five in the morning. She told Papa, "Well, it sounds like Maria is taking the garbage out like she is supposed to do."

When we got up in the morning, Maria had not only taken the garbage out, but she had also broken into Mama's linen closet and taken all the bed sheets and blankets and some other things that Mama had under lock and key. Mama cried a lot over that, but later in the evening she brought up her favorite proverb, "It's okay to lose the rings as long as we don't lose the fingers."

Mama still gets emotional over stuff that happens, but then quickly turns it around to the positive side, which is good. Otherwise, she would go crazy.

It was so scary the other night when I heard Mama screaming as she ran down the hallway and into the dining room next to the bathroom. She was crying as she grabbed Papa. "I just saw my father in the pantry room, just standing there." Papa hugged her and tried to calm her down. Then she took some more medicine that she gets from Uncle Augusto to help her calm her nerves.

I didn't say anything, but I believe that Mama has hallucinations. Every time she says something hurts, the doctors don't believe her. They tell her it's all nerves. They have her on all kinds of pills so she doesn't complain. I hate pills, needles, and doctors, but not Uncle Augusto.

I am looking forward to summer so that I can go to the *Feira Popular*, a very famous Amusement Park. Every year, we spend at least one afternoon there. We never have enough money with us for rides or to buy cotton candy or even a clay toy, but I enjoy seeing the other people screaming as they ride down the roller coaster. Most of all,

The Journey of Innocence

I can spend hours watching the motorcycle man going around and around inside his cage without falling off his bike. That proves that gravity exists. If Mama goes to the *Feira Popular*, it's usually at night with Papa. But once in a while, she will go with my brothers and me. She will buy us cotton candy, which I really like a lot, and I am allowed one ride. My favorite is the merry-go-round.

I love the smell of cotton candy, hotdogs, and the clay pottery brought in from the countryside. Pottery has a certain smell that I love. I don't know how to explain it.

Max-Leão and I are attending a home-study group at the house of a retired teacher. It is very close to where Grandma Rica used to live. Mama is worried that, if I don't brush up on Geometry, Arithmetic, and French and Portuguese grammar, I am going to forget everything by the time I get to go to high school. The classes at the home-study group are like a refresher course. Max-Leão comes with me because he is not a good student in high school and can use all the tutoring he can get. It takes us about 45 minutes to walk there from our house, but I like it because I get to chat with Max-Leão. They teach us Arithmetic, Drawing, Geometry, History, and French and Portuguese grammar.

Our teacher Julia is an assistant to the old teacher, and she is in charge of three other kids besides my brother and me. She is a young girl with lots of facial acne. She wears dresses that are very low cut and tight, which makes her breasts stick out just like the beautiful German actress Romy Schneider, her favorite actress. Julia is very romantic and loves romantic movies. During our two-hour lunch break, I look forward to sitting next to her as she describes, with the flair of a storyteller, the whole movie starring Romy Schneider that she saw over the weekend. It's better than going to the movies. Sometimes it takes more than a week for her to finish the story because she describes every scene with perfect accuracy, paying special attention to all the details, no matter how small they might be. If any of us likes a particular part and wants to hear it again, she is more than happy to repeat it.

Max-Leão and I were walking back to our house from the home-study group. We were talking about the power of the mind, and he said he wondered if that is possible.
"Of course it is possible. I do it every day. I can make anything happen!" I said, bragging about something that I knew nothing about. I just wanted to impress him.
"You can't do that," he said. "You are lying!"
We were just crossing in front of a school where kids were running down the steps. "Okay," I said to him. "Do you see that kid in the white uniform? Watch him. He is going to fall down the steps."
I pointed my finger at the boy. The boy tripped halfway down the steps and fell.
We didn't stop. We kept walking rapidly. Max-Leão became very quiet, and so did I. Max-Leão was impressed, but I knew that I had lied. I could not possibly have guessed the boy was going to fall. It simply happened that he tripped at the moment I pointed at him. It was just the luck of the draw.

Summer of 1957

I am supposed to believe that Max-Leão writes short stories and poetry about life. He is twelve years old, hates to write, and has had no life experience of any kind. I know that he is not writing this stuff. It has to be a ghost that has possessed him because he knows as much as I do about sex. That means he knows nothing. Supposedly he wrote, *"Women— women are born to be an instrument of possession, like the flowers being sold, like the long and time-consuming kisses, like the rose that upon being held is*

The Journey of Innocence

soft but frail; petals fall to my feet." Give me a break!

This was a real strange day for me. I went to the bathroom this morning and blood was coming out of my vagina for no reason. I debated what to do for a while, and finally gave up and called Mama. I felt so ashamed having to tell her that I was bleeding from there of all places.

She was not surprised and said, "Finally I can give you my present." And she left, running down the hallway.

A few minutes later she came running back with a huge paper package tied up with a rope. I thought, *What a weird time to give me a present, as I am dying.* I opened the package. It was one dozen square cotton towels, the ones she had been sewing for some time. How in the world did she know that this was going to happen to me? I was very impressed by her intuition. Then she told me that all young girls start bleeding at twelve or thirteen years old. It's called *menstruating*, and that is how they become women. It's absolutely normal to bleed every month for about five or six days. Now I really have to be careful, she told me. If a boy comes up to me and kisses me, I will become pregnant and a baby will grow inside my belly. Her advice was for me to stay away from boys and wait until I am married to get pregnant. Then she showed me how to fold the napkin and pin it to my underwear with two safety pins, one in the back and another in the front.

She took me into the sunroom and handed me a brand-new big metal bucket, saying, "From now on, this is your own personal bucket. You put cold water inside and your napkins get to soak in the water for a few hours. Then you take the napkins out and rinse them again in the bucket till the blood is all gone."

This is so disgusting. Being a girl is really the pits. I wish I were a boy instead.

When I was younger, a friend from school told me that her brother's penis would expel whitish fluid every so often. She knew about these things because her mother used to get upset and yell at her brother when she would make his bed and find the sheets all sticky. As far as I know, my brothers don't have that problem. Not every boy has that happening to him. I think that, if I had a choice, I would rather have a discharge of white sticky stuff once in a blue moon than a bloody mess every month for the rest of my life.

Last week, Mama gave Rosa, our maid, some money to spend with us at the *Feira Popular*. It was enough for one ride for each of us. I picked the twirling ride. It goes around and around, and you get sucked into the railing on your back due to the force of gravity. I believed it was going to be a pleasant ride, but I didn't like it at all. It made me dizzy and sick to my stomach. They had to stop the machine and let everybody next to me out because I threw up and the wind blew the vomit around. They screamed at me, and everybody was angry, but it was the guy's fault for not stopping the motor when I started to yell, "Please stop! Please stop! I am going to throw up!" Nope, they didn't believe me.

We have gone back to Eiriceira. It was a unanimous vote, as we all like this little fishing village a lot more than Costa da Caparica, even if it is for only one month this summer. I will never see João again. I believe it's better this way. After all, I must sacrifice myself because this is true love, like Don Pedro and the Spanish princess Donna Inez. They both lived hidden in a villa in Coimbra, because his father, the King of Portugal, did not approve of Don Pedro's choice. There was a possibility that someday she could become the queen of Portugal when Don Pedro took over the throne, and that could never be allowed to happen. So, his father the king paid two criminals to kill Donna Inez while Don Pedro was away from the villa. They killed her right in front of her children. She cried out for mercy, but they had been paid good money for killing her. Don Pedro went crazy when he learned about what happened to his beloved, the mother of his children. He hunted down the two men and proceeded to kill them personally by ripping the heart out of one through the front of his chest and the other one through his back. Later on, when Don Pedro became the king, he had the body of Donna Inez taken out from the grave and seated on the throne and everyone paid homage and kissed the hand of his dead beloved. Then he made special arrangements for Donna Inez to be buried again. He buried her and made sure that her tomb would face his when he was buried so that, when they returned again at the end of the world, the first thing they would see would be each other.

It's too bad he stayed crazy and wasted his life drinking and hanging around with the people of the streets, never to do anything else with his life, except drink, suffer, and cry. The villa where Donna Inez was murdered became known as *A Quinta das Lágrimas,* the Villa of Tears.

All the friends I had here in Eiriceira have not returned this summer. Even Madalena will be leaving in two weeks. I heard her father telling Mama and Aunt Heydee, who was visiting us, that he knew Madalena was a virgin because, when she pisses, it comes out delicately, not hard and loud. If she ever lost her virginity, he would immediately know from the sound of her peeing that she was no longer a virgin.

I am glad that he never heard me, because my peeing can be soft, but sometimes, if I'm holding on for a long time, it is loud. I am a virgin like Aunt Heydee, who has never been married.

Aunt Heydee came by to visit us for two days, and as always, something wonderful happens when she is around.

She took my two brothers and me for a country hike! I had never been on a hike.

We went up the road and into some farmland, and then she pointed to the field, "Look, corn to take home!"

We looked at her surprised because it was not ours to take. "Yeah, behind a fence!" said my brother José.

"Yeah," she said, "except these two corns are sticking out of the fence." And she pulled them out. We all ran down the hill laughing and when we got home, she boiled the corn and split it into six pieces among all of us. I love corn!

Papa visits us on weekends. He gets here late Friday and leaves Sunday evening. Mama and Papa invited me to go to the movies with them. The last time I remember going to the movies together was a long time ago to see "Snow White" for my birthday. But this weekend, what I thought was going to be great turned out really dumb. It was an American movie starring the blonde American actress Lana Turner. About halfway through the movie, the actors, young teenagers, were having a party when the parents were not home. They were drinking and some were kissing and dancing in very close embrace and I thought, *Wow. My parents are really getting cool.*

Then Papa said to Mama, in his very German accent, "This is no good for our young daughter. They are going to start fornicating in this scene. Let's leave right now."

Mama agreed.

How could they do this to me, in the middle of a great American movie? Here I was, thinking they were taking me out like a grown-up, and instead I was being treated like a child. So what? They were kissing each other. Big deal. Now I will never know the end of the movie. When are they going to treat me like an adult, like a human being, with rights?

The Journey of Innocence

One of our beach neighbors came by this morning with her granddaughter, who is only three years old, in her arms. She told us that the little girl has anemia, and she is going to die very soon, maybe in a month or two. I stared at the child who was smiling at everybody. I don't understand why God allows her to be born and die so soon. I guess that nothing lasts forever, not even a little girl for her grandmother's sake. I'm not going to let this bother me. I can't help her. I don't care anymore.

I spend most of my time sitting on the sand and staring at the ocean. I like watching the waves and the way they hit the rocks, then intertwining under them with such force that they shoot straight up into the air, each wave trying to out-do the previous one.

I like to dream and see the sunsets. I am awake to everyone who goes by because my eyes are open, and they see my body sitting on the rocks or below on the soft sand, but I'm not there in spirit, only physically. I'm getting so good at it that I can do it even when there are people around me. It feels good to be by myself. I don't need anyone or anything. I am not happy and I am not sad. I am here and I am not, just like the little girl who is going to die very soon.

That was some incredible storm last night. I woke up hearing the sound of wind and ocean hitting the rocks and moving them below us. It was louder and deeper than thunder. It felt like the earth was moving. Our house is right on the tip of the cliff, I woke up wondering if we were still on the cliff or floating on the ocean. We went to look outside our front door, and the beach was gone. The noise we had heard during the night was from a huge storm that came and took all the sand off the beach and brought in huge rocks. There wasn't a grain of sand to be found. It had all been swept clean. There were only rocks, rocks of all sizes.

The owner of the beach was sitting on the ground crying. He had lost his livelihood, because he cannot collect rent for the cloth *cabanas* when there's no sand to stick them into. There is no beach to speak of anymore.

Everyone felt very sorry for him. Mama and the other women promised him that we would stay until the end of the month and still pay for the *cabanas*, even though it was very uncomfortable for us to sit on stones.

The good side to all of this was the enormous world of sea creatures that appeared before our eyes. Lots and lots of seafood to be cooked daily, and the most beautiful seashells we have ever seen were found between the rocks. Mama is going to use them to sew as decoration for my clothing and to make necklaces for everyone. Max-Leão, José, and I get to pick up a lot of crustaceous sea creatures. We put them into our beach pails and take them home to be boiled in salty water. At night, my brothers and I sit on the steps outside the house, and with a pin, we pull the tender morsels out of the shells to eat the delicious bits of the ocean. I love the taste and fresh smell of the sea.

Good news! A German company has hired Papa as their representative in Portugal. Now we can start paying back all the money that Aunt Heydee, Encarnação, and Uncle Augusto loaned us through the years. Papa will have his own office, and Mama will be helping him at work when we get back to Lisboa. She told us that Papa was chosen from among hundreds of other men because of his honesty and high morals. The company sponsors Portuguese and foreign artists who paint with their mouth or feet because they have no hands or arms. The German company uses the handicapped artists' work for postcards and calendars, and uses the money they receive to help these artists and their families with income. Everybody benefits from it—the artists, our family, and many Portuguese employees who

The Journey of Innocence

will have steady work and benefits. Most important, Papa will be getting paid a regular salary every month.

Mama already made all the arrangements for when we get back to Lisboa. The plans are set for a bathtub and a full-time maid once again, and I will be going to a private all girls high school. I will be starting this October. It is expensive, but necessary if I am to stay untouched by a goy until I marry Cousin Alberto from North America. The high school is right across from Encarnação's house, a few blocks from where we live. This will be very handy on cold winter days when I have to walk back and forth in the rain.

I am very happy that soon I will be in a real school. I will be wearing a white uniform, which is very good because my clothing is very meager. Mama also likes the idea of a uniform. I won't need a wardrobe to go to school. I only need a decent pair of shoes.

Since our sandy beach has washed away into the ocean, I have been walking more often to the tourist beach, which is just past the beach used by the fishermen. Nobody uses their beach because you might step on a fishing hook or a dead fish. We all know that this beach belongs only to the fishermen arriving with their fresh catch very early in the morning. There is no pier. They leave their colorful fishing boats of all sizes against the back wall where the tide is not supposed to reach, and they leave their nets drying all over the sand. Throughout the day, you are guaranteed to see a few old fishermen in their typical fishing gear sewing their nets by their boats, pulled along the seashore.

It's very hard for me to get up super early in the morning just to see the fishing boats coming into the bay. I did it once with Max-Leão, and they gave us a couple of sardines for helping them pull the nets ashore. I don't like sardines. They are too fat, and as always, oily or greasy stuff makes me nauseous.

Mama loves sardines, and so do her sisters. She told us about the time when she was with her sister Heydee spending the summer at the beach. Like us, they had helped some fishermen pull the fishing nets in. A couple of handsome fishermen not only gave them some sardines afterward but also prepared a small fire and broiled the fish right there on the sand.

Mama and Aunt Heydee were young and very beautiful, and every man who saw them would fall madly in love with them; the fishermen were no exception. Two handsome fishermen sat next to them on the sand and were talking to them. Aunt Heydee became so absorbed in the conversation that she didn't notice that Mama was eating the sardines, chewing the fish heads, sucking up all the juices, and then throwing what was left of the fish into the bucket right next to her, which had some water in it. As the sardines were being put into the bucket of water, their heads would swell again, and Aunt Heydee—who had only goo-goo eyes for one of the handsome fishermen—wasn't paying attention to which bucket she was taking her sardines from. She was taking the sardines from the wrong bucket and chewing on the same fish head that Mama had just spat out. As much as I love chewing on fish heads myself, I have to admit this story is the grossest I ever heard.

There is only one story that's even more disgusting than the sardine story. This is actually not a story. It is a famous Portuguese joke based on a true fact that in order to go to medical school you are either rich or starving to death because you can't afford to pay for food after you pay the tuition. Also, it could never be a true story because it is just too disgusting to be true, and I only laughed the first time I heard it. Max-Leão told me about it. Two very poor medical students attending the University of Coimbra in the north of Portugal were dissecting a human body in the lab. When they opened the dead man's stomach, they found it to be full of rice. The dead man's last meal had obviously been rice, and it was still warm. The sight of warm rice made the two hungry medical students' mouths water.

Manuel said to Mário, the other student, "There's a phone call for you out in the hallway. You better go and get it."

While Manuel was out, Mário used his hands to dig the rice out of the dead man's open stomach. Suddenly Manuel came back and realized he had been tricked when he saw Mário with a mouth full of rice.

Exasperated because he wanted the rice for himself, he said to Mário, "How disgusting! How utterly disgusting! Eating the rice from a dead man's stomach! It makes me want to puke."

Mário realized that Manuel was right and got sick to his stomach. He started to throw up back into the dead man's stomach, and then he walked away to clean himself.

Manuel had done well at tricking his friend out of the room, and with a big smile, he began eating the puked rice from the cadaver's stomach.

When we got back to Lisboa, Mama sent Papa with me to buy shoes and a raincoat for when school starts. Now, that was some trip to downtown Lisboa. He took me to the best store, the one where tourists buy their stuff. A lady came up to us, and he said, "My daughter needs a raincoat for the winter. Show me the best one you have in this store."

She did. She guaranteed that not a drop of water will go through this type of gabardine material and it will last forever. It is double-faced. One side is light gray, mostly for winter use; the other side is a soft cool blue, more for the spring look that was my fancy that day. It fits perfect. And it has a belt to match both sides. Finally, I can show my waist. Everything else I have to wear is big and wide, to last years and years. The shoes are made of real leather and they don't really fit comfortably on my big feet, but the lady said that they would stretch the more I use them.

Papa was happy with his purchases, and so was I. When Mama saw the bill with the amount he had paid, she almost fainted. She said she would never, ever again send me out with Papa to buy anything because he had just blown a small fortune. If she had known he was a spendthrift, she would have taken me herself instead.

Thank God she didn't. I love the raincoat. And the shoes, according to the saleslady, won't hurt my feet once they are broken in.

We are so modern! We have a brand new bathtub and a heating system above it which, upon lighting with a match, heats up the water for a bath. Papa was very patient at showing us how to use it. Papa also bought a washing machine! The fun starts when the clothes go through the wringer to take the water off. They come out almost dry. No more twisting by hand.

The maid called it *sissy stuff*, as she would rather wash everything by hand the old-fashioned way.

If technology keeps going like this, who knows what the future will bring. In another ten years, we will be visiting other planets. I want to travel in space so badly!

Autumn of 1957

I am so glad I was not born a princess. I know that miracles can happen and sometimes a person can become a queen or a princess by marrying someone from royalty. I hope that will never happen to me. What's the use of being rich when you have to constantly watch what you do and say in public, and every move you make has to be dignified? I saw poor Elizabeth II of England when she was visiting our country this year, and she looked like a stuffed doll smiling and waving her hand back and forth as she peeked out of the old coach during the royal parade down the *Avenida da*

The Journey of Innocence

Liberdade. I can only imagine how smelly and hot it must be inside an old coach built in 1820. The poor thing. She would have been better off walking.

I have been to the Coach Museum several times, and I always leave with a headache from the impregnated musty mold of the antique coaches. Even so, I have to admit that I like seeing them and playing in my mind the ways of yesterday, when you couldn't travel too far without a horse. Some of these coaches were enormous, like monsters, and after one trip they were done for.

I have read many books concerning the lives of the aristocratic, and it's not a pretty picture. I would never want to be a princess because I would have to follow the laws and rules of behavior as dictated by the royal people and their ancestors.

Mama vomits a lot. Trying to lose weight is not easy for her. She eats her meal, followed by, "I'll be right back." And she runs to the bathroom and vomits all the food she ate. I can hear her vomiting into the toilet. It sounds horrible. It must hurt her throat every time she does that. I don't like to vomit. She bought some Italian sticks made of hard dried bread and has been eating them instead of real bread, but it doesn't seem to help her to lose weight. It's horrible to see her suffer like that on account of food. I wish I could help, but I don't know how. It makes me sad when I don't have a solution to a problem.

I started the all-girls private high school across from Encarnação's house. This is really the best school I could ever imagine. I am so happy with the school, my raincoat, and the new shoes. There are about five or six girls per class, and the teachers know each of us by name! There's a teacher for each subject, and each teacher loves to teach her subject. I am even enjoying science. There's a lab for science experiments. There's sewing, gymnastics, and ballet classes. Portuguese, Latin, French, and English are the languages. I don't care for French, but I love English. I can't escape taking Algebra, Geometry, and Geography, but World History makes up for all the subjects that I don't like. I have counted on my fingers twelve different subjects at school, and I love every one of them, even if I still have lots of difficulty with Arithmetic and Algebra. Anything with numbers is a nightmare.

    The classrooms are so small that, no matter where I sit, I can hear and see a lot better. The girls are very grown up, and most of them have boyfriends. They go to parties at each other's homes, and they have their own little cliques to which I don't belong because I am different. I have no boyfriend, no parties at my house, no friends, and no freedom of any kind. Even though we all wear the same uniform, they can tell that I don't have pretty clothes bought from fancy stores like they do underneath. My clothes are made at home. I wear my hair straight because I get a headache when I use hair curlers. I don't go to the beauty parlor because Mama can't afford to pay for it, and besides, every time I get my hair curled, they burn my hair, my scalp, and the top of my ears with the chemical they use for making the hair curl. The beauticians say I have delicate hair and I am allergic to the chemicals touching my skin. At school they call me *existentialist* because I am different from my schoolmates. Even though I was born in Portugal, my last name makes me a foreigner.

I walked home repeating in my head over and over again the joke I heard in school today. My friend Beatriz is the one who told me, and I thought it was really funny. I waited until everybody was seated for dinner so that I would have a nice-sized audience. My intent was to impress Mama and Papa with my humor, because a few years ago Papa was very impressed with my tongue clicking at the roof of my mouth. Both of them were amazed at my creativity and had

The Journey of Innocence

laughed heartily. I wanted to make them laugh again.

We were all about to start eating the vegetable bean soup when I said, "There was this young girl sitting on top of a tree. She wasn't wearing underwear because she was very poor and couldn't afford to buy it. A man walked under the tree, looked up, and felt sorry for the young girl. He said to her, 'Here pretty girl, take this 25 *centavos* and buy yourself some underwear.' She ran home happily to tell her mother what happened. The next day, the mother figured that would be an easy way to make a living so she got herself on top of the tree without underwear and waited patiently for the same kind gentleman to walk by under the tree. That day it happened he was walking by and happened to look up at the tree. When he saw she was not wearing underwear, he said to her, 'You poor woman, take this 50 *centavos* and go get yourself a shave.'"

I barely made it to the punch line trying to control my laughter.

Papa didn't laugh. He got very angry. "This is a very offensive joke to tell your parents."

Mama seemed to have a smile on her face, but added, "You shouldn't tell jokes like these at the table. It's in very poor taste."

Papa stopped eating and continued to lecture. "An educated and proper-mannered girl would never talk like that. Verónica, you have disappointed me."

My tears fell in the soup, and I swore to myself that I would never again tell a joke or open myself to them. This is a lesson to learn. They are my fuddy-duddy parents, not my friends.

According to Mama, calf brains are guaranteed to help increase intelligence and clear the thought process during school exams. I don't know if that actually makes me smarter, but Mama says eating them is good for my brain. I personally don't believe it, but I like their taste when they get stewed in wine sauce. The other thing that makes me laugh—and I only take it to make Mama happy—is the medicine that she gives me in a tablespoon before I leave the house to take the tests in school. I entered the kitchen one day and saw her preparing the concoction—sugar and water! I know I am not smart, but I'm not that stupid either. She says it's a calming medicine from Uncle Augusto's medicine cabinet. She doesn't know that I saw her making it. Mama likes to use psychology, but it doesn't work with me. She lies.

"Ah, Burt Lancaster, now that's a man who takes my breath away," said Mama as she delicately sipped the tea from her china cup. Aunt Heydee and Aunt Simy were visiting us. They were all having tea and butter cookies.

"Oh, no," said Aunt Simy. "For me, there's no one like Kirk Douglas and his cute, dimpled chin."

"All American movie stars are handsome," said Aunt Heydee in all her wisdom.

Mama turned to me and asked, "I am curious, Verónica. Who do you like as a man?"

"Jerry Lewis!" I responded without blinking an eye and knowing well in advance that was not the answer they wanted to hear.

"Why, in Heaven?" said Aunt Simy, looking at me as if I were an oddball.

"He is a twit, a nerd," they said almost unanimously. Their faces showed complete disappointment.

I had to explain. "He makes me laugh!"

"That's not a normal man. How can a girl your age like a man who acts and looks like a clown?" said Aunt Simy.

And then, to my surprise, Mama defended me. "It's okay that she likes Jerry Lewis. She is still at the age of innocence. She enjoys his humor and appreciates it. That's fine, Verónica." And she smiled at me.

My goodness. Mama sometimes is truly a wonderful

person. She has moments when I could kiss her, but I didn't. I am not going to show any weakness toward her. Every time I do, I am sorry later on. If I stay hard on the inside, she can't hurt my feelings. I am so confused.

My friend Amelia and her family went back to Africa. We cried a lot this morning as we hugged each other and said goodbye forever. I will miss them, their perfume, their gay, lively attitude, the loud African music, and, most of all, Amelia. She will live forever in my heart.

Winter of 1958

I like storytelling, and I don't mind when a story is told over and over again. But there are a few corny ones that Mama is always more than happy to tell, like the "Ten Little Friends." There was this woman who had gotten married. When her husband would come home from work, she had been sleeping all day and was too tired to do any housework. The poor husband would come home for lunch, and she was still sleeping. He would come home for dinner, and she had done nothing all day but sleep. She didn't do any housewife duties. Dinner was never ready, and the house was always dirty and dusty. She was just plain lazy.

Then one day a fairy godmother appeared to her and said, "What's your wish?"

And the woman said, "I need help to take care of the house and have everything done by the time my husband gets home—the dishes cleaned, the food ready, the clothes ironed. You know, the usual housewife duties."

And the fairy godmother said, "Okay, my dear, your wish is granted. I will give you ten little invisible magical friends to help you with all of the chores, but you must get up early and help them. Otherwise, they will not help you either."

The next morning, the woman couldn't wait to get up

early, as the good fairy had advised. She made her husband breakfast, and after he left to go to work, she started dusting. Then, after washing the dirty clothes in the tub and hanging them outside to dry, she put them away to be ironed in the afternoon. She arranged some fresh flowers on the table after preparing lunch, and she got all cleaned up for her husband, who was delighted to see lunch ready.

Then he went back to work. She did the dishes and scrubbed and waxed the wooden floors and did the ironing and made a gourmet dinner after dusting the furniture and washing the windows. She noticed that by that evening she had done all her duties. The ten invisible little friends were definitely her best friends. She had everything done at the end of the day, just like she was supposed to. Thanks to her ten invisible friends, she was even dressed pretty and her hair looked really nice and she didn't smell of onions or garlic—only perfume. When her exhausted husband got home that night, she had his favorite drink ready for him. This went on day after day, month after month, and year after year. They had five children, and they all lived happily ever after. Who were her ten friends? Who could have possibly helped this woman to become a good wife and later a good mother, one might ask? Well, I have to pause and give it some thought as if this is the very first time I heard the story. I make believe that I am thinking about the answer—that's half the fun, and then Mama lifts her hands in the air and opens her fingers wide, saying, "Her ten little fingers, of course!"

Mama took me out for a surprise. She would not tell me what it was all about. She loves mystery, and she kept saying, "You will see. You will see. Be patient!"

We reached the fourth floor of an old apartment house around the corner from where we live, and a very old woman dressed in black from head to toe opened the door and let us in. Her place was exactly the way I imagine a

The Journey of Innocence

witch's house to be. I felt like I was inside a dark forest, smelly and dusty, with lots and lots of costumes and hats and everything one can imagine from days of forgotten times, the times of queens and princes and fairy tales. Nothing looked real. In the kitchen, she was probably brewing magic potions. The aroma of her cooking was unrecognizable. Hanging on the walls and all over the tables and chairs and everywhere were costumes, masks, and hats in complete chaotic disarray.

The most elaborate and expensive wardrobe was hanging along the left side of the long room, and it covered what was once a window. Mama told her that she was on a very tight budget and asked her to show us the least expensive outfits. It all looked good to me. I picked a gypsy outfit from the inexpensive rack. Mama agreed. The price was within her budget. It's going to be *Carnaval* in a few days, and I will have a real costume, like all the other kids. This is the real thing!

Mama had everything planned. She had matinee tickets for all of us. My makeup was a real workout for Mama and Aunt Heydee. It wasn't easy to make my straight hair get curly like a gypsy would wear around her face. Red lipstick, green eye shadow, black eyelash coloring, and of course, the most important part of all of the makeup, the *piece de resistance*, a black mole on my right cheek drawn carefully with Mama's personal black pencil she uses for drawing her own mole when she goes somewhere special with Papa. When they finally were finished with me, Mama took a deep breath of contentment. She said, "So, this is the way Verónica will look when she gets to be an adult. Not bad with makeup."

I think Mama enjoyed seeing me look pretty.

We all had fun costumes. Max-Leão was a pirate with an eye patch, and José a cowboy. Aunt Heydee made her own dress out of something, nobody knows what or how, but she looked like a queen. Even though *Carnaval* is meant to be for kids only, there's no law that says adults can't have fun. In Brazil, adults get all dressed up and celebrate *Carnaval* with a huge parade. Mama didn't want to go with us. She had only five tickets, and she sent the maid with us instead, to watch us. The show was an American musical, and it showed the way Americans live, always singing and dancing every time they go out to a restaurant or out into the field to work on the farm.

Intermission was horrible. The kids and the adults with them were throwing little bags full of hard corn tied to elastic strings so that they could hit you in the head and immediately retrieve the bags before you could catch them. Each hit was very painful. The bags of corn felt more like stones. I didn't have corn bags to fight back, so I was at their mercy. If that's entertainment, they must be mad. It wasn't a laughing matter. I could feel the lumps starting to form on my skull. I promised myself that I would never again go to one of these *Carnaval* events with other kids. I'm too grown up for that. No wonder Mama didn't join us. She is smarter than I give her credit for.

Aunt Heydee agreed with me that getting hit over the head over and over again with a bag of dried corn was a cruel and childish way to enjoy the *Carnaval*. She took my picture outside the theatre and told me I looked too beautiful to go home. She sent my brothers home with the maid and took me to her favorite dance hall so that I could show off my outfit. She said I could go with her, but I was not allowed to dance. Because of my age, I was not allowed to enter the dancehall. She got me to sit on a fainting couch outside the main ballroom. From there, I was able to watch her dance. Aunt Heydee can dance to any tune. She has a natural beat.

I sat there thinking about Mama when she was young and used to come to places like this with her sisters. She has told us several times about the young man who came up to her and said, "Would you like something to drink?"

The Journey of Innocence

And she said, "Whiskey!"

He came back with a whiskey, and then asked her to dance with him. She said, "No, I do not want to dance with you!"

And when he asked her why not, she responded by saying, "Because you are not my type, and I despise you."

I don't like that story. It bothers me that she brags about this event and she is even proud of being arrogant and harsh as a young woman. I hope I never become like her.

I decided not to think about things like that. I watched all those grownups twirling under the shiny crystal chandeliers and white stone pillars that reminded me of an old Greek palace. A man came up to me and asked me to go inside with him to dance.

Feeling my cheeks getting red with embarrassment, I told him, "I am sorry, but I'm not allowed to do that. I'm only here because I am waiting for my Aunt Heydee, who is dancing over there." And I pointed to her.

He said he was going to be right back.

Not ten minutes passed by and Aunt Heydee came up to me and grabbed my hand. "C'mon, let's get out of here," she said hurriedly. "If your mother finds out that I brought you to this place, she will have my head."

I started to tell Aunt Heydee about the man who had approached me, and she cut me off saying, "Yeah, I know all about him. He is a lawyer. And he had the balls to tell me that he had a lot of money and would pay anything to dance with you. I told him that you are only thirteen years old and not for sale."

I have stopped eating chocolates and potato chips since the beginning of the year. I get 30 *escudos* per month as my allowance. I don't go to the movies. If I go twice in one month, I don't have any more money, and my goal now is to save enough money to buy a birthday gift for Papa in April and hopefully for Mama next December. I am on a mission. I have my eye on a small diamond pin for Papa's tie and a colorful, real stone broach for Mama. This is going to impress them both. I know they love me, but when they get these presents they will love me even more. I get a regular paycheck from working weekends and evenings at Papa's office. I work all of the weekends. The more hours, the more money I can put together. I need a lot of money if I am to buy the gifts. I address and stuff envelopes with postcards and calendars and information on the artists. People are amazed at how these artists paint beautiful artwork using the brush with their mouth or feet. Some were born without arms, and some lost their limbs in a car accident and have become wheelchair-bound, without any other means to make a living. Papa and the German company make a living from giving these people a second chance. Life can be brutal unless we make the best we can with what God gives us daily.

For the last three months, I spent most of my morning weekends at Cousin Leonardo's library. He is a distant cousin of the Ezaguy family, which is probably the reason I had never heard of him or his wife until Aunt Heydee arranged for me to come to their home and use their private library.

It was my intention to read all of their books until last week, when their two sons and daughter came home before I left. I felt out of place in my meager dress, and I was also afraid to say something stupid. I tried to leave, but they insisted that I stay and have lunch with them. Their maid brought us hot milk with toast and cheese. They were as nice as they could be toward me, but I knew that I didn't belong. I made every effort to eat my sandwich and not drop any crumbs on the white tablecloth. Then Miguel, the younger boy, said something really funny as I was drinking my milk. I couldn't help laughing along with them, except that the unexpected happened. The milk came pouring out of my nose. Everybody was laughing at me. I tried to laugh, too, while I was crying on the inside for being such a jerk.

Aunt Heydee told me that they were asking about me and wondering why I had stopped going to their home. I told Aunt Heydee that I finished reading all of their books.

Spring of 1958

I don't like Portuguese music. The *fado* music is sad and depressing. The Portuguese are never happy when they sing. It's always the same old story, someone they love either died or is cheating on them. I'd rather listen to rock and roll. I love Elvis Presley, Big Joe Turner, Chuck Berry, Bill Haley, Paul Anka, and so many I can't even count on my fingers. They are all great. They make me move, and I feel happy from my toes to my head. When I hear their music on the radio, I can't sit still.

The two most painful events in my life are menstruation cramps once a month and my birthday celebration. In my family, everything is always a big secret. Everybody most likely knows what's going on, but it's still kept a secret. So, Aunt Heydee takes me to a movie matinee. That's her present for my birthday, but I'm not supposed to tell anyone because she wants everyone to think that she is on a very fixed income, which *everybody* already knows.

Then Mama comes to me and whispers, "I'm going to take you to the midday movie matinee, but I don't want you to tell anyone. Most of all, don't tell your father, because he is going to take us both tonight to the movies for your birthday!" Three times in one day I sit on a chair. It is a total of almost six hours, and that's when my tailbone hurts. Since I fell on my back in Eiriceira, sitting for too long is very painful to my tailbone. I am keeping my fingers crossed that, when I turn fifteen years old, there will be a surprise party for me with balloons and a birthday cake covered with fifteen candles. Also, Mama will give me a beautiful dress with a wide skirt like Encarnação's daughters wear and high heeled shoes. And in the evening I will be allowed to go dancing, and I will meet a handsome young man. We will fall in love and get married, and we will live happily ever after.

I was going for a walk to downtown Lisboa. I had just turned the corner of our street to go down to the *Praça do Chile* to take the trolley when I was inundated with a glow of sunshine. The air became like a transparent gown that covered me with life from inside my soul to my skin and hair. I know that, scientifically speaking, there's no explanation, but it was like being lifted by angels. I knew that God was once again very visible to me, as life itself. Wow! What a feeling. It lasted just a few minutes, but I was smiling the rest of the day. Too bad this feeling doesn't happen more often. I love it. Love it!

Mama came home very excited and told us that she had visited a fortune teller and was told that her three children would be like stars, each going in a different direction.
    I don't understand why that was such good news, unless she is happy that my brothers and I are leaving home. What I wonder is, where are we going? The gypsy didn't say. I don't believe they can tell the future by looking at one's hand. It all sounds to me like psychology talk. They always say the same stuff, "You have someone special in your life. You have lost someone special in your life. Watch out for someone who envies you, they will try to hurt you. You will be going on a long trip—soon."
    This gypsy reading was different from the usual mumbo-jumbo they always say. Maybe there's something true about it, and my brothers and I will be going in different directions. I hope not too far from home.

The Journey of Innocence

Mama made me take José to the hospital for his asthma treatment, which consists of me sitting with him in a closed airtight box with other asthmatic people. Then they pressurize the compartment, as if we were flying in an airplane. This is supposed to help José breathe. I cried with the pressure in my ears. It hurt like hell. Mama was very nice about it when I told her. I don't have to do it again, but I have to take José for breathing treatments with some smelly stuff that's supposed to help his lungs. I am not his mother. Mama should be the one going with José, not me. The smell makes me nauseous. I want to throw up every time I go with him.

Mama started sending the maid with José for the breathing treatments at the hospital. Thank God for that. I don't know how José or the maid can stand that smell.

If I am going to enter the second year of high school, I will have to pass an entrance exam on all the subjects I have taken this year. This is the only way to graduate from one year to next. It is a very demanding experience. The oral and written exams are given at another school, so there's no funny business with our own teachers giving us a good grade and passing us. I have been doing slightly below average, and for me that's maximum because I am not as smart as Max-Leão or José. I don't even come close to Max-Leão's photographic memory or José's genius with Arithmetic, Physics, and Geometry. I'm barely passing everything by the seat of my pants, and that's because the teachers are very good and the classes are small and intimate. If it weren't for every single one of them being such good teachers, I would know absolutely nothing, just like when I was in primary school. The four years that I attended it were a waste of time. I never had any idea what was really being taught, and I never got a good foundation. Wearing glasses now helps me to see what's written on the blackboard, but I consider myself to be a terrible student and taking tests is pure torture. It's pathetic that during the oral exam your family can come into the school and watch you make a fool of yourself. I made Mama and Aunt Heydee promise they would sit quietly in the last row of the examining room.

For dinner last night, Mama had the maid prepare calf brains stewed in wine just for me. When we left the house this morning, Mama gave me a spoonful of the usual magic potion she calls *brainpower medicine*. She is a great believer in the power of suggestion, that's for sure, but I know better than that. I am going to fail the tests miserably no matter what I eat or drink. Some things are just too hard for me to do, and taking tests is one of them.

Three professors sat at a long desk, and one of them called my full name, pronouncing it with difficulty. I had been watching each student get up and be questioned. They would go up to the blackboard, pick up a piece of chalk, and wait until one of the examiners gave them an algebra problem. They would write down the solution to the problem. Then they would answer a few more questions and wait until one of the professors said, "Thank you. You may return to your seat."

So, I got up, but I didn't go to the blackboard. Whatever they were going to ask me, I already knew I would not have the answer, so I stood close to their desk and smiled at them, saying to myself, "What the heck am I going to do now? Please, dear God, help me."

One of them said, "Go to the board and write down the solution to the problem I am going to give you."

I smiled again and didn't move an inch. I couldn't, because I was paralyzed with fear.

She said, "Are you hard of hearing?"

The one sitting in the middle said, "Didn't you see her name? She is a foreigner! Don't ask her to write, ask her to

The Journey of Innocence

tell you the answer."

She did that, slowly and louder, as if that was going to make me understand her any better. With my fingers crossed behind my back, I looked at them, and with the most innocent look on my face, I jabbered out, very sure of myself, the sounds of an instantly made-up language, "Oinkra, bingsy ah harling lonk zap, yahr, toom!"

The examiners asked each other, "What did she say?" All three of them were intrigued. All three of them were actually puzzled.

The examiner at the end of the table repeated the algebra question once again, looking straight at me.

I raised my hands up as if I was describing it along with my words in a manner that I hoped to come across as starting to get impatient with their ignorance of my language, and I spoke a lot faster this time, "Oinkrabings-yahharlinglonk-zapyahr-toom!"

"It sounds German," one of them said.

"Are you German?" asked the examiner on the left.

I was quick at answering, "German, yah!" I said, remembering how Papa had tried to teach my brothers and me a few simple German words one evening with no success. Frustrated, he had announced in German, "Yah." And then in Portuguese, he added, "My children, you sure are retarded." Then he lifted his arms in the air and left the room as he gave up on us.

"She looks very confident of herself and seems to know what she is saying," said one of the professors smiling at me as if he understood my dilemma. I stood there, looking straight at them and telling myself, *keep smiling and don't faint.*

They talked among themselves and were convinced of my knowledge, but in another language. "Thank you, Miss Wartenberg. You can sit down now," they said almost in unison as they smiled at me.

I couldn't move. My feet were glued to the ground I was

standing on. I questioned what they said with my eyes. The one closest to me repeated, "Sit down." She pointed to her own chair as she got up and sat on it again.

I went back to my seat. I got 18 out of 20 in my exam. I have never had 18 in any subject, not even history. My normal score is 11, a *passing* grade on anything I do.

I did get Mama and Aunt Heydee's full admiration for my ingenuity. When we left the school, Aunt Heydee said, "You are truly my niece. I am Napoleão #1, but as of today, you are officially Napoleão #2."

Mama agreed. I am going places someday.

Summer of 1958

The book *I Killed my Son* by my brother Max-Leão was published. At first Aunt Heydee did not believe that it was my brother's writing, but she loves my brother so much that it didn't take Mama long to convince her. Her doubts were unjustified; after all, writing runs in our family's blood. Aunt Ligia is a writer. Cousin Augusto was a well-known writer, and there is a street in Lisboa named after him. He was very famous. Even Uncle Augusto, Mama's brother, wrote poetry prior to going to medical school. He wrote the lyrics for much of Mama's original music. All the critics are in an uproar because my brother is only twelve years old but writes like a playboy. They call him a *child prodigy*.

I love sugar as much as I love salt. Codfish is salty, but it's not my favorite food unless it's made *Gomez Sá* style, with potatoes and onions. We have codfish just about every day. Meat and chicken are only for special occasions. They say that there are at least one hundred different codfish recipes. My least favorite is boiled codfish with potatoes, carrots, and cabbage, and then served sprinkled with olive oil, lemon juice, and finely chopped garlic and parsley. This has got to be the most boring food in the world. And that is Mama's favorite dish, which means we have to eat it, too.

I like what Papa says. Food is to be enjoyed for its texture and taste and presentation, and to eat like an animal without appreciating all of these factors and the components that go into making it special is like turning your back on a sunset.

I really like *tremoços*, a small salty yellow bean usually served free at the taverns in Lisboa. Aunt Heydee told me that this type of legume is also called *lupine bean*, and she believes that they were most likely introduced to Portugal when we were under the rule of the Roman Empire.

Over the years, I have developed a very efficient technique for eating *tremoços*. First, I put an incision on the outer skin layer with my front teeth, and then I "pop" the deliciously salty seed directly into my mouth. When I was younger, I would enter a tavern and grab some *tremoços* from a small dish on the counter. They want their customers to keep drinking as they develop a devouring thirst for more cold beer because of the salt. Lately I have been feeling too old to steal *tremoços*, so, when I am in the mood for something salty and very inexpensive, I buy a small bag from a street vendor or at the grocery store. Without salt, food would have no taste.

Once upon a time, there was a king who wanted to know how much his daughter truly loved him, so he asked her. She told him, "I love you as much as salt."

He was really upset with her answer, because to him salt had no value whatsoever. Out of anger, he threw her out of his kingdom. She was lucky he didn't kill her. To prove how useless salt was, he gave her all the salt he had in storage to take with her. He didn't think that salt was important until he got his next meal. He spat out his first spoonful of soup, and when he got to the stew, he realized how tasteless it was without salt. He immediately came to the realization that he needed salt or he was going to starve to death. His people were also very upset and wanted a new king, someone who had salt to share with them. Without delay, the king sent out his emissaries to look for his daughter since she had taken all the salt with her. When they found her, they told her that the king, her father, was very sorry and was willing to accept her back if she could only return with the salt. She did, and they lived very happily ever after.

We have returned to Eiriceira for our summer vacation, but we are staying at a modest house very close to the more modern beach, the one with resorts and lots of tourists. This beach has sand. The other small beach where we used to go to is still bare of any sand. Our rental house is right next to a park overlooking the ocean. The park has a roller skating rink, swings, and steps that go down to the cliffs below us where the lobsters are kept alive for the restaurants above to use. When one walks above the rocks, it's really neat to see the lobsters underneath our feet in their manmade homes built into the rocks. The metal bars above the lobsters' cages remind me of the *Torre de Belém*, the Tower of Belem, the prison where political prisoners are still being put inside dungeons. Here the lobsters love the high tide, but the men put in the bottom of the Tower of Belem are not sea creatures and they drown. The tower just happens to be conveniently located next to the River Tejo.

My private arithmetic teacher's son was only eighteen years old when he was taken by the government's secret police. Someone tipped them off that the boy had Communist books at home. They broke into my teacher's house and took Raul away. It's been a year now, and she still has no idea what happened to him. She thinks that Raul might have been sent to one of our African territories, like Angola or Mozambique, and put into jail. She keeps telling me, "I wonder if I will ever see my son again."

I don't believe she will see him again, but I didn't tell

The Journey of Innocence

her that. Our President Salazar is a good dictator. That's what everybody says out of fear. I am sure that my teacher's son is dead. Most likely he drowned in the Tower of Belem. Why spend for a ticket to Africa when they can kill him closer to home? Mother Nature takes care of the political prisoners, and the government officials can wash their hands. After all, is it their fault that the water rises with the tide and above their cells? *Ooops! Soooooorry!*

This new beach in Eiriceira is too big for me. I don't know anyone here. I spend the days sitting on one of the swings at the park and reading. I realize that I am too shy to talk to strangers, and I'd rather read and stare at the ocean. I can stare into anything and block everything around me. I can disappear anytime I want. I just concentrate until everything around me is gone and I just float away.

I have read all of the books I brought along with me from home so that the summer won't be boring. Some of my favorites, I have read over and over again. They are *Alice in Wonderland, David Copperfield, Oliver Twist, The Count of Monte Cristo, Arabian Nights,* most of *The Adventures of Sherlock Holmes,* and so many more.

Someone told me there is a lady on the other side of town who rents out used books, mostly romance novels, for 10 *centavos* each. I am dying to read a romance novel. With my allowance, I will be able to read ten books this month.

I read faster than I thought. I already rented five more books. Mama gave me some change to buy ice cream. When Mama is happy, she shares some of her money with me. I filled my bedroom bottom drawer with six bags of potato chips and two chocolate bars. The chocolate will not last more than a day.

I tried to roller skate. It's not easy. I have to hold on to the railing around the skating rink. I do not want to fall. Falling on the slippery rocks a few years ago hurt my tailbone really bad. I still can't sit for hours and hours on a hard chair without feeling pain. I can't afford to fall again. I am very careful now. Aunt Heydee is a good skater. Some kids were making fun of her and laughing because her clothing is very flamboyant and not for her age. She started to talk to them, and by the time she was done chatting, they asked her to join their group. She is an amazing person.

I was sitting on the sand this morning by our beach *cabana* while reading one of my romance novels. Mama appeared out of nowhere, grabbed the book out of my hand, and said sternly, "Let's see what it is that you are constantly reading." Just my luck, she opened to the page where it described a passionate kiss between the two main characters. Just my luck, of all the pages she could open to, she reads that one. She called it *pure trash* and said now she knew why I was so uncivilized. She would not give the book back to me and prohibited me from reading any more novels.

I was sitting on the sand and acting like I was staring at the ocean, but I was actually deep into an adventure of love and danger. A handsome pirate had kidnapped me from my parents' home and was taking me to his hidden island somewhere in Hawaii. I was debating in my mind if I really wanted to get away from him or get to know more about my future boyfriend, the pirate.

    I was pulled into reality when Mama abruptly interrupted my fantasy. She said, "I have gone through a lot of work trying to find you a friend." Then she pointed to a young woman sitting by the ocean. "Over there. Her name is Clara. Go talk to her. She is looking for a friend."

    I could just imagine Mama talking to a complete stranger about me. "My daughter is a nerd. She has no

The Journey of Innocence

friends, and she is obsessed with reading trashy novels. Can you help her? Please, please!"

I got up against my will and walked over to Clara. I sat down across from her and said, "My mother wants me to talk to you."

She was twenty-three years old! She asked me if I had a boyfriend. She must be kidding! She didn't say much after that, and I didn't either. Mama always passes me on to others to take care of me, like when I need to go to the dentist. Aunt Heydee is the one who goes with me. I doubt that this woman on the beach and I will ever be friends. She is old. We have nothing in common to talk about. Clara was just as uncomfortable as I was, and seemed relieved when I finally got up and said goodbye.

This afternoon I had to go to the Costa do Sol Hotel to meet with Clara, the woman from the beach. She was having lunch with other women her age. Mama told me she went through a lot of trouble to set me up for this meeting at the hotel. It was for my own good, because she wants me to stop acting like an unsocial animal. It's obvious that I will never be able to read a romance novel again. From now on, I will have to write my own love stories inside my head as I make believe that I am paying attention to the jibber jabber around me.

When I got to the lunch meeting at the hotel, they already had finished their food. There was a small plate of ice cream that they told me to eat.

"No, thank you," I said.

"All kids love ice cream!" said one of them.

I looked straight in her eyes and lied, "I don't like ice cream." How dare she call me a kid?

They kept insisting, and I kept refusing. Finally the ice cream melted. I felt bad that I had not eaten it, but I also felt proud that I'd stuck to my guns. I am not a kid. If I choose not to eat ice cream, that's my prerogative. It's bad enough that I had to sit a whole afternoon with a bunch of older women who talk only about boyfriend experiences.

The end of this summer has been lonely and boring without books to read or anyone to talk to. My brothers are gone to do their boy stuff, and I am left alone. Except for watching the sunsets while seated on the swings, I have nothing to live for.

Today a man stopped by the swing where I was dangling and said, smiling, "I see you on the swings every day. You must really like it."

I didn't know what to say. I shook my head "yes," and then I ran home. I have to look for another place to hang out. He might come back, grab me, and then squeeze me like a lemon. We are going back to Lisboa in one week. I am staying away from the swings from now on.

Autumn of 1958

Good news from North America! Next spring, Aunt Nelly, Mama's sister, is coming to visit us. A few months ago, her husband died from cancer. The story goes that it's been close to thirty years since she left as a young girl to marry her third cousin, Ralph, who was a pharmacist. Cousin Ralph lived in New York. He was visiting Portugal for a few days when he met Aunt Heydee at the temple in Lisboa. Aunt Heydee found out he was single and alone, so she did what any kind person would do, she invited him to come home for dinner with her family that evening. It turned out that his great-grandfather was the brother of Aunt Heydee's great-grandfather, on her dad's side, which made them cousins. Two days later, Cousin Ralph returned to North America. About a month later, Aunt Heydee received a letter from Ralph asking for her hand in marriage. In a moment of true love and devotion to her family, who needed her more here in Portugal than abroad, she sacrificed herself. She sent a letter back saying, "Thank you, Cousin Ralph, but the one you must be asking the hand of in marriage has to be Nelly. She is the most beautiful of all my sisters and also the most intelligent."

Soon Aunt Nelly got her papers in order and was waving goodbye to her family and crying as she boarded the ship to the USA. Her mother and father were never to see her again, a small price to pay because her life was going to be easier and a lot more fruitful in North America.

Aunt Heydee cried a lot when Cousin Ralph died. He had been more than true to her over all those years, not only being a good husband to her sister Nelly but also sending her a twenty-dollar bill every single month. Once a month, she blessed his name.

In preparation for her sister's visit, Mama is having the kitchen walls painted white. The smaller front room facing the street will be Nelly's bedroom while she is staying with us. Max-Leão and José will move to the big front room with the balcony, and I will be sleeping in the room next door to it where I will have no privacy. I will have two doors that people can walk through at any time. Except for the lock on the bathroom door, none of the locks in our house work.

"So, Verónica, tell us about your boyfriend," Mama asked during dinner.

"What boyfriend?" She had to be kidding.

"Someone told me about him," she said, winking at me. "It's very sad that you never confide in me, your own mother, and I have to find out these things from other people."

I was shocked. "I don't have a boyfriend," I said, surprised at her remarks.

"Yes, you do. You have a boyfriend! Now tell us about him and stop lying about it."

My eyes started to tear as I tried very hard not to cry.

Papa came to my rescue, "Let's stop this nonsense right now. If Verónica says she has no boyfriend, she doesn't have one. Verónica never lies. Daughter, I believe you!"

Wow, thank you for believing in me. You may never show any affection and for the most part I am scared of you, but sometimes you are a real Dad to me. Thank you. Of course, I didn't say what I was thinking.

I have two girlfriends in school, Beatriz and Laura. Beatriz and I have one thing in common: we are the only two girls in school who are not Catholic. She is Protestant. We both get excused from religion class for an hour twice a week. Beatriz and I get to talk about our lives in the school's garden. She is always telling me that I am lucky to be a Jew because we were already persecuted. Now it's the Protestants' turn, and some day she will wind up in a concentration camp for Protestants. I told her that, because we are good friends, if that happens, she could hide in my house with her family.

Laura, on the other hand, became my friend because we walk home together. She has to pass my house first on the way to hers. We always leave school together and talk about the girls who are snobs and arrive at school in their chauffeured cars. I really don't care. I have been alone all my life. This is no different, but it gives us something to talk about, I guess. Laura wears too much makeup, and she uses the wrong color of face powder, which makes her skin very pale. I don't have the courage to tell her that she doesn't look real. I also think that her skin pores can't possibly breathe normally under so much makeup, but I don't have the courage to tell her my worries. She dresses very proper and wears her blonde hair up and twisted into a bun on top of her head in the style of today's fashion. I wear my hair straight down most of the time because curlers give me a headache. When I want the "curly" look,

The Journey of Innocence

I use newspaper strips to curl my hair. It lasts about two hours before it goes straight again. Laura is also very skinny. I don't think she eats much. She doesn't like school and intends to get married as soon as she is allowed to start dating. Her parents are not making her marry anyone in particular, but they are strict and she is not to date until she is eighteen years old.

A chicken and a turkey disappeared from our backyard. The household is in an uproar because we don't know who could have stolen them. The police were called, and there were no clues. This means we don't have the main course for New Year's dinner.

Winter of 1959

Papa gave me a book by the American writer, Hemingway. "From now on, you will read only classic books, the kind a young lady should read, with quality writing. Your mother told me about the silly girly novels you have been reading. They are no good for you, and they put crazy ideas in a young girl's head. When you finish this one, you let me know and I'll get you another book."

I was thrilled to have a new book to read. I said thank you and ran into the sunroom to read the first pages.

Mamma mia! I am stunned that Americans are so talented at writing music and yet, not when it comes to books. This is the worst I have ever read. I have been skipping pages as I read this guy's book. Ernest Hemingway has very poor skills at writing, in my personal opinion. He uses little paragraphs, not enough description, and lots of bad words. Talk about trashy stuff! My romance novel's worst moment is a kiss, which drove Mama nuts. I am not going to say anything. We will see what books Papa comes up with next. I would rather have books about Egyptian, French, and Portuguese history. I'm going to go bonkers reading this boring *American literature*, as Papa calls it.

Max-Leão was on national television. He was the guest star of the evening talk show, and I was very impressed how he was able to pull through it. Poor thing, he must have been so scared. We never talk about his writing. I feel this is a taboo subject, and I don't dare to bring more pressure into his life. He has enough discomfort already inside his ears. Mama keeps saying that Max-Leão is very loving because he gets on his knees and puts his head on her lap when she is seated. He told me that the reason he is always hugging her that way and putting his head on her lap is because the pressure of her hands over his ears helps to ease the pain. I believe that Mama is aware of that. Otherwise, why would she press her hands over his ears?

An English woman came to my school. Miss Alexandra something. She was an agent or a scout of some kind, trying to find ballerinas for her school in London. She came up to me, and as she touched my legs, she commented on my strong legs and good posture. She asked me how long I had been dancing and if I wanted to be a professional ballerina. I had to control my emotions when I told her that I would love to be a real ballerina. Either she or the school's principal called Mama that day, because Mama told me that "no" was the answer when I got home. I was not going to England. I am her only daughter, and I am too young to be far away from her. I was not surprised. These are not her plans for my life.

This afternoon, Max-Leão and I were walking a few blocks from our home on the *Avenida Duke de Avila* when a group of schoolgirls dressed in their white uniforms saw us. One of them screamed to the others, "It's Max-Leão! It's Max-Leão!" And they came running down the hill toward us. Max-Leão grabbed my arm and yelled, "Quick, let's run for

The Journey of Innocence

our lives. They will kill us if they catch us."

We ran like bats out of hell around the street corner and took refuge through an open apartment door facing the street. We locked it from inside and waited a while until the mad group of girls had gone by yelling his name. Finally, silence told us it was safe to leave. I wonder what they would have done to him and to me as his sister if they had caught us. Being famous can be a curse!

Someone snitched on my brother José. We found out José was the one who kidnapped the chicken and the turkey. He had hidden the birds in his friend's backyard because he didn't want them to be killed. He even paid from his own allowance for their feed and care. Everyone was touched by this act of kindness, but that didn't save the chicken and the turkey from their cruel destiny. We ate them—except for José, who got out of eating the birds by getting sick with an asthma attack that took him to the hospital. He is now taking experimental drugs to see if they help his asthma.

When I got home today, I heard that Max-Leão was doing a science project for school, by locking himself in the bathroom and covering all the holes under the door and window so that oxygen couldn't get in. He had made too much smoke by burning some stuff and was discovered just in time. The details are not clear if he was found unconscious. The whole thing is hush-hush, as with everything that happens in our family. "Max-Leão has no future in Portugal, and Israel is not the answer either. He will wind up killed in one of their wars," Mama keeps saying over and over again.

After his second published book, Max-Leão received a personal letter from the Israeli government inviting him to become a citizen and to live there. Mama was horrified by the idea that he would be nabbed into the military and die with a bullet in his head if he went to Israel. Papa is to get in touch with his family in England and send Max-Leão away as soon as possible.

Papa cracks me up sometimes. When there's no one in the kitchen, he sneaks to the refrigerator and takes out a raw egg. He puts a pin through it and sucks out the contents. Next he carefully puts the empty eggshell back. When Mama or the maid goes to the refrigerator to use the eggs, they can't figure out what happened to them. I am Papa's partner in crime. My job is to stand by the kitchen door and whistle at him if anyone is coming down the hallway. It took months before they caught Papa red-handed, sucking on an egg. He got a real kick out of the whole thing. I think it's funny, too. What's not funny is when he goes into the kitchen to make soup. It doesn't even matter if it is instant soup mix, the latest in prepared foods. No "real" man goes into the kitchen to cook. The maid says only queers go into the kitchen, and every time he makes soup the maid giggles and laughs and makes fun of Papa behind his back. Mama finally convinced Papa to make soup only on Sundays, when the maid is off. Most likely, the whole neighborhood knows by now that Papa likes to cook.

I know a little now about queer men. Mama explained that they are men who don't like women, only men and boys. A man will trick young boys into having sex with him by letting them put their penis into his anus. Then the man waits until the young boys really like having sex that way and tell them, if they want to do it again, they have to let him do it to them, too. I imagine it must be very painful, probably as bad as putting the penis into a vagina. She also told me that all queer men have a depraved look about themselves. Many times I have stood on the balcony of my bedroom having fun watching the people in the street go by, and I have noticed that the men visiting the queer neighbor next door don't look any different than anybody

The Journey of Innocence

else. I have a feeling that this is another gossip story that the neighbors and Mama have made up.

Mama asked me to write some poetry, as she wanted to know if I have any talent as a poetess. I got some paper, sat at the desk in my bedroom, and wrote a few scribbles throughout the day.

I gave her these few scribbles at the end of the day: "Do you think that death might be easier than life?" I have wondered about that often enough, and then, thinking about love and how lonely I felt, I wrote, "I learned to love, and then I learned all about suffering." I went on further with my thoughts: "There's only a shadow between the two of us, death, but, if you choose to go with me because you love me, then love will conquer death."

After lunch I added, "When we are together, my dream turns to reality. When we are apart, I am left in the abyss of darkness." "How can you curse the stars that prophesize your own destiny?" "Man is just dust, they say, but I believe they forgot to add that he also has a heart full of dreams and ideals."

For the next one I pulled on all my resources of thought, as I wanted to shock Mama. After all, if Max-Leão's books were all about sex and passion, I could do the same: "Give me just one hour in your arms. Let me feel the sexual ecstasy of love, and then I will leave satisfied because I have learned what is the essence of life itself." I was happy with that one.

Mama took my scribbles with her and came back to my bedroom not long afterward, saying, "You are definitely not a poetess." And she added, "Don't worry. I'll give them back to you later."

I really tried to write poetry to make her happy, but I couldn't. I'd rather write stories: children's stories and detective stories, the scarier the better.

I don't like poetry because it only expresses what is in

the poet's mind, a swirl of thoughts that can be misunderstood or interpreted differently by the reader. I'd rather have straightforward words that say everything with a clear purpose. Poetry is a lot like Arithmetic: *gumbo, blah, blah.* I hope she throws what I wrote away.

Papa gave me another book for my collection, *The Diary of Anne Frank.* I cried as I read it last night, and before I went to sleep, I promised myself to try my best to understand Mama. If either one of us dies or we both die, we will never see each other again and I don't want to be like Anne Frank. I don't want to lose Mama. I love her. I just don't understand her. It is so hard for me to connect with her, but I am going to try my very best and be good, the way she wants me to be.

I would love to be an archaeologist—either that or a ballerina. If I had to choose, I would pick archaeologist. Papa gave me a new book, *The Egyptian* by Mika Waltari. This is my very favorite book. Once I started reading it, I couldn't stop. I have read it twice, and it literally puts me in Egypt.

Papa and Mama have no idea that *The Egyptian* is a real adult book. The main character is a young Egyptian doctor named Sinuhe who falls in love with a beautiful but heartless woman who makes her living by lying down with men. She is only out for one thing, making money. Sinuhe is very angry with her, and in a moment of madness and jealousy, he gives her a special concoction that puts her to sleep. He personally takes her to the house of death, where professionals take the guts out and embalm people to be put inside the pyramids, as is the Egyptian custom. But what he didn't foresee is that she woke up before they cut her open. The men inside the mortuary fell in love with her and wanted her for themselves, so she used the same technique of getting presents from the ones who could afford her.

With her charms, she not only got away alive but also became very rich because they were all paying for her services. And Sinuhe goes on to describe how he treated the Pharaoh for headaches by drilling a hole in the Pharaoh's skull.

This book is about the strange Egyptian way of life, their old religions and culture. I was reading it last night in the dining room, and once again I was so lost into the story that I didn't even notice that it was getting dark in the room or that Papa had walked into the house. He came into the dining room where I was seated with my head basically under the table, where I held the book on my lap. He turned the light on. I didn't expect it, and as I lifted my head to look up, I hit my nose on the hard wood tabletop. Papa said, "Daughter, you are going to be blind reading in the dark."

He is a good father. The other night as I was dozing off, he walked into my bedroom. He reached for my blanket and covered my feet, and then he said in his harsh German accent, "Daughter, you better cover your feet while you sleep. You are going to catch a cold sleeping that way." And he walked away. I don't get hugs or kisses from Mama or Papa, but I love and appreciate words that show they care.

What a racket at school today! I sat in the corner of the classroom and looked at the brainless girls in Geometry class. They were crying and crying over some guy in North America who was going to be put to death in the electric chair for killing a couple of girls.

"Imagine," said one of them, "the poor man is nothing but a tortured soul, abused as a child by his family. What do you expect?"

I don't care how abused he was as a child. I was happy that he was being executed, but I didn't say anything. They were hysterical after reading the story in the *Diário de*

Noticias— most likely it was written by communist writers who hate Americans and will do anything to make them look like mean, selfish capitalists taking over the world, when the truth is that Communists are the ones who want to take over the world. I know that because Mama's brother, Uncle Abraham, is one of them, and he doesn't even hide the fact because he never got a proper education and believes anyone with more money than him should share it with him and others less fortunate.

I don't agree with him. If I had a good job and worked hard at being successful, I'd deserve my paycheck. I should not be forced to share it with someone who is lazy and doesn't want to work or does something else for a living.

Spring of 1959

I got into trouble at school, but I didn't get suspended. That would mean that my parents would lose my tuition for the month. I got reprimanded instead. I was never so embarrassed in my life. I got caught during class break playing the paper spin game with a couple of classmates. Every girl my age plays this game. You spin the handmade paper top on a flat surface, and if it falls on the number you picked, you open it to unfold the answer to your question. In this case, I had written on the inside of the top: *He loves you. He doesn't love you. He wants to kiss you. You want to kiss him. You will be getting married soon.*

I got into trouble for that because I got caught. I never get away with anything, but everybody else does. The principal said she was totally disappointed in me. Until now, she had thought that I was a very proper and dignified person, but I am nothing more than a silly schoolgirl. Well, I *am* a schoolgirl, darn it. Even my own mother thought it was funny. When I told her what happened in school, she laughed about it.

Big deal, indeed. They are lucky that my Cousin Carlos

doesn't go to their school. Nobody knows how he got up there, but he climbed the high school cafeteria wall and broke off the clock's hour arm. Time is standing still in his high school until they repair the old clock on the wall. Cousin Carlos also likes to inflict pain, and I don't like him. He is a bully. When he comes over our house, he likes to pinch me. Then he has the nerve to ask, "Does it really hurt? Tell me Verónica, how much does it hurt?" He is fat, has reddish hair, and sweats a lot. King Henry VIII probably looked like him when he was younger. Cousin Carlos is too strong and big for me to fight him off, so, when I see him, I stay away from him. He wants to be a doctor like his father. The family thinks he is a genius because they found him sewing a tail that he had previously cut off back on a cat.

"He will probably become a darn good surgeon when he gets older. He has done that several times and is getting good with the stitching," said Aunt Heydee in admiration of her nephew.

Sick little bastard! He is more like a Dr. Frankenstein if you ask me.

I heard Mama telling Aunt Heydee, during one of her visits to our house, how much she admires Burt Lancaster's masculinity, and his acting, too, of course. Mama added, "I can't help it if am a romantic. When I met my Joaquim (she doesn't like Papa's German name *Hans*, so she calls him *Joaquim*, the Portuguese name for Hans), I fell in love with him immediately, of course. I remember fantasizing—you know—he would lure me into his arms and take me to a little village somewhere out in the country, where we could make passionate love."

Up to this point, Papa had seemed to be busy reading his newspaper. He lifted his head and said, "Branca, are you telling me that you wanted to have sex with me before marriage?" Mama didn't expect that question. Papa continued, "If I had known at the time that *that* was all you wanted, I would have had my way with you and would not have needed to marry you. What a fool I was!" And then he started laughing, and so did everybody else.

I wondered if Papa was saying the truth, though. Aunt Heydee has told me several times, "Why would the milkman buy a cow, if he can get the milk for free?"

One of the girls in our school who always arrives in her own private chauffeured car has been found to be pregnant and won't be returning to high school. The stories are varied. Some think that she was fooling around with her chauffeur because he is the only man who drives her around. They say the chauffeur is very handsome. Others who knew her personally say it was one of her brother's friends. Either way, it doesn't matter. She is going to be a mother, unless she does like Rosa, one of Papa's employers. Rosa is married and has a son, but she doesn't want any more children. Every time she gets pregnant, she goes to a special doctor and aborts the baby. She doesn't even bother to tell her husband.

Mama is looking for a new place for us to spend our summer vacation. This time, she wants to try the countryside. It's horrible. I don't like the boring countryside. I prefer the beach, but she says her brother Augusto told her the countryside is good for the nerves and a lot more relaxing. She has taken me along from town to town while she is checking out houses for rent. There's always something that doesn't meet Mama's requirements. One house is too big, another is too small, another is too expensive, or the owner of another one has sons or a son my age. I always sit quietly in the corner of the room as Mama pleasantly interviews each landlord and their family. This morning, she finally found a house that was to her liking. I sat there listening to her, keeping my fingers

The Journey of Innocence

crossed that this was the one we would be moving to during the summer. "So, will you be living close by with your family?" Mama asked the landlord.

"Yes," said the woman with a friendly smile. "Our other house is right around the corner."

Mama was on a mission as she asked with the same caring smile, "How nice. And do you have children?"

"Yes, one very handsome boy. His name is José. As a matter of a fact, he is your daughter's age. I am sure they are going to get along just great."

As soon as I heard that, I knew we were not going to be renting the house from this woman.

When we left, I tried to use psychology by asking, "Wasn't the house beautiful and the lady so friendly?"

"Yes, to all that, but I know exactly what you are thinking about," Mama assured me. "You would like to meet her son who is the same age as you, but that is never going to happen."

I hate my mother!

Papa was very surprised with my gift for his birthday, a small diamond pin for his tie. It was a very small diamond, but he acted like it was the biggest diamond in the whole world. He hugged me, and his eyes were teary. I could see that he was moved because he said, "Daughter, you are my pride and joy. Thank you!"

It was worth saving all my money for a year just to hear him say that.

Today I was taken by surprise when a man on the street corner opened his gabardine and flashed his private parts while smiling at me. I stopped and stared at him for a moment because he had no hair down there and I thought that all adults had pubic hair. He stopped smiling and seemed upset that I was more curious than anything else, but my first thought was, *Poor guy. He has a small, defective, pink penis.*

  He rapidly closed his raincoat, as if suddenly ashamed of himself, and walked away from me. I just stood there not knowing if I should yell for the police or ignore the whole thing. I opted for acting like I had not seen anything, but when I got home I had to tell someone what had happened and Mama was the first person I saw. She told me that some people are mentally sick, and they get a kick out of showing off their sex organs. That is what I call *nuts*!

Tomorrow is my birthday. I am going to be fifteen years old. I have no doubt in my mind that this time there's going to be a surprise birthday party. I wonder what it's going to be like. It's not every day that one is fifteen years old. This is a very magical number. Most likely, I will get unique presents and a big, tall birthday cake. I will get new clothes made of taffeta and lace, like the ones Encarnação makes for her daughters. There will be a lot of colorful balloons decorating the house, and I'll get a radio of my own. I will be so happy. My life will be different from now on, because I will be treated like an adult. I am going to sleep now and dream about tomorrow's festivities.

I saw three movies today, the early matinee with Aunt Heydee, midday with Mama, and the evening one with both my parents. Once again nothing different happened. After the usual dinner of codfish boiled with vegetables, the family had the usual rice pudding for dessert. I was given a cupcake with a candle to blow out, even though we now can afford a *real* birthday cake, and that was the highlight of the festivities.

  There was no dancing or singing, just another uneventful birthday of getting a skirt and blouse that Mama made and I refuse to wear. The skirt has yellow roses, purple roses, and red roses, all on a vivid green background. Anyone can see me from miles away. And then, to add insult to injury,

Mama also made, from the same ugly material, an ornamental pin that is supposed to look like a rose to be attached to my new orange and purple shirt. I'd rather die than be seen in an outfit like that. I know that I hurt her feelings, but the gaudy rose pin she made, with tiny balls hanging out of it, is beyond anything I can possibly endure.

Max-Leão heard me crying in my bedroom and sat next to me on my bed. He said he didn't know why I was crying when I had gotten such an original and beautiful outfit. He likes it so much that he wants me to wear it when we go out together so that everybody thinks that I am his girlfriend. He was trying to make me feel better, but it didn't help. Mama probably told him what to say.

I am going to sleep tonight and freeze myself in a cocoon covered with bricks, completely sealed from the outside world. I will stay this way as a fifteen year old until the day that I am an adult and happy. Only then will I come out and start living again.

I will never again try to cheat in school. It was a waste of time, not to mention my nerves were shot worrying that I would get caught. I wrote some of the main rivers of Portugal on the left palm of my hand for the geography test, and I wrote some of the basic ideas on the palm of my right hand for the algebra test. I have trouble memorizing. I have the brain of a bird, a small bird most likely. But I was so scared that I would be caught that I didn't even have the courage to open my hands while taking the tests. Afterward, I ran to the bathroom to wash the ink off the palms of my hands and realized that nothing I had written, not even one of them, was the answer to any of the questions. If I had been caught, I would have been harshly punished for nothing.

I love dreaming about love. I do that whenever I feel lonely, like before falling asleep, when I am sitting at a coffee shop, and even in school. I look straight at the teacher and don't even see her. I look straight past her and into my own world. It's amazing how much I can hide by looking like I am paying attention, and yet—I am not even there.

In my big mansion, there are guests staying overnight. I can't sleep. It's a very hot and humid summer night. Dressed in my long, silk, yellow gown, I walk downstairs and open the French doors to the garden. A light breeze caresses my body as I breathe the pure oxygen of the mountains around me deep into my lungs. Suddenly, I feel that he is there: the man I love. I don't know if he really loves me, and we have hardly had a chance to talk since the party last night. My parents kept me busy in the kitchen helping prepare dinner. I know he is there because he can't sleep either, because he was thinking about me and would like to kiss me. I see the flicker of his cigarette lighter as he approaches me.

"You are so beautiful," he says as he comes closer.

I am in a trance. I can smell his aftershave cologne. The soft breeze gives me a chill.

"You are cold," he says as he puts his cigarette out. "Let me put my arms around you."

He holds me by the waist and then, very softly, his hand moves away the small curl of hair that has fallen over my face. His hand caresses me ever so softly. His face is very close to mine, and our lips meet for the first time. It is a passionate kiss, just like in the novels I have read.

Sometimes my lover and I meet at a dance, at someone's house, or even in the street, but the happy ending is always the same, a kiss of love. My lover has no real face. He is a love spirit created out of my loneliness. Nobody knows about my made-up lover.

My favorite subject in school is English. I love History and

The Journey of Innocence

Ballet, but English is like sunshine, happiness, ice cream, and strawberries! I melt in the English language! *Love*, what a word! *Kiss*, another word for lips and touching. *Moon*, the dark nights are lit by the *moonlight* while two lovers *kiss* in *love*. *Chewing gum. America. Cigarettes. Oklahoma*, where the cowboys meet the girls and everyone is happy, singing and dancing until they fall in love and get married and live happily ever after.

Summer of 1959

Horror of horrors! I made the mistake of not wearing underwear when I went out today. It's Aunt Heydee's fault. She is always bragging that she doesn't wear underwear during the hot summer months. That way, she keeps cool when she walks outside. So, I tried it. My luck. As I was almost home, right in front of our front door, while I was waiting for the downstairs door to open after I pressed the buzzer, a strong gust of wind came toward me and swirled my wide skirt up. I was naked to the world as all the men and women passing by stared at me and smirked. Now they know where I live. I hope nobody saw my face. I am not going out for a few days.

Aunt Heydee is a very petite woman who has been shrinking as she gets older. She is old, but still very beautiful. She has big green eyes, and her smooth light skin complements her blonde hair, which looks very natural. Her beauty secret is the daily use of almond oil on her skin, washing her breasts with cold water every morning to keep them from sagging, and using lemons to help maintain the blonde hair color. She puts fresh lemon juice on her hair, and once in a while she uses peroxide to lighten it even more. The sun always helps to speed up the process. Her special title of *Napoleão* is fitting. Everybody agrees that, if she had been born a man, she would have conquered the world. I admire her tenacity more than anything else. Anything she puts her mind to, she does, and nothing is impossible for her. Her age is not important since there's no way she is going to tell us. If she were to tell us, we would learn only that she is older than what she was thirty years ago. Therefore, it is simpler to say that this story happened a few years back in the past, somewhere in time.

One day, Aunt Heydee was looking through the newspaper and read an announcement that President Salazar would be a guest during a big political function. It was going to be the event of the year, the ball of your dreams, with dancing most likely to waltz music, chatting and flirting with some of the top-notch men in government, mixing with royalty, eating caviar, and drinking bubbling champagne from crystal glasses. Aunt Heydee decided that she was going to attend the event. It didn't matter that she had not been invited. The only apparent difficulty was to find something to wear that would fit the royal occasion. She only had plain clothes, basically clothes that were more like Cinderella's wardrobe before she married the prince.

So, Aunt Heydee was seated in her dining room and feeling sad when suddenly, on looking up, she noticed how splendid the old golden brocade curtains hanging in the window looked. Yes, they were old and dusty, but their possibilities were left to the imagination, and *that* is something Aunt Heydee had a lot of.

She asked Grandma Rica, her mother, if she could borrow the curtains for the evening, and went right to the old Singer sewing machine, where, in a jiffy, she created a masterpiece. A few golden ropes here and there, but no one was even going to dream that she was wearing her curtains.

She took the trolley as far as she could, and then, around the corner from the *Palácio de Queluz*, she picked up a taxi for her grand entrance. A doorman awaited the arrival of the evening guests, and when she entered the man at the door dressed in red and gold uniform simply asked,

"Madam, gold or silver invitation?"

"Gold, of course," she said with a glorious smile and without blinking an eye. No one dared to question her as to whether she actually had an invitation with her. She looked like royalty. The handsome man at the door was more than happy to offer her his arm and took her personally to the "gold room" where she spent the evening dancing and talking to everyone she met. And yes, she danced with the vice president of Portugal, but only because the president was not able to attend the soiree.

We are spending the summer in a little town called Malveira. I don't know why we are staying here when Mama said a few times already that the name of the town is like a curse of bad things to come because it reminds her of *maldição*, the Portuguese word for curse. Malveira is very isolated, and the only fun thing to do is to walk to the so-called town, which is a street with a grocery store and a coffee shop. That's it.

At night, Max-Leão, José, and I like to stand at the window in the hallway upstairs and look outside. We are trying to spot a werewolf, a witch, or even a ghost. Anything scary would bring some excitement into our lives. After we get tired and sleepy from looking into the dark woods that surround us, we each go to our bedrooms. Most of the time, I'll sit on my bed and read Portuguese history books. I love reading Portuguese history in this old house. It fits the house we live in, old and dark and in the middle of nowhere.

In this forsaken place, I only have two choices to keep me from going insane: reading or writing. There's nothing else to do here. In Costa da Caparica or Eiriceira, I could walk along the shore or take a walk through the village and hang out by one of the coffee shops at the center of town where the residents sit and watch the tourists go by. There are no tourists around here. We are the only city people. I am not allowed to walk alone into the woods around Malveira or go up one of the hills in the distance, much less into the quarry where I went a few times to play with stones. Mama told me that last week a girl was raped in the woods and then dragged to the quarry where no one could hear her scream for help. She had been found dead. The police are still looking for the criminal. I don't know what to do except read and write. But I get tired of sitting because my tailbone hurts from all of these hard, wooden chairs.

So, this week I dared Max-Leão to take a walk with me on the highway. I dared him to see how far we could walk from where we live. We walked all morning, and when the sun came up on us like a burning oven, we didn't stop. We were going to walk as far as the other side of the world. By the end of the day, our feet were killing us, and we knew we couldn't make it back home. We were exhausted when we stopped at the next town's tavern. They let us use their telephone to call home to see if someone could pick us up. Nope, no one was going to come and get us, and we were told to walk back home. The bartender felt sorry for us and drove us back in his car. It was a miracle that he felt sorry for us.

After this experience, the idea of running away is gone for me, at least not by trying to walk as far as I can. You can only go a couple of miles and your feet start to kill you, not to say anything about nighttime, when it's cold and the wolves are roaming the fields. I should have learned from Mama a few years back. She used to hit me a lot then, and one day she was really angry and grabbed me by the hair and pulled me down the hallway to the front door. She opened the door and said, "Get out of this house now. I don't want you here anymore!" I cried and cried, mostly because, while I was crying, I was thinking, *I can never leave because I have no place to go, and she knows that.*

The Journey of Innocence

Aunt Heydee was visiting us for the weekend, so I decided to unveil the beginnings of my first detective story to her and Mama. I invited them both to the coffee shop down the road, where my inspiration had grown out of complete solitude and boredom.

I took a good look at them and prepared them by saying, "Get ready to be startled by detailed descriptions of crime scenes."

I immediately started to read the first page.

"It was a dark night, as dark as the deepest well made by the devil himself. Detective Peter Smith tried holding his breath as the sewage stink crept up his nostrils and filled his lungs. His tall, skinny body was literally covered by the oversized gray gabardine that made him almost invisible as he walked firmly through the thick fog, which seemed to be there just to blind him without mercy. Slapping his wet muddy shoes through this narrow slum street of London, a rat ran between his feet."

"Stop!" Mama cried out. "What a heavy, depressing ghastly story for a young girl to write. I can't stand it. Your writing is going to give me nightmares. You should be writing about love, not about dreadful things like crime, and who knows what you wrote on the next pages."

"You don't want to hear the rest of my detective story?" I asked, knowing well in advance that I had hit a nerve.

"No," said Mama getting up from her chair. "I've heard enough."

Aunt Heydee didn't say much, only winked an eye at me, but before we all left the coffee house she whispered in my ear, "In my opinion you are a very talented writer. Don't stop writing even if people think it's too morbid. What do they know? You are Napoleão #2. Don't forget that."

I had cut deep into their minds, and the person I mostly wanted to stir was Mama. So what? She didn't like my writing. I was not surprised by her reaction. Impressing her with a story, even if it was a sinister one, was for me a great accomplishment.

As always after lunch, everybody goes into their bedroom to take a nap. I don't like napping, so I have kept busy, taking a fast twenty-minute walk as I breathe in slowly and deeply the awesome smell of the eucalyptus field I cross in order to reach the coffee shop in town. I don't even know why it is called a town. Maybe it's because the houses are closer to each other along the highway. It's a real small, dinky coffee shop that doubles as a tavern. The place is big enough for four very small, round, wooden tables with two hard wooden chairs each. There are no windows. The light that comes in is filtered through the beads hanging from the top of the two entrances. There are no signs like "in" or "out," but you know that one doorway is to come in and the other is to go out. I learn these kinds of things by watching the customers. I am there every day, sitting at my usual small, round, wooden table by the entrance. I act all grown up with a cup of coffee next to me, as I write my detective story and sip the coffee ever so slowly so that it will last for hours.

Three boys about my age walked into the coffee shop. One of them turned out to be a real jerk. He seemed normal until his eyes met mine.

"What do we have *here*?" he said, putting his hand to his chest. "A flower in the middle of an oasis?" And he pointed at me, as if he had found a treasure that I was not aware of. The other two boys were laughing at him, as the young fool acted as if he had just seen the love of his life. He threw himself on the floor, and then got up dramatically and banged his body into the front of the wooden counter where the owner stood. He was staring at the theatrical madness, not quite understanding what it was all about. "I want her to be my wife," said the kid, once again putting his hand over his chest as if he were having a heart attack. "I am in love!

The Journey of Innocence

I am in love! I am in love!" he kept screaming as if he were out of his mind. His friends were laughing while they tried to restrain him.

I felt embarrassed and also scared. I picked up my papers, and was ready to leave when the owner put his hand firmly on my shoulder and said, "No, you stay. They are the ones leaving now, or I'll break all three necks with my bare hands."

They left, dragging the crazy boy with them. I waited a while for the coast to clear, and then I went home. I was never so humiliated in my life. I know that I am just an average girl, and for this boy to put on such a stupid act was an insult. He was definitely making fun of me. Now I feel ugly and very sad.

A letter arrived today. It's from the boy I met at the coffee shop. He asks Mama to allow him to visit me, and says that he would like to apologize for his behavior toward me and would like to be my boyfriend. As if that wasn't enough, he went on to say that he couldn't forget me since he saw me. I can't forget him either. How can one forget somebody that embarrassing?

Mama asked Max-Leão if he knew the boy. He did and had been meaning to tell us today that the boy, Artur, lives up on the hill and is very rich—well, at least his parents are very rich, and they have a huge swimming pool on their property. Max-Leão knows Artur. They are acquaintances, and yesterday when they were talking, Artur found out that Max-Leão is my brother and invited Max-Leão to come for a swim in his pool.

Mama told me not to worry about the crazy kid on the hill. She would answer his letter, and send it not only to him but also to his family in a way that would stop him from ever bothering me again.

Max-Leão wouldn't stop teasing me, making me feel guilty. I am depriving him of swimming in Artur's swimming pool during the hot summer days ahead. I don't care if he is rich and has a pool, I am not going to sacrifice myself like a virgin on a mountain of fire so that Max-Leão can keep cool this summer. Besides, Mama is on my side this time. When she finishes writing the letter to him and his family, I am sure that he will feel like I do, miserable.

I don't know what to think. I am very scared. Aunt Heydee called us this morning to tell us that our parents are both in the hospital. They were on their way here from Lisboa when a car hit Papa's motorcycle from behind. They were both thrown off the motorcycle. They are both in the hospital. Mama is in a coma and might die. I have been praying for them. *Please, dear God, don't let my parents die.* I can't stand this thought.

Papa came home. He has lots of bruises all over his face. He called me to his side and said in a very weary voice, "My daughter, from now on you are in charge of the household. This is the amount of money I gave your mother every month. You are to pay the bills and oversee the maid and handle what meals are to be served daily."
"I want to see Mama," I said assertively.
"She can't have visitors, but you being the eldest I guess you have that right. Your brothers will have to stay here. I will take you with me tomorrow morning to the hospital, but you will have to come back alone, by bus. I have to stay in Lisboa because of work at the office, and I don't want to leave Mama alone at night."
I could see that he was tired and thinking out loud as he said once again, "As the eldest, I guess you have the right to see your mother." And he cried. I cried, too, with Max-Leão and José. We don't want to be orphans.

It was weird to see Mama lying in a hospital bed, unconscious. She was bruised all over, her head was covered with bandages, and she had a cast on her broken leg and another on her broken arm. Aunt Heydee explained that Mama had been thrown from the motorcycle and rolled about 20 meters before going into a ditch. She had hit her head several times along the way. She was bleeding inside from concussions to the brain. Nothing could be done for her. Papa encouraged me to go back to Malveira that day, but I insisted on staying the night with Mama, which allowed Papa to go home and get some sleep. He thanked me for it and showed me the straight armchair where he had been spending the nights. If by any chance Mama were to wake up from her coma, I was to run immediately to the front desk and get a nurse. Mama is in a private room, and that's why they allow a family member to stay the night.

I found out that I couldn't sleep seated. It felt like the longest night of my life. Every time I dozed off, my neck would be hurting as well as my stiff back. Daylight finally came through the window shades, and I got up from my chair of torture. Mama didn't wake up. She was still in a coma, but she was breathing so I decided to take a quick look around the hospital. I left her room and went down the hallway and up and down some stairs. I was looking for a door that would open to somewhere, not really knowing what I was looking for. I saw a door. I opened it and walked in carefully. A man was lying down in a white metal bed, just like Mama. He saw me and said, "Hello, come on in."

I got scared and ran out as I heard him pleading, "Please don't go. I won't bite; come back!" I went back to Mama's room feeling guilty for being so nosey. He could have been the criminal from Malveira that everybody was looking for, or even worse, a dead man lying on the hospital bed, waiting to be buried. I get goose bumps just thinking about it.

I took the bus back from Lisboa to Malveira. A boy sat next

to me. I was nervous, because I rarely have someone of the opposite sex and about my age sitting next to me. I could tell my face was going red, and I didn't have anything with me like a book that I could stare at, so I stared out of the window the whole time. But it was a long trip, so I got my potato chips bag, and before I took a chip out, I nervously offered him some. He said politely, "No thank you." He wouldn't look at me either. I could tell that he was as uncomfortable as I was. One stop before Malveira he got up, took a look straight at me, smiled, and left the bus. I took a deep breath of relief, but before the bus took off he rushed back into the bus and very shyly handed me a piece of paper. I wasn't going to read it, that's for sure. I was worried that it might be his name, telephone number, or say something silly like he liked me, or that I was ugly and he hated potato chips. I was afraid to find out. Whatever he had written, I was afraid to find out. I opened the window, and as the bus took off, I threw the still-folded note out of the window.

Now I feel retarded for having done that, but I would have died of embarrassment if he had asked me to be his girlfriend.

Something weird happened in Malveira while I was visiting Mama in the hospital. The night that I was away, our house got broken into. In the morning, the maid found Max-Leão in bed with his legs tied and his hands also tied behind his back, his mouth was taped and bound. It was too dark for him to see the assaulters, and they had blindfolded him before he had a chance to recognize anyone. The dresser drawers in his bedroom had been pulled apart as had the ones in my bedroom. Someone had been looking for something last night. José and the maid slept through the whole thing. I think they were robbers, but Max-Leão, José, and the maid think it was probably the crazy kid from the hill looking for the love letter he sent me. Nothing was missing. I am so lucky that I wasn't home last night.

Until we get back to Lisboa at the end of the month, I am going to lock my bedroom door from the inside, and every night I will push my dresser against the door with all my books on top of it. A robber will not be able to come in without making lots of noise, which would wake me up in time to scream loud enough to wake up everybody at home.

We have been eating like kings every day. I told Isabel, our maid, that we want fried potatoes for lunch and dinner while Mama is in the hospital. The little birds Max-Leão and José catch outside with their slings are to be fried and served that day. If we don't have enough birds, we will have steaks instead. We don't want vegetables, but freshly made tomato sauce with sliced onions is a must at every meal. And green soup is welcome every day for dinner. For breakfast, I asked Isabel to make coffee with lots of milk, a soft-boiled egg, and rustic bread with butter and cheese. Midday, between lunch and dinner, we have a tall glass of milk with coffee. We put bread into it, mash it with a spoon, and add lots of sugar until it turns into a tasty, soggy, sweet coffee cake.

Mama is no longer in a coma, and she should be here with us in a month, about the time we are going back to Lisboa. I can't wait for Mama to come home. She is going to be so proud of me when I give her the money I have saved while she was in the hospital. Papa gave me too much money to run the household.

Mama came home, but she is still very sick. She lost a lot of weight, and she faints all the time. She needs a lot of silence around her; otherwise, the headaches get worse.

Mama thanked me for giving her the money I saved while she was in the hospital, and asked me not to tell Papa about it. Otherwise, he will give her less money each month, and this is the money she uses for buying us special goodies or anything she needs without having to beg for extra cash. She added, "I am going to teach you how to budget a household and save money from what your husband gives you every month. It's always a good idea to have a little extra for a rainy day. All smart women prepare for the future by having a little nest egg saved."

Autumn of 1959

When girls become women, they bleed, and when boys become men, they have to get initiated into manhood by going to the house of prostitution to learn about having sex with women who do that for a living. I don't know which is worse—probably bleeding because you also get belly cramps with it. Max-Leão was given some money and sent to the house of prostitution as a fourteenth birthday present from our parents.

Aunt Heydee, Mama, and I waited for him to come home and tell us all about it. We were all curious. I don't know if Papa is really aware of all of this since he was not with us waiting for my brother to come home.

Max-Leão came home about four in the afternoon. He had been gone for over three hours. "Tell us all about it," was the instruction. He mumbled something about a naked woman lying in bed asking him to take his clothes off and to join her. At that point, I was asked to leave the room. No matter how much I begged to stay, Mama sent me out of the room.

Mama has pain all over her body, and her bruises have not healed yet. She is most happy when my brothers and I take turns pushing a wire in and out of her leg cast. That's the only way she can stand the itching.

Mama told me a secret that I am not supposed to tell

anyone, or people might think she has gone crazy. She saw Jesus when she was in the hospital. He sat on her bed and talked to her. He was very nice and soothing and held her hand. He sat on her bed, kept her company, and gave her hope for the future.

I think Mama is having stronger hallucinations after getting hit in the head.

Lucia, a Brazilian girl, joined our class last month. There were bets that she would never be able to catch up with us because Brazilians are not as smart as Portuguese and their education is not up to our high standards. But she has not only caught up to us, she passes all tests with high honors. She is very quiet and hardly speaks to anyone. I admire Lucia mostly for being able to live with her cracked lips. They are chapped badly from the cold, but she won't bite the skin off. It's amazing to me that she has such self-control that when a skin is hanging out her bottom lip she won't pull it off with her teeth.

One of the girls in class must have felt the same because I heard her going up to Lucia and saying, "Lucia, how can you stand your lips that way? Why don't you peel them?"

"It doesn't bother me." And Lucia went back to reading the book on her desk. What a geek!

Mama has to live in complete silence. She can't even listen to music anymore because of horrible headaches. They are so strong that she faints from the pain. This happens three and four times a day since the accident this summer. Even though she got a head concussion and they were afraid that she wasn't going to live because she was in a coma for three weeks, the doctors are now saying, "It's all nerves and in her head and she has a hysterical personality."

Of course it is in her head. Theirs would hurt too if they had hit their head on several rocks while rolling on the hard ground about 20 meters from the motorcycle. Anybody would be in pain for a long time if it had happened to him or her.

So, they give her "medicine" to calm her down and to sleep. These drugs are a lot more potent than what she used to take before the accident. Mama keeps them in a large shoebox that she carries under her arm from room to room so she doesn't have to walk far to get to them. Her brother, cousins, and personal doctor give all these medicines to help her stay without pain. Mama's leg has not healed properly, and it's weak. She must have broken her foot also, because it doesn't work right. She trips a lot over her own feet. She also has gained a lot more weight since she came home. She hurts all over. She has told me that she has developed sensitive spots all over her body since the accident.

Mama was very touched by my birthday present. She even cried from joy. She was born on December 15, but she celebrates her birthday December 5 because she is used to it. December 5 was the date of my grandma's firstborn. As a memory and respect for the dead baby, her parents changed Mama's birthday to the 5th. I think that was a horrible thing to do, and I don't understand the reasoning, but I have never said anything about it. Mama seems to be perfectly happy with December 5 being her birth date. I gave Mama a beautiful gold pin designed as a basket filled with little flowers made of small, colorful precious stones. She was very impressed that I had been able to save all my money to buy her the pin. I feel so good about myself. I feel like I can do anything and nothing is impossible as long as I put my mind to it. I like making my parents happy.

Max-Leão and José are jealous of me because Mama gave me her radio for Chanukah. It pays to be the eldest. I get priority on inheritance gifts. My brothers like music, but

The Journey of Innocence

Mama knows that I *love* music. José is into Geometry and Arithmetic, Max-Leão is into cars, and I am the music lover. The radio is to be used only in my bedroom, which is now up front facing the street. If Mama is home, I have to listen to music very low, but that's okay. At least I have music, rock and roll music. American music is the best music in the world.

I am so lucky that I was not riding with Papa on his motorcycle the day they got hit. I would have died, of that I am sure. Like Aunt Heydee said, Mama was lucky to be heavy, because it kept her from rolling even farther into the distance. If it had been me, being that I am lighter, I would have rolled into the next town like a cannonball at one hundred kilometers an hour. One hundred kilometers an hour is how fast they were going when they got hit. It's a miracle that both my parents survived.

Winter of 1960

Mama sleeps in the farthest room of the house, away from noise and light, next to the bathroom and the kitchen. The city noises keep her awake at night. I love the sounds of the city—cars honking, brakes trying to stop in time before the cars plow into each other, and if no one really gets hurt, the drivers cursing at each other, blaming one another. A lot of times the police have to intervene, or the two motorists will kill each other in hand-to-hand combat. This happens about three or four times a year right around the street corner from where we live. It's a tricky corner, and the hill is steep. When you get to the top of the street, it's hard to see the oncoming traffic in either direction. Many pedestrians have been injured or killed while crossing it because cars have the right of way. I usually walk to the next corner and then cross to the other side. I never play with fate by crossing straight across. When Max-Leão and I were kids, we sat on this street corner a few times to see first-hand two cars crashing into each other. It never happened while we waited, only after we had left the site.

Besides hearing the sounds of the traffic outside, I also hear when the garbage men come by our street. They like to throw the empty metal cans back onto the cobblestones. They make enough noise to wake up the dead, but it lets me know I still have two more hours of sleep before I have to get up to go to school. I can also hear the neighbors screaming, so I know who is fighting with whom, and it's usually the couple straight across from my bedroom window. Most of their fights are due to the wife's jealousy. She is constantly accusing her husband of cheating on her as he walks in drunk late at night. He punches her around, but she doesn't leave him. I don't understand her.

The lights from the cars going by hit my bedroom window like flashlights on a dark road. They make all kinds of light designs on the bedroom walls and ceiling. I love my bedroom, and I love my radio and listening to American rock and roll, the new music that has developed in the last few years, but I also have a weakness for Bach.

Aunt Heydee says that Bach is one of the most difficult classical composers to understand and appreciate, and she can't believe that I like him. But I do. It sounds like rock and roll music to me, in a classical way. I tried to explain that to her, but she didn't believe me. Nobody really understands me. I don't like Portuguese music. The *fado* has no beat and is depressing. Bach and American music make me happy.

I have to be very careful when holding onto Mama's arm. When we go out to the movies, I am very careful so she doesn't get sore from the pressure. Since the motorcycle accident, she seems different. She goes deep into thought, as if she is meditating. On the other hand, she takes me with her when she goes out, and she is a lot nicer to me

The Journey of Innocence

now. I love going out with her. Slipping my arm around hers feels so warm on a cold winter day. I feel close to her that way. She can't walk too far, one block and she starts to hurt all over. It's also hard on her legs. She walks slowly now, not like she used to. We take taxis every time we go out. The insurance will pay for it when they give her the financial settlement for the pain and suffering she is going through. That's what the lawyer my parents hired to represent Mama has told them.

What a day! Mama took me to a French beauty shop in downtown Lisboa. It is the most chic beauty shop in all of Lisboa, probably in all of Portugal. Only rich people, foreigners, and probably movie stars go there, it is *that* expensive. She asked for their best stylist. She wanted to see what could be done to make me look better.

A very tall, skinny young man with oily hair and the body movements of a ballerina looked at me as if I were some jungle animal that had been forgotten by time. He grabbed my face and pulled my hair in different directions. His little brown eyes were shining with glee when he asked Mama, "Can I do anything I want with her?"

"Yes, by all means."

He took me into a private room and told two girls, as he tossed them some nail coloring, "You already know what I want her nails to look like."

They must have read his mind. One got on her knees, grabbed my feet, took my shoes off, and put my feet into a container with hot sudsy water, while the other pulled a chair next to me and started working on my hands.

He returned later, looked over my nails approvingly, and clicked his fingers at me—as if I were a dog—to follow him. He pointed to a chair in front of a mirror. He then turned my chair around with my back to the mirror. He cut and cut and brushed, and then he clicked his fingers again, speaking like a broken record, "Makeup! Makeup!"

The same two girls brought him a box of colors. He painted my face. I still had no idea what he was doing to me, and then he called Mama into the room.

"Oh, my God," Mama said as she entered the room, "Verónica, you look like Cleopatra!"

He turned me to the mirror. *Mamma mia*, was that me? With green eye shadow and red lipstick and hair like—I just didn't know what to think. I didn't know that I could look this different. I don't know how much Mama paid for all that work, but it must have been a small fortune.

We left the beauty salon, and as we walked the street, people were turning to look at me. I felt funny, not comfortable. We took the trolley, and a man looked up and said, "Cleopatra for sure."

Mama was not happy about that remark. "This is going too far. It's going to go to your head. I don't want you to think that you are going to look like this tomorrow. Enjoy it for today."

Then another man came into the trolley and, looking straight at me, said in the very typical honest Portuguese way, "Very beautiful, but what's a young girl like you wearing all that make-up for? You don't need all that garbage!"

That did it to me. I was out of place. I knew it! I knew it! That's why everybody was looking at me. I don't want to look like someone else, not even Cleopatra.

When we got home, Mama was very straightforward as she told me, "Go into the bathroom and wash your face with soap. Then get your hair wet and parted to the side, the normal way, before Papa gets home."

I was glad to do that. I don't ever want to be someone else. Thank God, I am myself again.

Max-Leão and I have reached some maturity, because Mama now allows us both to go dancing on weekends at the Jewish Center. She had two dresses made for me from the fashion magazine the seamstress brought with her. I picked a light blue material and picked the model who looked closest to Audrey Hepburn. She was wearing a simple dress with a round white collar and long sleeves with white cuffs to match.

Mama said she was disappointed in my choice. In her opinion, it was a boring dress that didn't do anything for me. But I'd felt it did a lot for me, and it was the look I wanted. The other dress was her choice, purples and blues and fringes and ruffles. When I wore it, people commented that I looked like Sophia Loren, but I would rather look like Audrey Hepburn. Now I have three outfits in my wardrobe: the loud outfit with roses that Mama made for me, the sexy Sophia with the low-cut, ruffled top, and my favorite—the Audrey look—which is the only one I will wear to go dancing with Max-Leão.

When I walk in the streets, I get a line of cars following me. It's like a curse. I feel like Cousin Esther. I admit that I like it, because it means that these men must think that I am pretty enough to follow me, but I don't like it because I know that what they want is sex. They don't know me, and they don't love me, so I get mixed feelings about it. I feel like a real woman, but abused to a certain extent. They each slow down, put their head out of the window, and invite me for a ride. Big deal, they have a car. Do they really believe that I am going to go with a stranger so that I can be squeezed like a lemon? They cause traffic jams by slowing down the traffic, and when one gives up following me, another one takes over.

I told Aunt Heydee that I get pinched when I go out in crowded areas, and men press themselves against me on the trolley or bus and I can feel their hard private parts. The other day, a young priest put his hand on top of my hand when I was holding onto the bus railing so I would not fall when the driver goes for the brakes abruptly or around street corners at full speed. I thought it might've been my imagination, so I moved my hand, but his hand followed right after mine. I left the bus at the next stop and walked home. Aunt Heydee was not sympathetic with my misfortune. She said, "Priests are human beings like you and me, and most of all they are men. Imagine a man without a woman to love. That's loneliness!" Aunt Heydee has an incredible unlimited compassion for everybody. I will never forget the day she took me to a movie matinee and the man seated behind us slipped his hand through the seats. He put it softly on one of her breasts. She whispered to me, "There's a guy behind my seat, and he has his hand over my breast. The poor thing, whoever he is, I hope that touching my breast brings him comfort."

I was appalled at her way of thinking. "My goodness, Aunt Heydee, pull his hand off!"

"I can't do that. He probably doesn't have anyone special in his life. Besides, he is barely touching me. If this brings him happiness, let him enjoy it."

I don't understand Aunt Heydee in these matters. She is too nice. I would have picked up the man's hand and bitten hard.

I tried using the pity act the other day and it worked, but it took a lot out of me to do it. I was riding the trolley during rush hour. It was jam-packed with passengers, and some guy kept rubbing himself on me. I could feel his private part against my back, so I took a deep breath of courage and yelled out while pointing at him, "This man is squeezing himself against me and touching me in an indecent manner. Can someone help me?"

Two good Samaritans grabbed the molester by his coat and threw him out of the moving trolley before he could even utter a word.

It's been okay to go dancing on Friday nights at the Jewish

The Journey of Innocence

Center with Max-Leão. But there aren't that many boys attending, and the ones who show up are boring squares. I dance with whoever is available and dream about my future boyfriend, the one who will come my way some day. The best part of our night out is walking home, when Max-Leão and I take our sweet time. As long as we are back home by ten o'clock, our parents don't really care what we do. So, on the way home, we stop by the main road being worked on during the day, climb the mounds of sand to the very top, and then slide down. We try to stand up while doing that, as if we are skiing. Sometimes we throw a couple of *centavos* onto the railway to see how flat they get after the trolley drives over them.

About a month ago, a new boy came to the dance. He was tall, slim, and knew how to dance—a rarity in itself. While dancing, I tried not to look at him because his face was ugly with pockmarks, but still he was the best looking of them all. He always asked me to dance with him, but we never talked. I didn't know what to say, and he didn't have anything to say either, I guess. I have not seen him for the last two weekends. Probably his family moved out of Portugal. I don't know his name. We didn't have anything in common that I was aware of except that we danced really well.

~ Chapter Six ~

THE SPANISH LETTERS

1960

Spring of 1960

Mama gave me a large safety pin. A girl's best friend is a safety pin, she told me, and it works great in crowds of any kind. No one comes near me anymore. Well, they do, but they immediately move away when I stab their legs with the pin.

Aunt Heydee is my best friend, my only friend. I still visit Encarnação as often as I can, but she never goes out. She is home all the time. Aunt Heydee is *hip*. She is young at heart. She laughs and says silly things, and she always says something that makes me think and has meaning about life. She takes me to the coffee shops downtown, and we get to sit at the most sophisticated ones for hours and watch people go by. It's a lot of fun. She always makes friends with whoever is sitting close to us, most of the time people from other countries, tourists. She speaks so many languages that she can talk to any tourist.

 Yesterday she made me laugh because of the way she went up to the trolley driver and asked him to go faster or we would be late for an important appointment. She didn't

The Journey of Innocence

dare tell him that we were only trying to get downtown faster. When he said he could only drive the speed limit, she slipped 25 *centavos* into his hand as if she were giving him a million *centavos,* and smiled at him with all her charm. He speeded down the hill and down the avenida, ringing the bell all the way to our destination: the movie theatre.

Mama has been writing a lot of poetry since her accident. She writes every day. She carries paper and pen with her, and she is constantly writing. Papa says that the bump on Mama's head has awakened her artistic vein. She writes a lot, and everybody loves her poetry. Aunt Heydee believes that Mama should publish her works. I have tried to understand what she writes, but to me it's just something else about her that I don't understand. Her poetry is all about sexual innuendos and doesn't rhyme. I have come to the conclusion that I simply don't like poetry.

This morning, we all went to the airport to wait for Aunt Nelly. She is Mama's sister from North America. It was nice to see the whole family together and in an excited uproar when Nelly came down the steps from the plane. We were cheering and yelling her name, all excited to see her. She looked like she did in her pictures except that she was bigger—stocky, but not fat. I hugged her, and she kissed me, and I liked her immediately because she smiled a lot and kept kissing me and hugging me as if I were special in her life. She smelled like Wrigley's Juicy Fruit chewing gum. I heard Mama whispering to Aunt Heydee, "What do you think happened to her arms? They are so wide!"

Aunt Nelly was very tired and barely touched the special dinner we made for her of boiled chicken covered with homemade mayonnaise and a side vegetable salad with mayonnaise dressing. Only the soup was normal, collard green soup, my favorite. The use of mayonnaise and chicken is only for special occasions like holidays or when we are trying to impress someone. This dinner was very expensive, something we really can't afford daily, but it was a special occasion. We were obviously trying our best to impress Nelly with the French cuisine, but she hardly ate anything. She said she was getting nauseous and got excused from the table and retired early to bed. It was very disappointing.

We were all up early today to hear more from Aunt Nelly. She told us she doesn't like mayonnaise, because it makes her nauseous. Poor thing, no wonder she was feeling sick last night with dinner. She had a box of chocolate mints and shared it with all of us. She let me choose a pair of earrings from her personal jewelry box. I chose silver earrings with light blue stones. They are small and delicate. That would be something Audrey Hepburn would have used in one of her movies. I can't believe that Aunt Nelly is so kind and so very giving. Everything about her is North American. Even when she speaks Portuguese, she has an American accent. We are all so lucky to have someone like her visiting us all the way from North America, a country full of millionaires, cowboys and Indians, New York City, and Hollywood. She is my aunt, and she treats me like an adult. It's incredible!

Aunt Nelly is interested in talking to me. Whenever she goes anywhere, she wants me to go with her. She hugs me and kisses me as if we have always known each other. I love listening to her talk about life in North America.

This afternoon we all sat on Nelly's bed as she told us about her hard times. In the wintertime, she has to shovel coal under her house in order to heat it, if we could even imagine so much snow outside.

I have only seen snow once. I remember, because I was at Grandma's house. When I looked outside the window, I saw snow for the first time in my life—white, chunky, fluffy ice falling out of the sky. I remember my hands freezing until they were numb as I kept them outside the window.

Snow tastes like sorbet without fruit flavor. I had to walk home that afternoon, and I kept making little balls of snow and eating them. Then my hands and tongue got so cold that I had to stop until they got warm again. It wasn't a lot of snow falling, but it was enough for motorists to get out of their cars to scrape enough snowflakes to make silly fun things to place on top of the car roofs, and then drive around honking their horns for everybody to see their artwork. There wasn't much snow on the streets, but every ounce of snow that fell in Lisboa that winter day was used for eating or making something artistic on top of car roofs that paraded down the streets. I can't even imagine enough snow to make everything outside white and so cold to the point of making the houses need heat inside.

Aunt Nelly's husband, who was a pharmacist, also worked very hard, but she had dinner ready when he got home and the house was always beautiful and decorated with fresh flowers. Mercedes, her mother-in-law, had lived with them and had made her life pure hell. She'd died from colon cancer about eight years before Nelly's husband Ralph also passed away from cancer. The theory was that Mercedes had colon cancer because she ate hot peppers all the time and had burned her guts out. Nelly's husband tried everything he knew as a pharmacist to save his mother. Besides giving her medicine, he gave her gold shots. They didn't save her, but he believed they did prolong her life.

Nelly's husband made good money as a pharmacist, so she never had to work. She was a housewife and mother, and that was plenty of work. She never had maids. They are very expensive in North America, and only rich people can afford one. Nelly and Ralph were not rich. Nelly did the family laundry and cooked and cleaned. That's why her arms are so big, from working so hard.

Mama and Aunt Heydee cried when they heard all of this and hugged their sister, feeling sorry for her because that was the kind of work that no woman should be subjected to unless she was a servant. Nelly was a young girl, a fragile flower, when she had left Portugal.

She asked them not to feel sorry for her because she had been the happiest woman who ever existed, and, throughout her marriage, each day was better than the day before.

Aunt Nelly had a vision when she landed at the Lisboa airport. She'd never had a vision in her life, and she was embarrassed to tell her sisters. She was afraid that they might think she was crazy. After she descended the steps from the airplane, she saw her mother's ghost standing there and smiling at her the way she used to. She freaked out when she saw that. Mama told her that this meant that their mother had come to greet her, and it could be only a good omen.

Weird, if I say so myself. I would not be happy to see a ghost, even if it was my grandmother smiling. I would be scared. Tomorrow morning, Aunt Heydee is taking her sister Nelly to Paris for three days. I'll miss them both.

They are back! It was a bit disastrous between the two sisters. I heard Nelly tell Mama that Heydee was heartless. When they got to Paris, Nelly was feeling faint, and her heart was giving her trouble. She didn't feel that she should go out that night. So, Aunt Heydee tucked her in bed at the hotel and said, "I am going to share my heart medicine with you. Here it is right next to you with a glass of water and the telephone number of a doctor, in case you get worse. I'll see you later."

I had to smile when I heard that. Aunt Heydee has never had a sick day in her life, and if she did, no one was aware of it because she never looks for sympathy. She is too busy

The Journey of Innocence

to even bother with her own heart.

When Aunt Heydee heard Nelly complaining about being left alone to die in the hotel, she reasoned with Mama. "I am in Paris, and I'm going to stay in a hotel room holding her hand? Not me! The medicine was right there next to her, and as everyone can see, she is still alive!"

I don't believe that Aunt Nelly will ever forgive Aunt Heydee.

"Poor Nelly," I heard Mama telling Aunt Heydee in the kitchen. "Imagine how she must have felt when his sperm fell inside her eye. Of course, she cried scared. She thought she was going to go blind. He promised that he would never again ask her to do that. Her husband must have been a very understanding man. He loved her very deeply."

They both agreed.

"Just the thought of it," said Aunt Heydee with a sigh. "What women have to go through to please their husbands." I wanted to ask them what sperm is, but I have enough brains to realize that they would know that I was eavesdropping and I would get yelled at. One thing was for sure, it has something to do with sex. My friend Julia from school told me that sperm is a man's form of menses and that's all she knows.

Nelly and I have good heart-to-heart talks. She told me that she noticed I am treated like a child. She told me that, in North America, girls my age are treated like adults. She told me how much she misses her husband and how they used to take long walks every night after dinner and talk about all kind of subjects. He was a very intelligent man. They were both in love with each other, even after being married for so many years. Both her sons are very handsome, and her daughter Ruth is also very beautiful. She is married and has a little girl whose name is Kim. Nelly feels lonely, and she would love to take me to North

America with her. She told me that she loves me, and she gave me her picture as a memory to keep for myself. I put it in a small frame and set it on the night table next to my bed.

Nelly shaves under her armpits! That is so American! She uses a dainty razor blade made for women. She told me that after using it a few times, she will throw the blade away. I have never seen such a thing. Papa has to make suds in a cup and uses a very sharp razor blade knife. He carefully stretches his skin between his fingers so he doesn't cut himself seriously, but he always nicks himself no matter how carefully he shaves his face. Once in a while, he goes to the barbershop. They put hot towels on his face, as they do to for all of their clients, to make the shaving smoother.

Nelly told me that all her clothes are bought in various department stores, where you can choose from hundreds of styles. Not here, I told her. We have to have a seamstress come to our house to make our dresses because the price tags in the clothing stores are very expensive and for tourists only. I do have fun looking through fashion magazines and picking the style of dress I would like to have, but it can't compare to going to a store and actually trying it on first before buying it. To top it off, the seamstress who comes to our house has horrible bad breath. While she is pinning the material on me, I have to hold my breath the whole time. Mama knows about it, but she says beggars can't be choosers. Maria Josefina is the least expensive seamstress we know of, and she does a great job at sewing the dresses. Her price fits our budget.

Nelly has a movie camera and has been taking movies of all of us to take back to America. We went to the beach yesterday, and she filmed Max-Leão showing his muscles as he lifted me up in the air. Max-Leão is into physical fitness, and he works out lifting weights every day to build

The Journey of Innocence

his muscles. He is very strong.

Nelly sure drinks a lot of soda. I don't like soda. It gives me bubbles in the stomach, and then I feel bloated. She can drink the contents of a whole bottle of soda right from the bottle, all in one shot without taking a break to breathe. It's amazing! Must be the way Americans drink soda. We always put soda in a glass and sip it, little by little. If we are thirsty, we drink water, but that's probably because we can't afford soda. Water is free.

Over the weekend, Nelly and I went on a mission. This is a secret between the two of us. She wanted to see if someone she really liked when she was a young girl is still alive. His name was Jorge João da Silva. According to Nelly, he was the most handsome boy in the village where she had spent the last summer before going to North America. They were in love with each other, but the affair never went any further because he was Catholic. She had thought about him many times through the years, and now that she is a widow, she wanted to see him again.

So, we took the train up north and went to the small village, Pedro da Cadeira. When we arrived, the people working at the train station knew exactly whom she was asking about. He was married and lived with his wife and family on a big farm on a hill. The train station manager offered to call him on the telephone. Aunt Nelly asked him to tell Jorge João da Silva that he had a visitor from the past, but not to give her name. We waited at the train station, and about half an hour later, a man looking like an older John Wayne came walking our way. The meeting took my breath away. They looked at each other and still recognized each other after thirty-four years. They ran toward each other, hugging each other as if the years had stood still. He took us to his house and introduced us to his wife, who offered us lunch and seemed very happy to see us.

It was a wonderful day, and also a sad day because in my heart I was hoping that he was still single and they could have gotten married. I don't care if he is a Catholic or not, and I have a feeling that, had Nelly found him a single man, she would have not cared about it either. Love would have conquered all. But at least now she knows that he is alive and happy.

Before getting on the train, Nelly bought some very ripe and juicy plums, and we ate them on our way back to Lisboa. When I got tired, she put my head on her shoulder and said, "Go ahead, little angel. Take a little nap and rest." I love the way she talks to me.

Here it goes again, the *déjà vu* feeling. I was in my bedroom reading *The Count of Monte Cristo*, one of my very favorite books, except for *The Egyptian* which is my number one favorite book to read over and over again, when Nelly came in and put the pictures of her two sons, Alberto and Gabriel, on my bed. She asked me the same question Mama asked me a few years back, "Which one do you like the most?"

Hmm, I thought to myself. *Doesn't she know that I am marrying Alberto? Why is she asking me this question?* I pointed to Alberto's picture without a word.

She smiled at me and said, "I was just making sure." I smiled back.

She is leaving tonight to go back to North America. I wish I could go with her.

My brothers and I were all in bed, as we are supposed to be by nine o'clock to get up early to go to school, when I heard Nelly asking, "Where's Verónica? I want to give her a kiss once again before leaving."

I heard Mama tell her, "She has school tomorrow. It's late, and she is already sleeping."

Nelly tiptoed into my bedroom, and I made believe that I

The Journey of Innocence

was sleeping, keeping my eyes closed. She bent forward and gave me a delicate kiss on my forehead. "Goodbye, darling," she said. "I love you." And she left.

I cried and cried, and told God if there was one thing that I wished for with all my heart it was to go to North America and live with Aunt Nelly, even if I had to sacrifice myself and marry her son. He can't be that bad since his mother is the most loving and caring person in the whole world. Then I thanked God for everything, as I try to do every night before sleeping.

I have a special prayer that I personally made up: Thank you God for everything you have given me. Please continue to protect us all and bless our family—and João from Costa da Caparica, whom I will never forget even though he was never my boyfriend. I still love him and wish him my very best.

Mama came to my bedroom a few days ago looking sad. She pointed to Nelly's picture on the night table next to my bed. "I can't help but notice that you put her picture next to your bed, and you don't have one of me, your own mother. I want you to know that she is not the nice person you think she is. She acted nice to you to cover her domineering personality. And besides that, she is also jealous of anyone who gets in her way." Then Mama left my bedroom.

I opened the top drawer of the night table and put Nelly's picture away. The only picture I have in my bedroom now is the one of my two young cousins who were taken to a concentration camp by the Nazis and killed in the gas chamber.

Mama dictated a letter in Spanish to send to my Cousin Alberto, asking if his mother, Aunt Nelly had gotten home all right since it's been a week and we have not heard from her. I thought the whole idea was dumb, and I didn't want to do it. "It's been only one week!" I argued back to Mama.

"So what?" she insisted. "You write exactly what I am going to dictate."

So, I did, and in Spanish! My goodness, I don't like Spanish and don't understand Spanish.

Mama said the English I am learning in high school will not be enough to make me a writer, and Alberto doesn't understand Portuguese.

"Makes more sense that we write in Spanish," she said again. "Nelly lived with her mother-in-law, who was from Morocco, and they only spoke Spanish at home. Therefore, Alberto most likely can read Spanish," she continued to reason. "If he doesn't understand Spanish, Nelly will translate for him."

Against my will, I wrote in Spanish: "Dear Cousin Alberto, I am very worried. Something horrible must have happened to Aunt Nelly. I have not slept for the last three days as I am concerned about her health. I know she has a bad heart. Will you write to me at once with news of her condition?" I signed, "Your worried and distressed Cousin Verónica."

I hate being manipulated by Mama to do things that I don't want to do.

A letter written in Spanish arrived the morning after I sent out Mama's letter to Cousin Alberto. Alberto had seen my pictures and the home movies that Nelly had taken back with her to North America, and he would like me to write to him because he liked me a lot. Obviously, the letter written by Mama in Spanish wondering about Nelly arriving safely had not yet arrived.

Mama said we should wait for his next letter before I answered this one. Then Mama gave me a little piece of paper that she had kept hidden since I was born. Supposedly, Alberto had written to me when he was twelve years old to congratulate Mama on my birth. On the other side of the small paper, he had written in English, "I heard

The Journey of Innocence

that you are a beautiful baby with green eyes and dark hair. Will you marry me when you get older?"

His mother must have forced him to write such a note. No twelve-year-old boy would ask a baby girl to marry him. Just in case he did do that on his own, even though I doubt it, I put his note proposing marriage away in my jewelry music box, as the first love letter ever received and read.

Another letter from North America arrived today. It was Alberto assuring me that Nelly was still living and doing well. Somehow I felt that he had written that letter with a touch of irony, as if aware of the game being played. But then he went on again to say that he had seen my pictures and the films that his mother had taken home, and he had found me to be very pretty.

I was going to write back in my best English, but Mama said, "No way." I was inept in doing such a thing. She was going to coach me on exactly what words to write back.

Her writings are all poetic, boring stuff that makes no sense. The only words that are mine are my signature. I feel so weird about this whole thing.

Summer of 1960

While on a trip to the Tower of Belem, when nobody was watching, I carved a little heart with the letters J and V on the trunk of a huge tree. It stands for João and me in love forever. I no longer remember his face, but it feels right to have someone in my heart.

Letters come and go, all between Alberto and Mama. I write what she tells me to write in Spanish, and then I sign it. I wonder if Nelly is also telling Alberto what to write, because in that case this love-letter exchange stuff is basically between Mama and her sister Nelly. I can't stand it. I want to believe it's him though. He has been sending me pictures of furniture and clothes all cut out from magazines.

He says he wants to know more about me. He wants to know what my favorite color is, and what I like to do as a hobby. The answers are never mine. It's all answered like a mad poet in phrases that make no sense and don't even rhyme. I really don't know much about him except for a couple of pictures he sent me. He is not getting any answer to his questions from me because Mama is on a mission of poetry in fantasyland, where reality is nonexistent.

Alberto has been sending me lots of pictures. My favorite one was taken ten years ago when he was in the United States Air Force and he is wearing his uniform. He was very handsome even though he is now older, twelve years older than I am.

We are living in the country again for the summer. This is another forsaken place, away from civilization, with woods and lots of eucalyptus trees all around us. But somehow I like it better here than at Malveira. They don't pretend to be a town because there's nowhere to go. We have a huge forest behind our rental house that makes up for us being out nowhere, and I spend the days lying in the hammock outside, reading my books in the shade of the trees. The next neighbor's farm is about a fifteen-minute walk, but we have no reason to meet them.

The letters continue to arrive from America, about one every two weeks. I am starting to get used to them. Someone cares for me enough to bother to answer the dim-witted letters Mama writes. Maybe he likes the letters he is getting. What a horrible thought if he is not writing at all. In his last letter, he asked if I would consider being his girlfriend. Mama said "yes," and wrote more Spanish love

The Journey of Innocence

poetry back.

Aunt Heydee came by this weekend and took my brothers and me for a country hike. I love being with her. She is what life is all about. We walked and walked, up the hill and then up a mountain—my very first real mountain hike. We got to the top, and I made a wish to God. I want to climb mountains, tall ones and big wide ones, so that when I reach the top I can see the earth all around me. I want to travel and see the world and have incredible adventures. In every country that has a mountain, I will climb to the top.

Aunt Heydee knows all about the meaning of life. As she stretched her arms out, she pointed to the land around and below us. "Take in the breath of life," she said for us all to hear. "Use your lungs and your eyes and all of your senses, and live each day as a gift to be thankful for."

A few weeks ago, Mama wanted to make sure that I was healthy. The result came back that I might have tuberculosis. They saw something on the film, and tomorrow I have to go back to the hospital and see Uncle Augusto for more lung X-rays.

Uncle Augusto didn't hug me. I was there alone in the big, cold hospital building with no one to hold my hand. I felt very sad and lonely. If Aunt Heydee had not been in Venice for her vacation, she would have been with me. They took a lot more X-rays, and Uncle Augusto had a concerned look on his face as he put his hand in front of him so that I would not come close to him. I must be dying, and worst of all, I am contagious. He would not even give me a goodbye hug. He sent me back home, stating, "Tell your mother that I will call her later after I have some time to look at your lung X-rays."

Good news. I am fine. What they saw on the first X-ray was simply a scar that healed from when I had tuberculosis as a child. But, like Mama said, I am still not as strong as other people. I will always be sickly and have to eat more than others; otherwise, it could revert again to tuberculosis and I will die, just like our young maid Olivia who worked for us when I was just a baby.

Mama is always talking about her whenever the subject of tuberculosis comes up. Mama loved Olivia. She considered her more of a friend than a maid. But Olivia was dying and used to cough a lot and spit blood. I probably caught tuberculosis from Olivia when I was a child.

Mama is on a mission to make me strong and healthy. She wakes me up in the middle of the night to give me pudding. I love pudding, but not in the middle of the night. She says she is sacrificing her own sleep by waking up to feed me, and the least I can do is be thankful. I have to eat a little something every three hours, as she says. She even bought corn flakes so that I will drink milk. She loves me when I am sick. It pays to get sick, that's for sure. I love corn flakes with hot milk and lots of sugar on top. But pudding, even if it's chocolate pudding, is more than I can stand in the middle of the night.

Since the motorcycle accident, Mama has developed a sixth sense. She is able to tell things that are going to happen in the future. She saved Max-Leão's life when she stopped him from going for a car ride with two other boys. His two friends were killed in a car accident. She also saved her brother Augusto's life by warning him not to go out on a certain day because something bad was going to happen. Besides poetry, she is now writing short stories, too. Mama has also started painting, which is really strange because she couldn't even help me draw a vase before the accident. Now she is doing all kinds of paintings with oil on canvas.

I am doing well. I am basically healthy except for the sharp

The Journey of Innocence

knifelike pains I have on and off in my legs. As Uncle Augusto says, I have rheumatoid arthritis, and I have to learn to live with it. There isn't much that can be done except rubbing my legs, taking sour medicine, and sitting outside in the sun. Nothing really helps.

Mama gave Max-Leão and me some money to take a bus to Eiriceira. She had to go to Lisboa to have José treated for asthma. The experimental drugs they are giving him now make him act weird, and they are not helping him with the asthma. Max-Leão and I decided to hitchhike to Eiriceira and save the bus money to buy goodies when we got there. It took us over an hour of standing on the road with our thumbs up. The young couple that picked us up told us we were foolish to travel this way because there were people out there picking up children to hurt them. We know all of that, but it's not going to happen to us. We are very careful. Besides, we already had plans to take the bus home before it gets dark.

It was a wonderful day at the beach. We bought a nice-sized watermelon from a street vendor, and we climbed the rocks with it and the lunch box we had brought with us. We set up our stuff and clothes safely under the shade of one of the rocks and ran right into the water, where we stayed for hours—until we had purple lips and were shaking cold.

With both of us seated on the rock cliff, we ate our codfish cakes and bread. We didn't bring any utensils to eat with because it was all finger food, so we didn't have a knife to cut the watermelon. The solution was simple. Max-Leão picked up the watermelon up and then smashed it into one pointy rock, thus splitting the watermelon into pieces. We used our tongues and teeth and hands, and we ate until our stomachs were bloated. Then, drenched in watermelon juice, we sat under the warm sun at the seashore and watched the waves coming toward us.

When we got home, we told Marcia, our maid, about our

adventure. She told us there was a party going on at the next farm with people our own age, and we should go and have fun. We washed up quickly and took a walk to the neighbor's farm.

It was a hot summer night, and everyone was dancing or talking in groups outside on the wide marble veranda. The lady of the house introduced me to a few boys and girls my own age. We were there, talking for about ten minutes when Inácio, one of the boys in the group, asked me to dance. He was just putting his arm around my waist when Marcia showed up all flustered and nervous.

"Let's go," she said, as she grabbed my arm and pulled me away from my dancing partner. I was so embarrassed. I felt like a baby being taken home by the maid as I mumbled an excuse to Inácio.

Mama had come back from her trip to Lisboa and had found out from Marcia that Max-Leão and I had hitchhiked that day and were now at a party.

She was not happy.

As always, I got blamed for it. As punishment, she said I was not allowed to return to the party because I was the eldest and should have had more brains than to hitchhike with Max-Leão.

Marcia felt really bad, but what she doesn't realize is that Mama would have found any excuse to get us out of the party where Max-Leão and I would be among people our own age. We were allowed to have dinner before we were sent to bed, but I wasn't hungry.

"Psst, psst," I heard Papa calling me this morning as I was going across the hallway. He was sitting alone at the dining room table and had just finished his usual cup of coffee and breakfast of one soft-boiled egg and two pieces of toast with butter. "Verónica," he whispered, as if worried Mama might hear him. "Sit down next to me, and listen to me. I want you to know that what your mother is doing, you

The Journey of Innocence

know—setting you up for a marriage with your cousin—someone you don't even know, is wrong in my opinion. She believes it is the best for you, but, as your father, I have doubts. What do you think?"

Caught by surprise and being pushed into thinking about a situation that I didn't want to face wasn't easy.

"I don't mind," I answered. Barely speaking, I mumbled, "It's okay with me." Then I looked away as if afraid that he could read my fears.

"Be careful, daughter," he said. "You just turned sixteen years old. You are still a child in my opinion. Make sure you love this person before you marry him. Marriage is a lifetime commitment. If you change your mind, I am on your side."

I didn't know what to say except, "Okay. Thanks, Papa." And I left the room.

Papa rarely talks to me. His concern took me by surprise. I was speechless, but what could I say? Have a heart-to-heart talk with a man I am afraid to talk back to and don't even know, except that he is my father and he intimidates me most of the time. Yet, I had to smile when I left the room, for Papa does care for me and he is worried.

There's no going back. My future is somewhere else. Like the gypsy woman foretold already, each of Mama's children is like a star. Each is destined to go in a different direction. My destiny is going to North America and being happy.

The turkey was served for dinner, but no one was able to eat a bite. We just stared at it and ate the potatoes and the vegetables instead. Since we arrived here last month, this turkey had taken a liking to Mama. The other chickens, ducks, and turkeys went on with their normal daily business, but this one loved "Mama Linda." Since the accident, Papa calls Mama *Linda*. She likes the new name, and we all make her happy by calling her *Mama Linda*, especially if we are trying to get on her good side.

When she walked in the garden, the turkey would run toward her and then walk along her like a pet dog on a leash. When she would sit down, he would lie down by her feet.

One morning her bedroom window was open and the turkey jumped on her windowsill and just stood there, staring at her. That really freaked her out. She no longer thought it was funny. After that incident, our maid felt that the turkey was possessed by some lost soul.

Aunt Heydee came all the way from Lisboa just to meet the turkey. After all, turkeys are stupid and have no feelings, just like the chickens and other animals we eat. That's why they get eaten. They are not smart enough to run away and hide. Uncle Augusto and his family paid us a visit, too. Everybody wanted to see the possessed turkey. But the maid got Mama all flustered, and the neighbors coming by got Mama to believe that killing the turkey would set the soul free.

So, it was done. Killing the turkey was for the best, they all agreed. But when it came time to eat the bird, one had to wonder if the soul was still inside, and nobody was going to take that chance.

Aunt Heydee is so smart. Besides Portuguese, of course, she speaks fluent French, Italian, Spanish, and English. She is a woman of the world. She has seen everything and done everything except being married. She won't budge on her requirements for the perfect husband, and she will not settle for anything less than what she feels she deserves. He must be Jewish. Otherwise, the family would dishonor her. He must be rich, because she has been poor long enough. He must be educated, because she needs someone she can talk to on her intellectual level. He must be a lot younger than she is, so that he can keep up with her active lifestyle. And he must be handsome, because getting married will be enough of a sacrifice for her, and the truth is that she would like someone who is pleasant to look at. Sensitive and loving is a must, yet he has to be masculine with lots of muscles like Hercules. He must own his own private home in the city for the winter months as well as a villa in the country for the summer months, and—at top of the list—he must love opera.

She has told me about her travels through other countries of Europe, from the caverns on the Island of Capri to the Swiss Alps, from Rome's Coliseum to Paris's catacombs, and even though she travels by herself, she has no problem making friends along the way. Every day is an awesome day of adventure and wonder. She is a self-taught French and piano teacher, and she dabbles successfully in oil painting. She never went past fourth grade, yet she is a self-made master of everything she does.

Yesterday, while we were seated on the hammock outside, she told me how much she appreciates beauty as well as what someone else might consider to be ugly. Everything has a place in the palette of Mother Nature, she said. As an artist, she sees men and women as an incredible creation, and through her drawings and oil paintings she has grown to appreciate all forms and shapes.

"There is nothing ugly in the world," she told me. "It's all perception, how you look at it. Life is very much like a diamond, and it shines as long as you keep it polished."

She always gives thanks to God for being able to see, feel, and touch.

When I return to Lisboa, Aunt Heydee is going to start taking me along with her on her weekend adventures. Mama said it was okay. I need culture in order to make a good impression on Alberto; otherwise, he's going to send me back to Portugal. Aunt Ligia came into my bedroom before we left Lisboa to spend our summer in the country. She tried to make conversation with me about different topics that, in her opinion, are essential between a man and a woman for a happy marriage.

I didn't respond well to her interview. Matter of fact, I failed miserably because I didn't feel I had much to say about anything, so I didn't. Aunt Ligia and I have never been in a close relationship. She is too nervous for me. Besides that, a few years ago when I started writing children's stories she accused me of plagiarizing the children's stories she had written and used to read to me when I was a child. I don't have any recollection of that happening. I must have been a baby. Anyway, she reported to Mama that I was completely without graces and my culture was equal to a rusty nail found deep in mud. I had nothing to offer a cultured man like Alberto, an American and an engineer. Aunt Ligia told Mama that she'd better do something drastic about my personality, which amounts to a flat expression of nodding, staring, and "yes" or "no" answers. In other words, I am boring. I knew that.

Autumn of 1960

We all said goodbye to Max-Leão last week. He was sent to England to become an architect. Mama cries a lot. I don't cry about it, but I miss him.

Papa's family is paying for Max-Leão's upkeep and overseeing his education in London. Mama says that a mother has to make sacrifices like this for the welfare of her child, and for the same reason she will be sending me away to North America as soon as Alberto asks for my hand in marriage.

Personally, I feel like Mama is trying to get rid of all of us, and I feel confused about my situation.

It's not the same without Max-Leão. I do not see eye to eye with José. Basically we stay away from each other because we don't have anything in common. Mama sent us out to

The Journey of Innocence

the movies a couple of times, and he always disappears around a street corner and gets lost in the crowd. I feel so stupid and abandoned when he does that, so I refuse to go out with him. Last week, when we went down the busy street of *Madalena*, which is known for crime and prostitution, he took a quick turn around the street corner and once again disappeared out of my sight. He does that all the time. I went to the movies by myself.

I told Mama about it, and he was excused as being too young and just a boy. He is spoiled and gets away with everything he does. He is supposed to let us know when he leaves the house, but he just opens the front door and yells goodbye as he slams the door behind him. He gives us no time to ask him where he is going. He is also very good at making money deals at school because our *escudos* have certain small-sized coins that have more value than larger-sized ones. He has convinced some students to trade their small coins for his larger ones. So, he gets into trouble at school. But Mama says that, if the kids in his class fall for the size of the coin instead of its value, then they deserve to be cheated out of their money.

The other day José made me angry, and I told him that I would never ask him to come and live with me in North America because he is a crook and a liar and he will be put in jail and then he will be going to the electric chair to pay for his crimes. I know it was mean for me to do that, but he is constantly irritating me. He is a pest!

I have thought a few times in the past, and still in the present, that, if I could find a way to leave this world, I would do it. I don't like anything about my life, but I am too much of a coward to take a chance at hurting myself. Poison can't be pleasant. I read the book *Madame Bovary*, and I didn't think it was romantic when she killed herself the way she did. I can't even imagine more stomach cramps than when I have my monthly period. I thought about jumping from a bridge, but it has to hurt like hell when you hit the hard ground even if it's just for a few minutes. Jumping from a bridge into the River Tejo was another thought, but, since I can't swim, I'd be swallowing water like the victims of the Inquisition when they had water forced down their throats until they died—and that has to be as nasty as that time when I was a kid and that beach boy dunked me under the ocean—not a very pleasant experience. I could try what Max-Leão did with his chemistry experiment in the bathroom, but I would have to make sure that no holes were left for the gas to escape, and with my luck, I'd be discovered and beaten to a pulp.

My future is locked with Aunt Nelly and Cousin Alberto in North America. They are the only ones who can help me, and I know because I tried to run away to Spain a few days ago and it was an eye-opening experience.

I went to a travel agency. The price of a train ticket is more than ten years of my allowance, not to mention that I would need money to buy food and rent an apartment while waiting to get a job. I am only sixteen years old, and no one is going to hire someone my age. I don't have any skills, except for stuffing envelopes and writing addresses like I do at Papa's office. I don't know anything else. School has not taught me anything that I can use in the outside world. I can't even be a bum living in the streets of Spain because, if other bums were to speak to me, I wouldn't even know what they were saying as I don't understand a word of Spanish.

I was walking home from the American Embassy, where I have been spending a few hours in the afternoons while listening to music records and reading books, and a boy on the street saw me and followed me home. Then, about seven o'clock, I heard the sound of a guitar and someone singing a love song. I looked out of my window and there he was, with a friend playing a guitar across the street and

The Journey of Innocence

facing our building. I went out into the veranda of my bedroom and smiled happily. He took a bow, acknowledging my presence, and threw me a kiss with his hand as he started to sing, "Your green eyes are like the sea. Tell me that you are the one for me. I love you. I love you. Let me kiss your sweet lips and show my love for you."

Rosa, the maid, was the only one home besides me and said, "I'll take care of them. Just watch, Miss Verónica." She took off from the veranda and out of my room.

I had no idea what she was going to do. I was standing at the veranda enjoying his singing until I saw Rosa return from the kitchen with a pail of water. She stepped onto the veranda and asked them with a big smile if they could get a little closer to the building so that we could hear them better. When they promptly followed her invitation, she lifted the bucket of cold water and poured the whole thing on the two boys. They took off, cursing at both of us. I will never know who my Romeo was. I doubt he will ever return to serenade under my bedroom window.

A package arrived today from North America. It is a silver engagement ring with six brilliant stones all around. Alberto had enclosed a little note with it. "Verónica, will you be my fiancé?"

Mama wrote back saying, "Yes."

Now that I am engaged and have a real boyfriend, I can show my ring to everyone in school.

My friends at school were shocked by the news of my engagement. Laura, who walks home with me, showed a lot of concern and offered me her house if I wanted to hide away. She told me that I was nuts to go along with this charade. What if Alberto gets here and doesn't look like his picture? He may be missing his legs or be blind or be very old or be plain nasty, smelly, and ugly, she told me. I assured her that he was on the level because his mother is my mother's sister and she is a wonderful lady. Besides, I am in love with him and I am not afraid, I told her defiantly.

"I will get engaged, too, then," said Laura, getting upset over the whole thing as if this were some kind of a contest between the two of us. "I am not going to let you go ahead of me and get married. I am not going to be an old maid."

I told Mama about what Laura had said, and Mama told me that Laura was not to be trusted anymore as a friend. She was obviously jealous, and that's why she said stuff like that.

Mama has told me that I will not be returning to high school in January. There's no need to learn any more school stuff. What I need is a different type of education, the kind that will prepare me for being a wife. She signed me up to start this January at a school that will teach me proper manners and how to cook French-style and sew pretty dresses for myself. As of January, it is official: Aunt Heydee is in charge of the cultural part of my education.

As soon as I got into school today, Laura grabbed me in the hallway to show me her diamond engagement ring. I didn't even know that she had a boyfriend. She couldn't wait to show it to me. She is engaged and will be married when she turns eighteen years old. I am very happy for her.

I said goodbye to everybody in school. From now on, I will be busy spending time with Aunt Heydee and getting ready for the future, which does not include anyone here. I am better off breaking my roots now and not holding onto anything or anybody. Encarnação is my friend, but she has her family and can't leave Portugal. Aunt Heydee is in the same predicament. She says North America is for young people like me. Max-Leão is gone, and José is just someone who lives here. I am alone. But I long for love, whatever

The Journey of Innocence

that is that everyone speaks and writes about all the time. Love is in songs and books, and it's understood that, once you find it, you will always be happy. I would like to be happy.

Winter of 1961

Aunt Heydee goes out every night to dance or hang out with her girlfriends at the coffee shops, but she doesn't suffer from getting into a cold bed when she comes home. The maid gets 50 *centavos* to sleep in Aunt Heydee's bed until she gets home. Then the maid goes to her bedroom, and Aunt Heydee gets to sleep in the warmed bed. Her bed is next to mine, and I watch her as she sleeps with a bunch of pillows so that her head is kept up and her face doesn't get squished down. She doesn't have a single line in her face. She attributes it to sleeping almost sitting and, of course, using almond oil on her skin every day. It works!

Alberto has sent me a home movie and more pictures so that I can get to know him better. There's a lot of snow where he lives. I can't wait to play in the snow and throw snowballs at him and make a huge snowman. When I go to North America, I am going to have lots of bubble baths like Doris Day, wear clothes bought in a store, have lots of ice cream whenever I want, and sing and dance every day with loud American rock and roll music.

Things in Africa are pretty scary and getting worse as more and more of our colonies are becoming independent from Portugal. There are lots of ill feelings as the African people are trying to get the white people out. Horrible atrocities are committed every day. The newspapers tell stories of crimes against white women and children who are in the way of black people becoming independent from Portuguese control. It's an ugly, nasty time in history, and innocent people get caught in between the ignorance and savage behavior of everyone on both sides. I hope and pray that Amelia and her family are safe living in Africa.

The *Diário de Noticias* blurted out an episode of utter horror. When an eleven-year-old black boy was walking in one of the streets of Lisboa, some men from a garage grabbed him as if he were a criminal from Africa. They got the gasoline hose and used it as an enema. They killed the little black boy. I cried before I went to sleep. I felt that I could also be a criminal very easily. If I had a chance to do it, I would have killed the men who tortured the little boy. I would like to kill them with my own hands, those bastards! From now on, I will never read the news.

In order for me to leave Portugal right after the wedding, all of the paperwork with the civil wedding has to be arranged ahead of time. The Portuguese and the American Embassy are working together, but very slowly. If I am to leave with Alberto and go to North America, I have to marry him by proxy as soon as possible. That means I will have to marry Uncle Augusto, who will represent Alberto here in Portugal. Because Uncle Augusto is a medical doctor, he has a lot of influence with the government and can speed up the needed paperwork. Otherwise, it could take years for me to be approved to leave. Being married to an American will also expedite the procedure. When Alberto comes to Portugal to pick me up, I will already be married to him legally. Alberto only has one week off from work, so everything has to be ready for the real wedding within a few days after he arrives, and hopefully we will be married religiously after three days so that we can have three days of honeymoon before leaving Portugal. I am nervous, but not scared. I am enjoying the attention that everybody gives me, and I am wondering what other wonderful things are ahead in my life.

The Journey of Innocence

The civil wedding went very well, even though the "real" groom was missing. Everybody got dressed up, and Augusto's wife Coty was there smiling throughout the whole event. So were their daughters Rica Gilda and Palomita, along with Aunt Heydee and Aunt Gimol, who is Grandma Rica's youngest sister. It felt like a real wedding with guests, flowers, and signatures.

Papa never smiled throughout the wedding, and Mama was very fidgety. I felt she was scared I would back out of this compromise. She doesn't realize that I will do anything to get out of here and go live with Aunt Nelly.

I wore one of the dresses Alberto had sent me, and I held a bouquet of flowers just as a bride would. Pictures were taken inside the courthouse and outside, and while we were out there posing for the photographer, a woman going by said out loud to her friend, "Foolish girl—obviously she is marrying the old goat for his money!"

We all laughed, having a good time. Aunt Coty was hysterical and laughed the loudest. The woman passerby probably thought that we were all bizarre.

It's opera season with Aunt Heydee. No wonder she is called *Napoleão #1*. She took me to the famous *São Carlos* Opera House, and she introduced herself as a journalist and me as her assistant. This is the way we get into the *hot spots* of culture without paying. I am not to tell Mama, as she would not approve. Aunt Heydee cannot afford a ticket at *São Carlos*. She has a meager salary as a private French teacher, and she saves every penny she earns to go on vacation during the summer months.

Her food is carefully planned daily, healthy but small meals. Her clothes are handmade from other people's hand-me-downs. She is a survivor in a tough world. She is a woman without a man to support her and take care of her. As she has told me so many times, "You either grab life by the horns, or you lie down and die. The choice is yours."

Things didn't go as we planned. Aunt Heydee and I got separated inside the famous glittery *São Carlos*. It was the opening night of a Portuguese opera, which meant overcrowding. Aunt Heydee was pushed along with the crowd to the seats below, and I was sent upstairs with an usher. I don't know for sure how it happened, but the usher took me to a private balcony, a few spaces from the presidential compartment. I could tell, because it was centrally located and had the Portuguese flag draped in front of it.

Meagerly dressed in my Scottish-pattern, brown, flannel dress, I sunk myself into the red velvet seat so that I would not be seen. Then carefully, I took a peek out of my balcony, trying to see where Aunt Heydee was seated downstairs.

I was afraid that someone would come upstairs, grab me by the hair, and throw me out of the theatre. It was obvious I didn't belong in this sophisticated gathering of men in tuxedos and women all glittered up with long beautiful dresses. Everyone was dressed for the opera except me.

The *São Carlos* is the most famous opera house in Lisboa, and probably the most famous in all of Portugal. It is a magnificent theatre with gold-encrusted balconies and huge chandeliers hanging from its painted ceilings, which depicts what seems to be famous opera scenes. Only rich people who love opera can afford the expensive tickets. I saw Aunt Heydee down below. She smiled at me and waved. I waved back. During intermission, I intended to run downstairs and join her. I was proud of being so close to the president's balcony, even though it looked as though he wasn't going to attend because it was empty.

The lights went out, the door behind me opened, and three boys about my age came in. They were as surprised as I was. One of them sat next to me, introducing himself as the son of some guy I'd never heard of, as if that was going to impress me. The opera had started. I moved my chair

The Journey of Innocence

away from his, but he moved his chair next to me, making sure his knee was touching mine. I kept moving until I was cornered at the wall. One of his friends said, "Why don't you leave the girl alone?" But he would not listen. He tried to make conversation and wanted to know if I had a boyfriend.

I told him "yes," and that I was getting married officially in May of next year.

He went on to talk about how one year was too long to wait and a kiss from me would not hurt anybody.

What a retard! My luck. I always get stuck with jerks.

Then he put his arm over my shoulder, saying, "Give me a kiss."

I pushed him away. "No, I don't want to kiss you."

He was not giving up that easy. "And why not?"

I didn't know what to say, so I figured that, if I shocked him, he might leave me alone. With a very dignified look, I said, "Because I don't know you, and I am Jewish!" I am such an idiot, but what else could I say?

After being taken aback for a bit, he remarked, "I don't care what you are, I will kiss you even if you are Jewish."

I pushed him away again the best I could. I was so nervous, I thought I was going to cry. I said, "I am not allowed to kiss someone who's not Jewish. It's against my religion." He came closer to my face, and I pushed him away with my hand once again.

He finally got upset and said, "Well, Miss Jewish Special, if that's the way you feel." And he moved away.

Lucky for him, because I was starting to consider the idea that I might have to punch him if necessary. I was embarrassed and a nervous wreck. I have to admit that he was very cute, but he was definitely a "teddy boy," the latest phrase from England to describe an immature, bratty, young villain.

The opera was boring and silly with a bunch of people screaming to the sound of a full orchestra, as if that could help the singers. Opera singing doesn't sound as natural and soul moving as rock and roll. I found out that night that nothing is worse to my ears than Portuguese opera. Opera is bad enough in a foreign language, but in Portuguese it's even more annoying than Italian. I hate opera. Intermission came, and I ran out of the compartment and down the wide, luxurious, golden-carpeted steps.

I took a deep breath of relief when I saw Aunt Heydee in the foyer. We sat together downstairs for the second part of the show. People seemed to have left for good during intermission because now there were plenty of seats available downstairs. "I almost fainted when I saw you up there with three boys. Are you all right?" she asked.

Still trembling from the experience I had gone through, I said, "Yes. I am fine."

She encouraged me to keep this whole thing between the two of us. Mama would have her head if she found out about this incident.

~ *Chapter Seven* ~

ENGAGED TO COUSIN ALBERTO

1961

Spring of 1961

The school I am attending now is definitely a bride's school. The girls seem older than I am, and they have a lot more experience about life. I just sit through the sewing classes and manners classes and cooking classes. The students have their own little clique, and I don't dare tell anyone that I am already married to my cousin from America whom I never met. I know I am not the smartest person, but I know enough not to say anything and be ridiculed. They call me an *existentialist*. When I was in high school, I was called that too. I take it as a compliment and an achievement, because everybody else is like a cookie-cutter copy of each other. I can be myself, and I don't have to explain why. I like being an existentialist.

I have seen movies with existentialists like me. They live in cities like New York and Paris, too. They go out at night dressed in black to dark, smoky nightclubs. Their hair is straight, and they don't wear makeup. They are natural and love natural things. They are in touch with the Earth and do meditation. They dance to jazz and try to understand the meaning of life. They are unhappy, like me.

I love using the school's modern bathroom because it has perfumed hand soap. I lock the door and start by washing my feet in the sink. All those years of ballet have paid off. I have no problem reaching the sink with my feet. After my feet, I wash my armpits. We don't have soft perfumed soap at home. I feel sparkly clean when I leave their bathroom. Sometimes someone will ask me what's taking me so long in there. I always say the same, "upset stomach."

The girls in this school are always acting like grown-ups and talking about world stuff. The other day, between classes, we were waiting in the hallway for the next class and they were talking about the Russian army and what would happen if they attacked Portugal. Some said they would rather kill themselves than submit to some fat Russian. Others were saying to act nice toward them, and then they wouldn't kill you after they raped you.
    I have to smile about all of this because, by the time the Russians get here to rape them, I will be in North America.

It's so much fun receiving presents from Alberto. I anxiously visit the mailbox every morning. When I don't get a letter, I feel disappointed. I love the cards he sends me. My favorite card is the one where a red paper heart pops out on a spring. He wrote, "In America, today is Valentine's Day, and you are my sweetheart." I like that name, *sweetheart*. *Sweet* is sugar; *heart* is love. *Sweetheart* is such a perfect word. Americans are so smart with their language and expressions of love.
    Every day I wear the earrings that Nelly gave me when she was here visiting us. They are the only earrings I wear.

Alberto is spoiling me with gifts. This week I got a box with two more dresses, summer cotton dresses. The seamstress comes over and fixes them to fit me better. I like Alberto's taste in clothing, simple and comfortable styles.

The Journey of Innocence

He also sends me cutouts from magazines with the latest American styles of furniture. He wants me to pick the ones I like and send the pictures back. This way, he learns more about my taste in furniture. I have fun marking a little cross on the pictures I like, and then Mama has me writing back to Alberto in her poetic Spanish madness.

Mama continues to dream of becoming a millionaire, and she is sure that, any day now, she will win the million *escudos* lottery. I don't believe in that stuff. She has been playing the same lottery number her father played for years when he was alive. Every week, she buys a lottery ticket. Even when we were poor, she always bought a ticket. She thinks that the day she doesn't buy it, that's going to be the week she will lose the "big one." Sometimes she wins a few *escudos*, and that convinces her even more that she is due to win the real thing any time soon. In my opinion, she is wasting her money on a lost cause. When she is not feeling well enough to go out, she asks me to go all the way downtown just to buy a lottery ticket from a specific guy who sells the tickets on a specific street corner.

I always tell her, "You are wasting your money, Mama, and you are not going to win."

She gets upset and tells me that I just took her lucky chance away by blurting out a bad omen.

"Okay," I tell her. "Don't get the ticket, then."

And she says, "No, I'll take a chance anyway, even though you bring me bad luck. Go, get the ticket and think positive thoughts about it."

It would be nice if she won the lottery, but I really don't believe that she ever will.

For my birthday, I got a funny greeting card from Alberto. A little bunny popped up with outstretched arms, and on the bottom it said, "I love you this much." A little package arrived the next morning. Inside, there was a gold bracelet with hearts all around. This is a love present, and I like staring at it and feeling the little hearts in my hands. I wonder if he really loves me. He must. Otherwise, he would not be sending me such expensive gifts.

When I go out, I make sure my left hand is in view for everyone to see. The love bracelet and the ring state that I will soon be married. Lots of work is ahead to make sure that all the papers are in order so that I can leave for America with him next year. Aunt Nelly will be coming with Alberto for the wedding. They are bringing the wedding gown I chose from a magazine Alberto sent me.

Summer of 1961

Since Mama was away with Papa for a weekend in Spain, I felt it was a good idea if I answered the letter I received from Alberto this morning. I wrote in English, "Dear Alberto, I love you, too, and I can't wait to see you in May. Love and kisses, Verónica."

When Mama came back from her trip, she was concerned that I might have spoiled everything with some silly girly stuff and that Alberto was going to change his mind about marrying me. In her opinion, I should have waited for her to come back from Spain.

Alberto wrote back saying that he was thrilled I had finally written in English and he would be a lot happier if I could continue to write in English. Mama immediately made me write that I was terrible at writing in English, and I promised that, from now on, I would continue to write my feelings of love toward him in Spanish.

Mama gets a real kick out of Alberto calling her *Brigitte Bardot*. At the end of each letter, he always writes, "Give B.B. a kiss from me." Mama doesn't look anything like B.B. I believe he is very diplomatic, and he is trying to be friendly with his aunt and future mother-in-law.

The Journey of Innocence

Mama came into my bedroom last night and said that we needed to talk. She stood by the dresser and looked down at me while I stayed seated on my bed.

"You must not let anything silly, like thinking you are beautiful, get into your head. You are an average girl. At your age, I was a real vamp." She took a long breath and continued, "One young man died because he knew I could never be his, so he killed himself. All of my sisters were pretty, but I was a real knockout."

I stared at her, nodding my head in agreement. I was wondering why she constantly makes me feel like a worthless nobody and what was she trying to tell me?

She finished, saying, "Remember, you are a plain girl, nothing special. You must accept that, or you will be very unhappy." Then she left the bedroom.

I don't know what got into her. Maybe she saw me pose in front of the mirror in my bedroom before I go to bed. I like to pose in front of the mirror, and dance and smile and act like an actress. I always brush my hair before going to bed. One hundred strokes is the requirement for shiny healthy hair, but I never count. I don't feel unattractive, and I truly believe that I am pleasant to look at. Maybe she is afraid that I am getting vain, or maybe Aunt Heydee told her about the man we met in the trolley a few days ago. He came up to her and introduced himself as a movie agent. He handed her a calling card and said very politely, "I couldn't help but notice your daughter. She is very attractive. Please consider bringing her to my studio. Just call my office for an appointment." He left the trolley at the next stop.

Mama never tells me anything straight. She always has to beat around the bush. This is why I have not told anyone about the two sailors who stopped in front of me as I walked past them in downtown Lisboa a few days ago. One said to the other, pointing at me, "My goodness. What an incredible creation. And to think that this girl is the product of her parents fucking in the dark."

This was the worst language I had ever heard, but, as I kept walking away from them, I couldn't help but smile as I realized that, from the sailors' blunt point of view, they had paid me a great compliment.

It's been a lonely month. Aunt Heydee is somewhere in Morocco doing her once-a-year, one-month vacation. It's hot and lonely in the city. We are not going away this year. We are spending the summer in Lisboa. I fill my days by taking a daily bus ride to the airport to stand by the fence and watch the planes coming and going. Other times, I take the ferry across the River Tejo. I don't look or talk to anyone. I just look at the world as if I were the only one, and I welcome its arms around me, protecting me from anyone that might want to hurt me. I get off the ferry, look around as if I am meeting someone, and then take the ferry back.

Mama doesn't have to worry about me going anywhere by myself. I have been taught well. I don't trust anybody, and I have gotten used to staying within my own boundaries. I am faceless. No one can tell if I am sad or happy. Feeling this way keeps me protected from the outside, dormant until I wake up. Soon I'll be married and happy.

A neighbor asked Mama, "How can you let Verónica, your only daughter, go to North America? It's too far away. Most likely you won't see her again. Aren't you going to miss her?"

Mama responded in the same manner as when she sent Max-Leão to England, "As a mother I must make sacrifices. I'd rather have my daughter far away and happily married than close by and without a future."

Everybody admires her utter sacrifice, and she is very self-righteous about that. She will not stop me from being happy even if she doesn't see me anymore. I can't wait to leave.

The Journey of Innocence

I saw a black person this afternoon, but it wasn't a good experience. I have learned that there's good and bad in people of all races. I was walking a few blocks from home and my right hand hit somebody between the legs. That's how close this black man was walking next to me. I said, "Excuse me," and I kept walking. Soon I realized that he was doing that on purpose, and once again my hand touched his leg. I stopped, and he stopped and smiled at me. I started walking faster, and he started walking faster along with me, as if glued to my side. I thought about using my safety pin, but he was too big and it would probably feel like the bite of an ant on his leg.

He must have seen my angry face because he didn't follow me as I ran the rest of the way home. I feel sad that some black people are as bad as white folks. I didn't tell anyone about what happened.

Autumn of 1961

Aunt Heydee is back. Thank God! I went out a few times with Aunt Morena last month, but I was embarrassed to be with her. She purposely pulls her skirt up as far as she can to show her legs while making "goo goo eyes" and smiling to any man sitting across from her on the bus or the trolley. It doesn't even bother her that she doesn't know them. She winks at men when they walk past her on the street. It doesn't even matter what they look like. She acts like a loose woman, and I can't help feeling ashamed to be with her.

Aunt Morena has told me stories about her dating experiences. She met a man at a dancing hall, and he asked her to go with him to his car. She did, because she thought he wanted to be with her to talk and get to know each other better. When he tried to take her clothes off, she fought him and he got angry and beat her. The police were called to the scene when people going by heard her screaming. She told me that she has to have a man in her life. She sure gets into a lot of trouble looking for love. In my opinion, she is too desperate.

This summer, Papa almost fired Aunt Morena because of what she did in his office, but Mama convinced Papa that all he had to do was move Morena's desk away from the window. Supposedly, while she was seated at her desk, she was lifting her skirt even further up than she does while riding the city's public transportation. With her legs open, she was trying to entice the man living in the third floor apartment across the street from Papa's office. This was going on for a while, until the man's wife started to wonder why her husband would come home from work and go straight to their balcony window. That's when she caught her husband red-handed staring at Aunt Morena's crotch.

Aunt Morena's alibi was simple. She was very hot, and the only way to cool off was to take her panties off and open her legs. It wasn't her fault that the neighbor was a Peeping Tom. She has told me several times that, after twelve years of waiting patiently for a divorce from her womanizing, alcoholic husband, she is very lonely.

The *night man*, as we all call him, is like the invisible man, and I wonder sometimes if he is from this planet. You don't see him while walking the streets, but you know he is there, like a salamander blending into the city walls. When Aunt Heydee forgets the key to the front door downstairs, she does her usual thing. She claps her hands a few times, and there, right out of the shadows, is the night man with all the keys of the block.

He hardly says much. "Good evening, ladies. Forget the keys again, *hmm*?" And after Aunt Heydee gives him 25 *centavos*, he opens the door for us.

It's freaky to say the least. I mean, what kind of a job is that, hiding in the night shadows and waiting for someone to clap their hands to get help opening the front door?

The Journey of Innocence

Freaky, freaky! And I should ask, who is paying him? He couldn't be living from the 25 *centavos* that Aunt Heydee gives him whenever she forgets her house keys.

Mama told me that I am not to go out with Aunt Morena ever again. She has been officially banned from our home. She was caught stealing money from Papa's office. She had been stealing since Papa hired her two years ago to do office work. Papa only hired her as a favor because she is Mama's sister and needed a job. She is not being sent to prison because she promised she would pay the monies she owes to Papa's company. The money was supposed to be going to artists without hands or arms who paint with their mouth or their feet and depend solely on the profit of selling their cards and calendars to make a decent living. This incident has put much shame on our family, and the name Morena is not spoken in our house. Papa will be putting the stolen monies into the company out of his own pocket, and Aunt Morena has promised to pay him monthly payments until it's all paid for.

Mama has cried a lot about this whole affair. Aunt Morena is not only man-hungry but also not to be trusted. She steals from her own family, just like her perverted son Leão, whom I saw stealing a silver ashtray from one of our cousin's houses when we were visiting them a few years ago when I was a kid. Mama told us that, after Aunt Morena pays Papa what she owes him, she will open our home to her sister again. Aunt Morena may be wicked, but she is still her sister. Having the name *Morena*, meaning *tan* or *dark*, must have been hard to live with, while my mother was called *Branca*, *white* like Snow White.

Names like Morena have an innuendo of negativity which can dictate someone's general characteristics as they grow up, said Papa.

I understand what he means to say because my name is Verónica, which will always be associated with Saint

Verónica, so I can never be a bad person—at least not with a clear conscience.

Mama told Papa how, as children, Morena was always treated as the black sheep of the family, no pun intended. She had grown used to being called "dark," and everybody had agreed that the name fit her because she had darker skin and was the ugly duckling. She never finished second grade. They treated her like a maid, sending her out to do errands for everybody. She had grown in the streets, being smart and corrupted by the people she hung out with. When she married a man who was not Jewish, that marked her even more as an outcast. When she moved with her husband to the island of Açores, everyone quietly agreed the farther the better. After Mama told this story, Papa felt sorry for Aunt Morena and said, "If you call a child names, that child is marked to be what they are called."

And Mama added, "My poor sister Morena. Her fate of what she became was sealed from childhood."

Mama and Papa have a lot of wisdom and understanding when it comes to life and the reason for people becoming who they are. I still think Aunt Morena should have gone to jail after stealing from people who have no hands and her own family.

Aunt Heydee takes me everywhere with her—to dancing halls, the theatre, the circus, museums, and art shows. I always look forward to going out with her. It's so much fun. She is my best friend.

Getting into the circus is a totally different experience than getting into the opera house. There's a lot more pushing and shoving with people who attend a circus. They are common folks and not as refined. When the main door opens, the line of people who've been waiting outside in the cold for about an hour becomes an anxious, agitated serpent of living flesh that is going to push through without consideration for anyone else, even if it takes a few

The Journey of Innocence

trampled bodies along the way. The idea is to show your ticket to the doorman as quickly as possible and run in to grab a good seat. There are no assigned seats. It's all first come, first served.

Aunt Heydee taught me how to use the mass of moving people to our advantage. The idea is to get pushed in along with the crowd, like riding on an ocean wave. You don't get off until it reaches the shore, which in this case is passing the doorman collecting the tickets, and then you get in without paying. This is very exciting, but I got caught once. It was one of those docile, family type of crowds that was moving too slowly, and the doorman stopped me and asked the deadly question, "Where's your ticket, Miss?"

My heart stopped, and my face flushed hot. I was surprised that he believed me when I said with a trembling voice, "My aunt has the tickets with her, and she is still in line."

He pointed to the side aggressively and told me to wait next to him. I knew I was going to jail. This was going to be the last circus I attended. Then a wave of saviors came pushing through, and I let myself float away with them. Before I knew it, I was seated inside the circus tent and saving the seat next to me for Aunt Heydee.

Aunt Heydee and I always prepare ahead as to where we will meet outside if we become separated inside. Twice I had the misfortune of finding all the seats around the circus ring already taken, and I had to go to the very top floor instead.

The tickets for the last row upstairs are the least expensive, and there's a good reason for that. Everybody has to stand up along the rail, crowded with a bunch of other people because there aren't any seats available up there. This is the worst place for seeing the circus. It's so high that I can hardly see the performers below, and to make matters even worse, I always get squashed against the railing by some guy who finds his way behind me and obviously enjoys putting his leg between my legs or pressing his private parts against my back. As soon as that happens, I take a deep breath and make a little prayer for God to give me the courage for what I am about to do. Then I reach for my safety pin and rapidly jam it in and out of whoever's leg is becoming part of my body. The man automatically moves away, giving me a dirty look, but he doesn't say anything. I hate to have to use the pin. I am always afraid a man will grab it out of my hand and stab my back with it.

I found out how old Aunt Heydee is. Mama told me how to figure it out, and it's quite simple. You go by the present year. Since it is 1961, she is presently sixty-one years old.

She is older than I thought her to be. Aunt Heydee would be upset if she knew that I know her age. Besides, she has gone through a lot of trouble to change her age to twenty years younger. All her identification papers, including her birth certificate, show that she is forty-one years old. Mama explained that Aunt Heydee used a special ink pen to change the numbers.

Winter of 1962

Dancing is when I dream of Alberto. Soon I will be dancing with him. I am allowed to attend Sunday soirees with Aunt Heydee so that I can learn to dance. Mama wants me to learn ballroom dancing, and because she cannot afford lessons, this is a good way to learn. Aunt Heydee always gets me in for a minimal fee because she knows the ticket man. I get to dance with many partners. I have no rhythm when it comes to dancing slow while being squeezed by some man who wants me to follow his steps. I am a terrible dancer, but the men don't seem to care. I step harder on their feet when they hold me too close and press me between their legs.

The Journey of Innocence

There is one young man named Luis who is studying to be a lawyer. He is very respectful toward me when we dance together. He keeps a space between us and doesn't squeeze me against him like the others. I dance with him most of the time. He likes me a lot, and he said I should dance only with him because he can teach me better since he has a lot of dancing experience. He has been trying to convince me that I am making a mistake by marrying my cousin.

He keeps asking, "How can you marry him if you've never met him?"

I always say, "I have seen his pictures, and he is my aunt's son. He loves me, so I love him, too."

I feel sorry for Luis because I like him, but he is wasting his time trying to make me change my mind. I am already promised to Alberto. There's no room for anyone else. Besides, Luis is a goy and also he is not my type. My type of man has to have knowledge of the world, not be afraid of anything. He must be an adventurer who can take me by his side, protect me, and love me. He has to be strong, yet sensitive. And most of all, he has to make my heart speed up every time I see him. I have not met such a person yet. I can only dream about him and hope that Alberto fits my expectations. I know he will since he is an American and all American men are very cool—like James Dean, Robert Wagner, and Marlon Brando. As soon as I dance with a new partner and he starts making advances or asking personal questions, I tell him that I am there only to learn to dance so that when my husband from

North America comes to pick me up I won't be so clumsy.

Mama told me to say that because I was unable to think of an answer of my own. At least it is honest. Of course, some of the men don't ask me to dance again after such an introduction, and that's fine with me. I don't have to hassle them away like some others who don't know how to take "no" for an answer.

The *school for brides*, as I call it, is just a place to spend part of the day. I find it to be a bunch of unfriendly snobs, and since the first week of classes, I'd rather stay to myself. Mornings are for learning to cook, and then, after the two-hour lunch break, we spend three hours learning how to make clothes by following paper patterns, cutting, and using sewing machines. The sewing teacher has an aversion to anyone who uses a thread longer than twelve centimeters long to sew anything by hand. She says only lazy women use long thread to sew. It's best to have short thread and to keep threading as needed. This sounds like a waste of time to me. When she is not looking, I use long thread. I sit way in the back so she tends to forget about me.

I started doing an embroidered white tablecloth with two shades of blue thread. I like it a lot because it gives me something to do besides reading when I am home. Papa says it's really nice work. He knows how to appreciate hand embroidery. His family used to have a lace and embroidery business on the island of Madeira in the Açores, where he was a representative for his father's German company.

After the morning cooking class, I don't stay for lunch with everybody else. Instead, I go into the pastry shop around the corner and buy my favorites, yogurt and fresh fruit, with the money Mama gives me to buy lunch at school. I still have change left to use for the movies, chocolates, and bus tickets back and forth to the airport. I feel very rich.

So far, I have learned to make the delicious and world-famous *Crêpe Suzette,* a paper-thin crepe that is flavored and flamed with tangerine and Curação liqueur. The secret to making a "real" *Crêpe Suzette* is in the Curação liqueur, which is made with *eau-de-vie* (brandy), sugar, and bitter orange peels. I tried three times to eat the school lunch made by our teacher, and it made me nauseous. He uses too

The Journey of Innocence

much butter and cream. It's really nasty. I think he is French, because it's hard to understand him with his accent and he talks fast and his voice is difficult to hear. Pedro the chef is tall and over-weight. He wears a starched, white uniform and a tall, white chef hat. By the time he is done cooking for the morning, his outfit takes on a different look; the apron gets sacrificed first, and then he starts wiping his hands on his backside. I feel sorry for whoever has to wash and starch his clothes every day. I know how it feels to iron Papa's shirts with starch, not my favorite work. Pedro also wastes a lot of food when he cooks. He breaks the eggshells with one hand and a large portion of the egg whites are still dripping from them when he throws them out. Half the potatoes he peels are gone with the skins. He cuts the base off lettuce and throws it out. Mama would have a fit if she saw that, as she loves the base of lettuce. He also uses too much butter between the layers of dough to make croissants. And now that I have seen how much fat is put in between the several layers of dough to make elephant ears, I am not eating them anymore. No wonder they charge so much for lunch at the school. It's most likely to cover the cost of the wasted food.

I was walking back from lunch to the bride school when I heard Luis calling me from across the street. He came over to me and we shook hands, and then he invited me to go to the coffee shop with him to sit down and talk. I got all flustered and didn't know what to do but cut the encounter very short. So, I waved goodbye as I ran down the street saying, "Got to go. Bye-bye."

I don't like to hurt people's feelings, but I really didn't know what else to do but run away from him. I feel so embarrassed. I realize I have no social manners, unlike the girls I know at school who have boyfriends and are comfortable talking to the opposite sex. I just don't know what to say, and I get flustered and confused. I feel inadequate and sad.

Lately Mama and I have been spending more time together. Now that we know I will soon be gone to North America, Mama has become nicer to me. I am starting to feel as though we are almost pals, even though I know better than to confide anything personal in her. We have been going to the movies more often, and today we even went to a restaurant for lunch. This was my very first time having lunch with Mama outside the house, a woman-to-woman type of experience. I feel so important being part of Mama's life. It feels good being with her, even though we have different opinions about everything. I don't disagree with her. I simply nod my head up and down at everything. I am afraid to jeopardize our time together.

I found out that Mama's favorite food to eat out is roasted chicken basted in spicy mustard. I liked the chicken, but the wine made my legs go numb. My head felt weird, and it was hard to breathe because my heart started to expand inside my chest and beat faster. That was a weird feeling! Mama said that I am allergic to wine, and therefore I should stay away from it. I can't agree more.

Mama can still embarrass me to no end. I have to grin and bear it for a little while longer. I can't really complain because she pays for my movies and has been buying me ice cream every time we go to a matinee. This afternoon, a young man followed us into the theatre and stood against the wall staring in my direction while the lights were still on. That doesn't bother me anymore. When men follow me, I ignore them and they go away sooner or later.

Mama said, "Watch him disappear from our sight." She removed her dentures, both the top and bottom. Between her two hands, she made them open and close as if they were chewing on their own, *clap-clap-clap*, in his direction.

He opened his eyes shocked, and as Mama had said, he was gone and out of sight before we could even blink an

The Journey of Innocence

eye. Mama laughed and laughed as I tried to disappear into my seat. I felt like Alice in Wonderland looking for a hole in my chair. It's bad enough when she takes her dentures out while having dinner at home and puts them neatly on a white napkin next to her plate.

She says her gums hurt when she chews with them. I think it's disgusting to put your dentures on top of the table where everybody can see them. And she wonders why I don't like to sit next to her. I don't understand how Papa can feel attracted to Mama Linda.

I am getting so pampered. Uncle Augusto's wife Coty invited me to go out with her to the best restaurant in Lisboa to have the latest new drink from North America. It's called *ice cream soda*. She has never taken me out before. The most experience I have had with her was while running errands from Mama to Aunt Coty's house. Then Aunt Coty would give me some fig cookies to take with me and eat on the way home. I felt guilty for a long time because I never told her that I don't like fig cookies.

Aunt Coty would ask me, "Did you like the cookies I gave you last time?"

"Yes, they were great," I would say to her, afraid of hurting her feelings. After all, she had told me that they were expensive cookies. On the way home, I would eat the cookie and throw away the fig filling. I love figs, but only when they are fresh and juicy—not made into a sugary paste.

Aunt Coty is always home. Sometimes I would find her in the kitchen in the middle of force-feeding one of her children, while they were crying and refusing to eat any more food. Other times she would be lying down on her bed reading fashion magazines. We never talked much, and in many ways I have always been a little shy of her because she is an adult, married to a doctor, and therefore superior in intelligence and status to everybody else I know. Besides all that, she is Spanish, and her accent makes it hard for me to understand what she says. I have a lot of trouble understanding Spanish. Uncle Abraham's wife Simy is also from Spain, but she is not as smart as Aunt Coty. She is still having trouble speaking Portuguese. I hardly understand anything she says.

So, Aunt Coty came to pick me up at home in a taxi and took me to the famous Imperial Restaurant right under the Imperial Movie Theatre. It reminded me of Papa's restaurant with a wide staircase going down and rooms sumptuously decorated and full of business people having their lunch. Aunt Coty asked me what my favorite fruit was, and I told her, strawberries.

The waiter brought us both a very tall frosty glass with a strawberry ice cream soda. I thought I was going to die. It was the best drink I have ever had.

Aunt Coty turned out to be a cool person. She actually talked to me as if I were an equal. She even confided that, once her kids are all grown up, she is contemplating with the idea of teaching French in high school. She wants to stay busy and feel that she is useful to society.

After this get-together, I look at Aunt Coty in a different way. I am not afraid of her anymore. She is like everybody else, and a very nice human being.

I lost my friend, the shoemaker down the street. He sits by his window facing the street, which is below the first floor and therefore at the level of the sidewalk, and works, surrounded by shoes of all sizes and colors. There he sits at his small wooden bench from morning until evening, diligently fixing the neighbors' shoes. Whenever he saw me going by, if he was not too busy nailing some heels to a pair of shoes, he would smile at me and we would talk about the weather and his dream. He was going to North America with his family someday, he would tell me, in case I had forgotten. I thought he would be happy to hear that in

The Journey of Innocence

May I am leaving for North America, so I took a walk to his shop to let him know about it. But, instead, he started yelling at me. He had been waiting more than twenty years to get a visa for himself, his wife, and three children, to go to Newark, New Jersey, in North America, and here I was, a young girl, leaving the country in a few months. Cursing me, he closed the window, and I was left there, startled and blinded by tears.

He had never been my friend. All those years, I had been a passerby, breaking his monotony with small talk. I am not telling anybody about this. I feel guilty for having told him about my happiness without regard for his feelings. I am ashamed for being selfish. I wish I were already out of here.

Mama took me to Chiado in downtown Lisboa to buy an underskirt. The smell of plastic is all over the stores in Chiado. It goes up my nostrils and makes me cough and sneeze, but I still like the smell. Plastic is the latest word in household items, such as cups and dinnerware. No more hand-embroidered tablecloths either. They are now made of plastic, but look so real that you won't know the difference unless you touch them. Besides, they are a lot less expensive. It is the modern way of life arriving at our markets, probably from North America, where everything is made not to last. You use it and then throw it away.

Uncle Augusto asked Mama if there was anything special that I need as a new bride.

Mama told him that I need an underskirt. She took me with her to look for the best, most expensive one. She told me that Uncle Augusto is paying for it. He can afford a good one, so we might as well get the best because it is part of his wedding present.

We found one—very, very beautiful. I will be able to use it with any wide dress skirt, and if I am lucky and the wind blows, I will be proud to let it show. I saw others that would have done just fine and felt guilty that we were taking advantage of Uncle Augusto's offer, but Mama was set on getting the best, and I didn't say anything.

Uncle Augusto was shocked and angry when he saw the bill. "This is a ridiculous price to pay for an underskirt. I hope Verónica really enjoys it, because that was the amount of money Coty and I were planning to give her. That's it from us." I couldn't say anything. As always, I get blamed for whatever goes wrong. I had been blamed for being greedy and the truth is that, even though I did like the underskirt, it didn't mean anything to me. This is the stuff that Mama does that gets me upset. Too bad that I have to take this underskirt to North America, I have no intention of wearing it. It will always remind me of Uncle Augusto being angry for being taken advantage of.

Since the motorcycle accident, Mama has been dreaming about the compensation money she will get from the driver who caused the accident. His insurance company should have paid a fortune, but the case was settled out of court last week. All Mama got was enough money to pay the lawyer and the expenses she incurred with extra drugs and medical bills. I had a feeling about it. I was there when the insurance company had their doctors examine Mama.

I heard them say there was nothing wrong with her as a result of the accident. What she has now is what she was going to have anyway, because she was predestined to have these symptoms. Being in coma and suffering from blood clots in the brain was not good enough. In their professional opinion, she was emotionally unstable and the daily pain and fainting was all part of her "nerves."

How could they possibly know that? Are they gypsies or witches who can read the future? Of course the doctors in our family could not testify on her behalf. It would have been inappropriate. The idea that the insurance company actually paid for all the medical receipts she kept was itself

The Journey of Innocence

a miracle. But I know that Mama was different before the accident. She never used to faint two and three times every day. Mama has become very sensitive to touch. Her legs hurt, her arms hurt, her whole body hurts all the time, and she is very weak and out of balance. If not careful, she falls when she walks. She can also tell when it's going to rain, because the broken leg talks to her. She will never be the same again. She is to live on pain medicine for the rest of her life. I don't understand her at all, but I do feel sorry for her because this accident made Mama Linda a very sick person, and the insurance company doesn't care.

We keep getting very sad letters from Max-Leão. He wants to come home. He misses us. He says he doesn't get enough food and goes hungry, and he is very cold in the winter. He would do anything to come home. He says it's so foggy in London that sometimes he goes around and around the block and he can't find the door to his apartment. That is what I call *British fog*.

He had to leave the apartment where he was living because his roommate, the son of the family he was renting the room from, was queer and would not leave him alone. One night, the boy even dared to go into Max-Leão's bedroom and tried to force him into sex. Max Leão had to fight him off with his fists. Thank God that Max-Leão had a little training in boxing before he left for England and was able to defend himself.

Mama and Papa feel very sorry for him, but they agree that he has to stay in England. No matter how bad it is, it can never be as bad as staying in Portugal without an education or a future.

My wedding is now confirmed for May of this year. Alberto is going to let us know the exact date in his next letter. We are keeping our fingers crossed that he comes over during the beginning or the middle of May, and not at the end of the month, because that's when I menstruate. We are too embarrassed to say anything and are hoping for a miracle.

The neighbor upstairs got pregnant while she was menstruating, and the baby was born underdeveloped. According to their maid, the neighbor's husband was too selfish and didn't care whether his wife was menstruating or not. I didn't say anything, but I am wondering how the maid knew that they had sex while she had her period. For that matter, how does the whole neighborhood know that for sure? If that is true, what a mess it must have been—and painful as hell, I am sure.

May is the only month available for Alberto to leave work. He will have ten days off, and he realizes that it's going to be a bit of a rush. To make up for it, we will have a real honeymoon when we get back to North America. We will be going for a whole week to the Pocono Mountains in New York. I didn't know there were mountains in New York. I thought it was just a big city.

Mama has been taking me along with her to visit a few rich people in the Jewish community still living in Lisboa. I feel so embarrassed and ashamed with this whole idea of hers. It's like begging from strangers. It makes no sense. They don't even know us, so why would they lend the dowry money to Mama? We have had no luck so far. Mama is about ready to give up. It will be a relief for me. I hate sitting in the living room of people I've never met, and smiling at them as Mama tries her best to tell them how much she needs a loan so that I can get married. Why should anyone care?

I wonder if Papa knows about this project. Nobody is going to lend her money. She has saved so far a total equal to one thousand American dollars, and I believe that is more than enough. Whatever it is that she saves by May will have to do. Alberto doesn't need money from my parents. He is already rich. He is an American and an engineer. I think that Mama is worried that, without a good-sized dowry, the marriage is off and she will be stuck with me.

Mama and I spend more and more time together. I do like that, even if I don't agree with her way of thinking and a lot of the things she does. This week we spent a few hours in downtown Lisboa going from one very expensive jewelry store to another. Mama acts like she is very rich, and asks the salesperson to show us the most extravagant tiara, bracelet, or diamond ring. Then tells the salesman that she is shopping around and will return in another week or so. She needs time to make up her mind, she tells the salesperson. It feels weird to me to waste these people's time, but on the other hand, I am with Mama.

Mama is always in pain, and walking is difficult. Since the motorcycle accident, she no longer wears her favorite, black, high-heeled shoes, only flat shoes made of soft cloth. They are the only ones she can walk in without having calf and foot pain. This afternoon, she almost fell when she took a step off the sidewalk. Good thing that I was holding her arm and was able to hold her up. She says she doesn't quite feel her feet, that they feel numb. It was lucky for her that I was holding her arm. We take taxis everywhere we go. It's too hard for Mama to climb the steps of the trolley. I am very sad to see what has become of my mother.

I saw Audrey Hepburn in the movie *Breakfast at Tiffany's*, so now I have an idea of what to expect in the city of New York. In North America, I will see lots of tall buildings, but also Cowboys and Indians, and I will meet Paul Anka and Elvis Presley and lots and lots of movie stars in Hollywood. I will be speaking English, my favorite language. I will be able to listen to American music all day long, not just at a certain time of the day on one radio station like here. I will be able to listen to the music as loud as I want and dance to it all the time. I hope Alberto likes to dance, too.

I found out that the English language in North America is quite different from the English the British use. I have been learning English incorrectly. Luckily for me, Mama found Lucia, a Portuguese woman who spent five years in North America. I must learn to articulate like an American, or Alberto won't understand me. I have been studying American with Lucia at her house now for a month. She also teaches a few American kids, but she told me in confidence that American kids are stupid because their education is below our standards.

Lucia asked me to help her teach, and she won't charge for my lessons anymore. That has been a lot of fun because these three kids, two girls and a boy, are real Americans with a real American accent, the way I will be speaking soon, when I am living in North America. She put me in charge of the young boy who is nine years old. I teach him to read English, which is a real joke with my accent, and to do very basic Arithmetic, which is simple, so I feel comfortable being the assistant teacher.

According to Lucia, everything in North America is done in a retarded way. The American workers have a low aptitude for multi-tasking. For example, when they put a book together in a factory, one person gets paid to design the cover, another to put it together, another to set up the pages, another to sort it out; in other words, to put a book together takes more than half a dozen people. Here, one person does everything. I think she doesn't like Americans. There's something about teachers and Communism. Every teacher I know calls Americans *capitalists*, *stupid people*, and *greedy people*. I don't know anyone who wouldn't give their right arm for the opportunity to go to North America. I believe they talk down about Americans because they are jealous, and they are the ones who are ignorant.

The Journey of Innocence

What a boring day it was. I had to spend the day, the whole day, with Aunt Simy. She is the one who married Abraham, my mother's brother. When she first met Abraham, she was a divorced woman who fell in love with him. She sneaked into his bed one night while she was visiting his family in Portugal, and she forced him to make her pregnant so he had to marry her. She is from a very rich family in Spain, but she won't help him with finances or go to work to help out. She feels that he is the husband, and therefore it's his problem, not hers. He works as a telephone operator because he had no further education than primary school. He is the only one who takes care of paying the bills. She is too selfish and greedy to part with some of her fortune. Mama and Aunt Heydee always talk about Aunt Simy and how she is mean to her husband. The worst mistake one can make is to get married for money only.

The real story, I will probably never know. One thing for sure, they constantly fight like cats and dogs, and Uncle Abraham attempted to kill himself various times, but without any success. One day, he lay down naked on the kitchen's cold tile floor in the middle of the winter in hopes of catching pneumonia. That way, she would finally suffer, watching him die a slow death, but all he caught was a nasty cold. He loves Communism and gets very excited when he talks against Salazar, our president the dictator. Uncle Abraham is consumed by politics, always talking about politics and the government and how wonderful Communism is and how we should have Communism in Portugal like in Russia where everybody has an equal share of everything. Aunt Heydee and Mama agree that the cause for his bleeding ulcers has to be from burning himself from the inside out. I find his conversation topics very annoying, too, and he always has a sad, gray look about his face, as if he were dying. When he comes over to our house, which is rare, I already know he is going to argue about some political stuff, so I leave the room. I can't even imagine how his daughters can live with him. Seeing how their parents are mean to each other, it can't be easy on them.

I am blessed because Mama and Papa are very loving toward each other. They only argue when Aunt Heydee says something hateful about Germans.

Aunt Simy is a short hefty woman with eyeglasses as thick as binoculars. They make her green eyes look like two little green dots. This has got to be the worst case of myopia I have ever seen. One of the most annoying things she does is, hold her hand open against her chest when she walks into our house and put her hand spread out behind her back as she leaves. It's called *los cincos*, a Moroccan superstition that as long as you keep one of your hands open on your body your enemies will drop dead if they are jealous of you. It drives Mama and Aunt Heydee crazy.

Mama and Aunt Heydee take *los cincos* as being an insult toward them, and they have been adopting the same motion back at Aunt Simy.

I find this behavior quite childish between adults, but I dare not say anything about it.

When visiting Aunt Simy in the winter, I always find her lying down in bed looking like a seal, wrapped in her mink stole, as she tries to stay warm. She called Mama this week and told her that, as part of her wedding gift, she wanted to teach me how to make her secret grape jam recipe, and that today was perfect for her because no one, including her daughters who were in school, would be home. After I swore to her at least ten times that her jam recipe would not be divulged to anyone, and then sweated over a stove mixing and mixing and mixing grapes and sugar, and grapes and sugar, I was finally let out of her house—five hours later.

My friend Encarnação gave me two very special gifts this morning: a little red handkerchief with mischievous

The Journey of Innocence

English words printed on it and *The Bride's Book*. Encarnação made me promise not to show Alberto the red handkerchief until we are on our honeymoon, then he and I can have a good laugh together.

I began reading *The Bride's Book* as soon as I got home. I have been reading it slowly and taking my time to understand each page, which is filled with the advice of the expert author. I don't want to miss anything important because, as Encarnação said, this book will teach me how to make my marriage successful. If anybody knows how to make a home happy, it is Encarnação. I only have until May to learn the whole book. It says that, as a future wife, I must listen to my heart and the little voices inside of me. They will give me a conscience and the common sense to know if I am doing the right thing, because the bride is part of a trilogy with wife and mother!

I am scared, but I have nowhere else to go and no one to share my fears with. I am only looking for love and happiness, that's all.

The Bride's Book is very straightforward. I must always be happy by acting happy and smiling to everybody, even when I am sad, because men like only energetic, healthy, happy women. This book has a lot of good ideas I was not aware of. For example, it's important to cover up our inferiority complexes or sad feelings by forgetting about ourselves and concentrating on the person we are with instead. I must learn to listen more and speak less.

That's no problem. I think a lot, but hardly have much to say. The book gives advice on how to stay healthy with exercise and eating healthy, like staying away from fat, fried foods, and sweets. I don't exercise, but I do walk a lot, and I have no trouble staying away from greasy, oily food because it makes me sick to my stomach. Staying away from something sweet like chocolate, now *that* is going to be a sacrifice.

The writer also gives a two-page list of basic needs for filling a hope chest, such as a dozen towels, a dozen sets of bed sheets, thirty kitchen towels, four aprons, and so on.

Thank God, Alberto wrote back saying not to bother with that kind of stuff. He has everything at home already, since he lives with his mother.

Mama brought in the seamstress with the bad breath, and she is making me two new dresses to take with me to North America.

I was looking through *The Bride's Book* to find out about the first night of marriage and what that's all about, but it doesn't say anything except two and a half pages of philosophical words like, "Don't take in your baggage, only dreams of happiness" and, most important, "You must not use purple or dark colors in your bedroom. They will take away the brightness of love."

The Bride's Book Encarnação gave me has become my "Bible." Important things to remember from it: When my husband gets home, I must have his dinner ready. I should be attractively dressed, smile, and keep quiet until he feels like talking. I must stay graceful and not bring up anything that might get him upset concerning silly, daily housewife problems; he has enough pressure and stress with his own job. I must keep his clothes clean and his shoes are to be shined every day. I must remind him to shave daily and have his hair cut when he needs it. And no matter how hard a day I had cleaning and cooking and taking care of the kids, when he gets home, I must be in my best dress, perfumed, and ready for love.

I'll be taking this book with me to North America, so I can refresh my memory by reading it again and again. If I follow the directions in this book, I will have a better chance of being happily married to Alberto, the father of my future children.

I dreamt last night that I had a baby boy with dark curly hair, and he just appeared in my arms like magic. He looked like Alberto's picture, but in miniature size.

Mama said it was a good omen and that my first-born would be a boy.

What I didn't tell Mama is that I am very scared of having a baby. I don't know how it's going to come out. I mean, I know from where it comes out, and *that* is what scares me the most. I want to be a mother, but I am not looking forward to the delivery.

~ *Chapter Eight* ~

THE WAY OUT

1962

Spring of 1962

Mama was seated in her rocking chair in the living room across from Papa, who was seated in his favorite armchair—because it's not only very comfortable but also belonged to his father. Over the years, his armchair started to fall apart, but Mama had it re-upholstered about a year ago for his birthday.

I was walking into the living room, and when she saw me, she said, "Verónica, I want you to sit on your father's lap and make nice to him."

"What do you want me to do?" I asked, scared and embarrassed with the situation she was presenting to me. I had never sat on Papa's lap before, so what the heck was she asking me to do?

"Sit on his lap, and make nice to your father," she repeated with an authoritative tone.

My goodness, I thought, *she has gone completely mad.* But being obedient as I am, I sat on Papa's lap and stared at her because I couldn't even look at him.

"Touch your father's face with your hand, and make nice to him."

The Journey of Innocence

I was scared now. "I don't know how." I said, wanting to cry.

"Just make nice to his face. Is that too much to ask?" she asked, obviously frustrated.

I stretched my right hand flat, keeping my fingers straight and rigid, and pressed it down on his face as if I was cleaning a chalkboard. Twice I swiped my hand flat, stretched-out across his cheek with my thoughts in a fog as to what to make of the situation.

Mama got hysterical. "Oh my God. What's Alberto going to do with her when she can't even make nice to her own father? What are we going to do, Joachim? She doesn't even know how to caress!" She was frantic with my inability to show any affection.

No kidding, I thought to myself, feeling like I was going to throw up.

Papa pushed me up and away delicately and said to Mama, "Don't worry about her not knowing how to show affection. I am sure that Alberto, who is an American and a man of the world, and experienced in matters of the heart, will be glad to teach his young bride what to do." And he went back to reading the newspaper.

I felt better after he said that, and I quickly left the living room.

Papa hit the roof when he found out that Mama had taken the tablecloth I had embroidered to a neighbor to have its border done on a sewing machine. He screamed and called her *stupid* for ruining what he felt was a work of art. He said the tablecloth no longer had any value.

"You don't sew a masterpiece by hand and then use a machine to finish it off! It's just not done." Papa very rarely screams at Mama, but this time he was furious.

I felt bad about it, because she was worried about my eyes. She didn't want me to lose the little eyesight I have left by straining over some silly cloth border.

She yelled back at Papa, "Joachim, the tablecloth is going to get stained over the next few meals, and then most likely it will be thrown away. It's worse for our daughter to ruin her eyes over it, since in North America tablecloths are made of plastic."

Mama is so genuinely concerned about my eyes that she made me put my hands on her head and solemnly swear that I won't shed any tears when she dies. She said that tears are salty and they burn the eyes. Besides, there's no point in crying over spilled milk. Once you are dead, you are gone and there's nothing that can be done about it. Crying will be a waste of time, and if I go blind, my husband will leave me for a woman with eyesight.

After Papa let out all his steam, he stayed seated in his favorite chair while holding the tablecloth in his hands as if it were a dead baby and shaking his head in dismay.

I am glad that I don't have to sew the tablecloth border by hand.

I stopped going to bride school. I am done with housewife education. This week was also the last time I saw Lucia, my private English teacher. She is very excited about my marriage and wants to go to the airport with the family and everyone else to see what Alberto looks like.

I spend the days saying goodbye to my surroundings, going for long, familiar walks through the parks, taking the boat across the River Tejo, and taking the bus back and forth to the airport. I also said goodbye to the people at the front desk of the American Embassy. No more listening to records of American plays, pop music, or light opera and reading their books. I am now well educated in the American way of life so that, when Alberto talks to me about theatre or music from his country, I won't be completely ignorant.

I went to the temple on Saturday and sat upstairs, looking

down at the rabbi as he sang with other male members. As always, I didn't understand a word they were saying, but it gave me comfort to sit there and listen. I sat quietly and stared at the walls. I wore the old brocade veil that Aunt Heydee gave me a month ago. I felt pretty with it on, and I was hoping that someone would come in and notice how holy I looked with my head covered. I felt the veil gave me a look of religious devotion. I stared at the ceiling and then at the empty chairs around me where the women usually sit. The house of God was empty, and it made me sad for a little while. Then I realized that the temple, with its warm walls surrounding me and protecting me from the outside world, was all mine. The future was promising, but I had no idea of what.

I was about to leave when a young foreign woman came in and sat next to my seat. She introduced herself as an American journalist.

This was my opportunity to speak English with an American accent, and so I did. When she found out I was getting married to my first cousin from North America, she took an interest in my life as if I were a very odd finding. She started writing my answers to her questions on a notepad. I was happy to talk to her. After all, I felt like my English was very good because she seemed to understand what I was saying.

After I left the temple, I got a feeling that I had talked too much. I decided not to tell anyone about my encounter with the American reporter. If Alberto reads her story in the newspaper in North America before he comes to Portugal, he might change his mind about marriage. Nobody wants to marry a blabbermouth.

We have a new maid. Her name is Maria Elena, and she is really nice. She has a very bright disposition, which matches her reddish-blonde curly hair, and she is easy to talk to. Maria Elena knows everything about sex because she is forty-two years old.

A few days ago, I was helping her to hang the laundry outside to dry, and she started telling me about her experiences with dating and men and what they want from a woman.

I got this gut feeling that somehow Mama was behind all of this sex education so that I am not stupid on my wedding night. I am thankful for that, but I wish that my mother was the one to talk to me. Of course, that is just an impossible wish. I already know how to cook, clean, sew, and even save money, but when it comes to sex I only know what I have learned from the girls at school, the movies, and the romance novels I have read. I've never heard the answers directly from the horse's mouth. I felt comfortable asking Maria Elena delicate questions because she went into detail about her personal life with different men she had been with.

I was curious, so I dared to ask the forbidden question. She told me that penises come in all sizes, depending on the man, just like some women have bigger breasts than others. She went on to explain how penises get hard and longer than their original soft size.

"How painful is it to put it inside the vagina, and does it have to be that way? Can't it be just kisses and hugs?" I asked, horrified by the idea.

She said, "If you are going to have children, there's no other way. And yes, most likely it's going to hurt the first time. Some women will bleed afterward, but after the first time, it will be less and less painful until it's the opposite. It becomes pleasurable, like when we touch ourselves, but it's even more enjoyable because you share the experience with the one you love." She went on about the wedding night, how I must be helpful, move my body, and even if it hurts, endure it until it's over. That's my duty as a wife.

I didn't tell her, but I am more scared now than before. I am hoping that Alberto doesn't like sex.

The Journey of Innocence

I got a letter from Alberto. It is now confirmed. He bought the airplane tickets, and Aunt Nelly and he will be here for the wedding on May 24. He took that week off from work purposely to come to Portugal. My luck, that's when my menstruation is due. It arrives like clockwork on the 24th of each month.

Uncle Augusto told us not to worry. He will give me a shot of medicine that will prevent the menstruation from arriving that month. I am an adult now, and even though I don't like needles, it's a good reason to have one. I only hope it works.

I got a big scare today. I didn't tell anyone my plans. Most of all, I did not tell Mama because I already know how she feels about death. Any time someone dies in our family, I am not allowed to go to their house, so that I am guarded from people suffering and crying.

During lunchtime, I decided to go to the Jewish cemetery and say goodbye to Grandma Rica. Aunt Heydee keeps telling everyone how wonderful it is to go to the cemetery once in a while and visit her parents. She even takes a blanket and a picnic basket with her, and she sits by their stone for a while, keeping them company, eating her lunch, and telling them all the latest news about the family and what's going on around the world and so forth. I have been there with Mama a few times to visit old relatives I never met and her parents' gravesites, so I felt that I had nothing to be afraid of.

I put a few stones in my pockets before entering the metal gates, like I had done before when visiting the cemetery with Mama. "Flowers don't last, but stones do," she told me.

I think that stones are also cleaner and a lot more respectful than dead flowers all over one's tomb. I went in and visited Grandma Rica's tomb, and after looking around a bit, I found Grandpa Leão's tomb. The letters engraved in the stone were worn out from so many years of being beaten by the weather. I went around the burial ground, being careful not to step over anybody's grave, and said goodbye to any name that sounded familiar. I left a little stone marker where Uncle Augusto and Aunt Coty buried their first child who died soon after being born.

Just when I thought I was completely alone and was ready to leave, alive and safe from ghosts, I heard a voice calling me, "Verónica!"

I thought I was going to die.

"Verónica!" The same tone of voice rang across the deserted cemetery.

I could not tell where it was coming from. I could not see anyone as the sun was in my eyes. And then again, "Verónica, what are you doing here?"

No ghost would make a question like that after my name. They would have said, "Boo." I looked up, and it was Aunt Simy, the one married to my mother's brother Abraham. She was visiting her mother Aziza's grave.

I felt so bad when Aziza died a few years ago. A robber followed her home and mugged her before she could climb the stairs to her apartment. He hit her over the head to rob her. She died on the way to the hospital. I really liked Mrs. Aziza. She was a very beautiful old lady, and she was always happy, always smiling whenever I visited her. I hope the robber who killed her gets mugged himself over some miserable *escudos* so he can feel what it is like to lose one's life due to someone's greed.

Aunt Simy hugged me and asked me how I keep so slim and maintain such a small waist.

I didn't know what to say. I don't do anything at all.

She reminded me one more time, "Now don't ever give anyone the grape jam recipe. That was my wedding gift to you and should stay that way."

I smiled at her and said with conviction, "I promise never to divulge the grape jam recipe to anyone."

The Journey of Innocence

And I hugged her as a seal of commitment. I was thinking, *I don't even like jam. Why would I spend a whole day over a hot stove making a pot of jam?* So, I hugged her once more and said with meaning, "Don't worry. No one will ever learn your secret jam recipe from me."

May is my favorite month of the year, not just because it's my birthday, but also because the sun makes me happy at this time of the year after a long, cold, and rainy winter. I just turned eighteen years old, and I know that I am an adult because I am getting married in a couple of weeks. Alberto my husband will be here soon to take me to North America with him. When Alberto and Aunt Nelly arrive, we only have three days to make everything fall into place. I will have to sleep on a small mattress on the hallway floor for those three days because my bedroom will be getting prepared for the reception. Aunt Nelly will be sleeping in the other bedroom up front, which will be especially decorated for her with lots of flowers. That is also the room we are using for me to be dressed in my wedding gown. Alberto is staying at a *pensão*, a cheap hotel, down the street from where we live until the wedding day. It would be considered in bad taste if he were to sleep in the same house as the bride.

Mama and Aunt Heydee have been making all the arrangements. Even the music to be played at the temple during the wedding ceremony has been carefully chosen so that it isn't too romantic or mushy. Aunt Heydee has put a lot of work into choosing bright and cheery tunes. She is concerned that the wedding ceremony along with the slow depressing music they always play at weddings might be too much of an emotional issue for Papa, who has a bad heart. According to Uncle Augusto and our Cousin Salomão, who is the head of the cardiology department in one of the hospitals in Lisboa, Papa's heart is worse than

Mama's, and they all wonder how he is still alive.

This morning we went to the temple to work out some very important details, such as where to put the flowers, the guests, and the tent. Papa came along with us, but he refused to listen to happy tunes for the sake of his heart. He was really annoyed about that, and felt that I should choose the ones I like, because it is my wedding and not his. Of course I picked the happy tunes, as I am not going to be the one to go on a guilt trip if Papa drops dead in the middle of my wedding because of some gushy silly music. I would have to live with that for the rest of my life. I went along with whatever Aunt Heydee had already chosen. Tunes coming out of a pipe organ, my least favorite musical instrument after the accordion, are not going to sound *hip* no matter what is playing.

I am enjoying watching Mama and Aunt Heydee get all excited as they make plans for the food being served at our house after the ceremony, the car rental, and who is getting the little bags of rice.

Haim, who is Aunt Ligia's little boy, and Palomita, who is Uncle Augusto's younger daughter, will be holding up the tail end of my wedding gown so it doesn't get caught anywhere as I walk up the aisle holding on to Papa's arm. I am not supposed to do or think about anything. Everybody insists that I have to stay fresh and cool for the wedding itself. They have everything under control. My job is to relax and enjoy the fun that's ahead.

Our house is ready to receive the wedding festivities. The walls have been whitewashed because paint is too expensive. New, brightly colored curtains have been hung in the living room, and fresh flowers have filled some of the vases that have not seen a flower since they were bought. The whole place is smiling.

It's hard to sleep when the mattress is too thin and the

floor is so hard. I was up at 5:30 in the morning. I am wearing the tight, sexy, pink, cotton American dress that Alberto sent me. I want to look as American as possible. He will be happy to see that I am wearing the gifts he sent—the dress, the ring, and the gold bracelet.

Encarnação took me aside and told me, "I am going to the airport, too, and if you don't like him or for any reason you want to cancel this whole thing, let me know and I'll take you home to live with me." She is my best friend.

We all went to the airport a little early to wait for Alberto and Aunt Nelly. Most of our family was there, except Max-Leão who is living in England. That means my parents, José, all my cousins, aunts, uncles, my two girlfriends from high school, Lucia, my American teacher, some neighbors, the maid, and best of all Encarnação. In case I have to run away, I can count on her.

I saw Alberto getting off the plane. He was tall and handsome, just like his pictures. He was smiling and that made me feel relaxed, like after taking one of Mama's calming medicines where you are too numb to have feelings or worries. I decided to enjoy each moment as the beginning of my destiny. There was no turning back. My future could only be bright from this day forward.

Everybody was waving and calling him, and then they pushed me to the front of the line. He was holding two pieces of luggage, one in each hand, and walking toward me. When he saw me, he dropped them both to his sides and ran to me. He hugged me and then he picked me up in the air as if I were as light as a feather. Everybody started to clap, and everybody around me was happy. It was an amazing feeling to be surrounded by happiness. I could not ask for more. We all went home in taxis. Alberto and I held hands, and he hugged me a lot, but we hardly spoke to each other.

When we got home, we were separated. I was taken to Nelly's room, where she showed me the wedding dress she had brought with her.

The wedding gown was made of white lace with brocade patterns intertwined with pearls. It was low cut, and had long lace sleeves and a long trail. I had stepped into a fairy tale, there was no doubt in my mind, and Nelly was my fairy godmother.

The seamstress with the bad breath was called in to make the gown fit a little tighter.

Nelly had brought many gifts for the family. Everybody was anxious to see what he or she was getting. Alberto and I hardly saw each other, but every time he saw me, he would grab me and lift me up in the air and hug me. I can't wait to be kissed by him on the lips like the movie stars.

At the end of the day, Mama sent the maid with Alberto to show him where the *pensão* was, down the street from our house. I wanted to go with them, but didn't dare ask.

Alberto and I have spent the day running from one municipal building to another to finish all the paperwork needed before the wedding. We spent the whole morning being sent from one place to another, across the city from one office to another, until someone took pity on us and sent us to the correct address. Alberto doesn't like his name. He wants me to call him *Al*.

In the afternoon, I had to go see a medical doctor to get the okay that I am healthy and can go to North America. The doctor made me take all my clothes off and lie down on a couch. He pulled the curtain around us and sat staring at me with his dark, beady eyes for what I felt to be a lifetime. He touched my breasts and said, "You are still a virgin, I can tell. So young and pretty and getting married—a child in a woman's body—hmm."

I could feel my face turning red, and I was scared that Alberto would pull the curtain and see me naked, so I nodded "yes" at everything the doctor asked me and stared away from him. That's the way slaves must have felt when

The Journey of Innocence

they were checked out before being sold naked in the open market. He gave me a clean bill of health, and in broken English, he blinked an eye at Alberto and said, "You are a lucky man."

When we left the office, Alberto was laughing about the doctor and called him an old pervert.

It was a busy day of showing Alberto the city of Lisboa, or I should say *Al* since that's what he wants me to call him. Tonight we are going to a nightclub in downtown Lisboa. I have never been to a nightclub before. It was dark inside and very romantic. The only light inside the club came from the small candle in the center of each small, round table. One could barely see much. I felt like a real woman going on a date except that in my mind I knew we were as good as married. I was very happy that the tables were small and we had to sit close to each other. I wasn't wearing my eyeglasses. Mama and Aunt Heydee feel that I will look ugly if I wear my glasses, and Al will take the next airplane back to North America. Men don't fall in love with girls with glasses. Al talked a lot, and I really tried to understand what he was saying, but it was hard to hear with the loud music in the background. So, I said "yes" and nodded to everything he said and smiled politely. They offered us some drinks, and I was surprised to find out that Al doesn't like alcohol even though he is an American. He only likes milk or soda. The waiter was annoyed when he brought us both two glasses of cherry soda. We didn't stay too long because tomorrow we have quite a bit of running around to do.

We have to see the notary, and all the paperwork has to be finished by the end of the day if we are to be married on the 24th. Having doctors and lawyers in the family has helped speed up the paper processing a lot, but there's still a lot of leg work.

Our first kiss was not what I was expecting. He took me home, and downstairs he held my face between his hands. I closed my eyes waiting for his lips to seal mine with the passion of the moment. He kissed my forehead and said, "Good night, my love. I will see you tomorrow morning." He saw my face, and I guess he assumed that I was worried about him getting back to his motel alone because he added, "Don't worry about me. I remember how to get to the *pensão*." And he kissed me on the forehead again, as if we were friends and not engaged to be married.

I was very disappointed, because I'd imagined my first kiss would be passionate and intoxicating like they describe the kisses between lovers in the books I have read. He is twelve years older than I am. Maybe I am too young for him. He probably sees me as a child, his little cousin. I am worried that there can never be passion between us. Instead, we are family—friends and buddies.

When I got upstairs, Mama was waiting for me at the door. She asked eagerly, "Did he kiss you?"

I nodded "yes."

"Was it wonderful?" she asked again.

"Yes," I yelled back at her as I ran down the hallway. "I am going to wash up and get ready to bed. I am very tired," I said as I closed the bathroom door behind me.

I stood staring into the three half-faces of myself coming at me from the chipped mirror above the bathroom sink. The colorful oil-painted flowers covering the cracks on my face failed to make me smile. Nothing was going through my mind.

I got up early this morning and was allowed to go by myself to get Al at his *pensão*. We needed to be at the notary by nine in the morning. I was a little nervous meeting a man in his room, even if it was Al, my future husband. I told myself that it was okay because we would be husband and wife in two days. I felt that, after last night's goodnight kiss, I could trust him completely. He does have a beautiful smile. Now I understand why his

The Journey of Innocence

teachers used to call him *Cookie* as a child.

He was ready and waiting for me, and he welcomed me with a big hug. We left the *pensão* holding hands, as if we had known each other for centuries. I was full of joy as we walked down to the *Praça do Chile*. I was feeling the rays of sunshine resting warm on our shoulders as if they would stay with us forever, thus promising many more wonderful, happy days ahead. As we walked down the street, I took a few quick shy looks at him while evaluating my situation. I was finally a woman, a real person, and an adult.

I guided him to the *pastelaria* (bakery) down the street, where they always have my favorite pastries, *pastéis de nata*, small round pastries filled with custard. I had to introduce him to the Portuguese desserts. It was going to be our breakfast. He ordered two large plates with two samples of each of the pastries enclosed in the glass showcases. I was shocked because there was no way in Heaven that I was going to eat more than two or three pastries with my coffee. I thought he ordered all of that because he was really hungry.

I found out that Al does not drink coffee or tea either—only soda or milk. I sat with glee on my face, staring at the two dishes full of delicious pastries. I was finishing my first *pastel de nata*, when he announced, "We better get going." As it is written in *The Bride's Book*, your husband's wishes are the law. I wanted to put the cakes in a box to take with us, but he said, "No need for that. I'll get you more later on."

What a waste, I thought. *Americans are so rich and spoiled*. But I didn't say anything.

Al tripped when we were running to catch the trolley, and because his arm was around my waist, I fell forward under him on the cobblestones, flat on my face. I was a sore puppy while we sat waiting for over an hour to see the notary. We were announced like royalty as we walked through a long room with palatial gold-encrusted walls and huge antique paintings. At the end of the room sat a small, pale, middle-aged man behind a huge, dark mahogany desk that was definitely too big for him. Al kept laughing about him and saying, "Who is he, the King of Portugal?"

The notary was very dry and would not even smile, as if we were keeping him from more important matters, but he did say, "Tell your Uncle, Dr. Augusto, that all the papers are now notarized and in order. You can leave for North America with your American husband any time you want."

Al kissed me on the way out, right on the lips. Not hard, just soft and very loving, and it felt perfect. I kissed him back, and I was happy.

To celebrate our success, Aunt Heydee recommended a very expensive French restaurant for dinner. She said it was ideal for two lovers. There was a problem though. After three years of French in high school, I still have difficulty with the French language, and Al speaks only English. I also found out that his Spanish is as bad as mine, even though he grew up listening to his mother and Mercedes, his Moroccan grandmother, speaking Spanish at home. Al knows two words in French, *oui* and *non*, and of course he likes Brigitte Bardot.

It was up to me to order dinner from the French menu. I ordered three different dishes, or so I thought. I never had the experience of ordering food at a fancy French restaurant. Actually, I had not ordered even at a regular restaurant. They brought us two small plates of chicken liver pâté with crackers, served on a silver cup. It was okay. We couldn't wait for the next dish. The second order came, and to our surprise two silver plates of liver pâté with crackers was served, this time decorated with a couple of lemon slices around the plate and two olives on the top. Al asked me, "Don't they serve real food here?"

I kept my fingers crossed for the next serving. The waiter commented in Portuguese to me, "You both must really love liver." And he put in front of us two more plates with a small ball of liver pâté surrounded by two thinly sliced pieces of French bread with some parsley on top as decoration.

I had ordered the same stuff three times in different sizes and presentations. We asked for some butter for the bread and left the liver. Al thought it was funny and didn't get mad. I liked the idea that he didn't get angry even though he was hungry. When we got home, I told the maid what had happened and she gave us cow's knuckle stew, the leftovers from supper that evening. We were both starving.

In the morning, I told Aunt Heydee how nice Al had been to me when I goofed up at the restaurant.

She smiled and said, "Let me tell you a story, so you are prepared for the reality of life. Once upon a time there was this girl who went dancing and met a boy in the dance hall. Because this was her first time dancing, she was very clumsy and stepped on his feet. She said to her dancing partner, 'Oh, I am so sorry.' And he said, 'My dear, I didn't even feel it. Matter of fact, your delicate feet felt more like a dove flying over mine.' Soon they got married, and after a few years of marriage, about ten years or so, she asked him to dance with her. It was their wedding anniversary. The same thing happened. She stepped on his feet by accident, and before she could even apologize, he said, 'Maria, you clumsy woman. Why don't you watch it? Your feet feel like a ton of bricks.'"

Today was spent walking along the River Tejo and downtown Chiado. We were on our way home when we met a young group of rowdy Communist students who overheard Al's American accent as he was talking to me. They thought we were both Americans. We had just crossed over the street from the American Embassy when I heard one of the boys say to the others, "Hey, those two lovebirds are Americans. Let's give them a beating."

Al didn't know what they'd said, and I wasn't even going to try explaining to the "teddy boys" that I was not American or translate to Al what I had just heard. I knew instantly that we had to run for our lives. I turned to Al, and with a strong look of conviction in my eyes, I yelled at him, "Al, those boys want to hurt us. Run with me as fast as you can."

He could tell I was serious and started running with me. We ran down the hill like a train without brakes. The boys were running after us screaming, "Yankees! Dirty capitalists. Go home!"

We could have won the world marathon as we ran into the American Embassy and told them what had happened. They said things are a bit difficult at present because of Communism on the rise and, with it, a lot of ill feeling toward North America. They took us through the back door like we were criminals, and offered to chauffeur the two of us in one of their cars. Al wanted to know if they were going to do something about those boys, but they said it was better left alone. Some of the younger people are fanatics and can go to extremes. They didn't look forward to having the Embassy bombed in retaliation.

We got home just in time for dinner. Mama insists that we come home for all our meals. Before we entered the building, Al bought flowers for me from a street vendor going by our door. I wanted to tell him that I don't like flowers, but I didn't want him to think that I don't like beautiful things. Cutting flowers should be considered a crime, because not only will they die in a few days but also they are extremely expensive. He bought all the flowers the woman was carrying in the straw basket on top of her head. He told me that he felt sorry for her head and now she could go home.

I explained to him that all street vendors carry their goods, such as fish, vegetables, and flowers, on top of their

The Journey of Innocence

heads. Once you learn to balance the straw basket on top of the head, it is advantageous to have your hands free. I gave the flowers to Mama from both of us.

While we were having dinner, Al got very upset when Mama rang her little metal bell to call the maid from the kitchen to come and fill his glass with water. "The maid is not a slave," he said. "She shouldn't have to come all the way from the kitchen to give me water. The water container is right in front of me. I can serve myself."

Al doesn't understand this is part of our culture. We always serve ourselves with water, but guests receive special treatment. Still, I was happy to hear that he doesn't like people to be treated like slaves.

After dinner, we retired to the living room area to talk and have tea and cake for a little while, and then we said goodbye since it was late. When Al left, Mama caught me in the hallway and said, "Your father wants to talk to you concerning what you should expect on the first night of your honeymoon. He is going to give you advice." Then she called out loud for Papa to come and talk to me, as he had promised her.

His face was one of, *Why am I doing this? I don't want it!* Mama squeezed his hands in hers, as if giving him moral support, and said, "Your father wants to talk to you in private." Then she pushed us both into one of the bedrooms.

We entered the room and stayed staring at each other for a few seconds. "Verónica, sit down," he said, pointing to the only chair available.

I sat on the hard, wooden chair by the bed. I looked up at him and was scared of hearing something horrible that I really didn't want to hear, at least not from my own father.

He took a few breaths and then, looking as much trapped as I was, he said, "My daughter, the secret to a happy marriage is the way you sew the buttons on your husband's coat." And then he continued, very sure of himself, "Yes, your mother drives me crazy. She can't sew a button properly. Do you know how many times I am at a meeting and the darn button falls off because it wasn't sewn correctly? It is very embarrassing, because it means that my wife doesn't love me enough to pay attention to my needs for the way I look. Use double string. Then reinforce it at the end by going around the base of the button. And then secure it with a few tie-ups. How difficult can it be? Do you think that I am asking too much?"

I could understand his frustration with the buttons, but what did that have to do with my wedding night? I said, "No, Papa, you are not asking for too much."

"Okay," he said relieved. "Now, we are going out of the room. If your mother asks you if I told you everything about tomorrow night, just tell her 'yes.'" And he winked at me.

When we walked out of the room, Papa took off down the hallway. Mama was waiting by the door. She asked, "Did your father tell you everything about tomorrow?"

"Yes, he did," I said, keeping my fingers crossed. And I kept walking down the hallway just as Papa had done. I hid myself in the bathroom, as I always do. This is the only room in the house with a lock. No more sleeping on the floor. Tomorrow night I will be sleeping in a real bed with my husband Alberto. I mean, *Al*.

"Cousin Esther is downstairs!" screamed José as he ran up the steps of our house to give us the news.

I had not seen Esther for a long time. I had my wedding gown on. I grabbed the long trail end of the gown, and with everyone else behind me, went to take a look. I saw a huge woman, out of breath, trying to climb the steps to our apartment. Next to me, Mama couldn't help saying, "My goodness, she is even bigger than I thought could be possible."

"No," I said in disbelief, "that's not Cousin Esther." But

The Journey of Innocence

Mama was right.

"That husband of hers kept his promise. She sure looks old and ragged," said Aunt Heydee. "He keeps her in the country where she has no other activities than to cook, clean, and have babies."

I met her halfway down the steps. She was out of breath from walking up the steps to the first landing and apologized for not making it all the way up to our apartment. She wanted to give me a hug and wish me the best. Then away she went, back to her husband who was double parked and impatiently blowing his horn. I felt I'd probably never see her again. It's so sad that people have to change. Life is a happy merry-go-round except when you are on the roller coaster and it's out of control.

In the kitchen, two maids and Encarnação were busy preparing dainty little sandwiches. Encarnação was in charge of the menu and making the wedding cake, too. Mama asked me to go to Encarnação and thank her for all the help she was giving us. I hugged Encarnação and said, "I love you. Thank you."

And she said, "It is my pleasure. Go my little one, go. And God bless you. All the food to be served after the wedding ceremony will be ready when you return, but I will not miss your wedding either. I'll be there. See you later."

We had to be at the temple at 11:30 in the morning, and then we were coming back to our house, where we would have the wedding cake and all kinds of delicious foods prepared for the wedding guests.

The small bridal bouquet of white lilies was very simple, but precious. Uncle Augusto decided to pay for the arrangement at the last moment. I have not seen Al this morning. He will be seeing me for the first time in the wedding gown when I arrive at the temple.

After the wedding pictures were taken inside the house, Mama kept her distance from me. A few times that I looked at her, she stared at me with a glazed look in her eyes. I had the impression she wanted to cry but her inner pride would not allow it. This was her triumph day. Her mission had been accomplished. There was no time for emotions of any kind except enjoying the moment.

Papa was wearing a black tuxedo and a bow tie. He pointed to his lapel with the small diamond pin I had given to him for his birthday as he said, "I am proud of you, my daughter. Remember that this diamond pin you gave me for my birthday will always be very special to me."

Mama was wearing a silvery, bluish, lace dress with a matching hat. Nelly's pink brocade dress also had a small hat matching the dress, which she brought with her from North America. She and Mama were dressed very much alike and looked very elegant in their outfits. They must have discussed what they were going to wear for the wedding when they wrote to each other.

I walked down the marble steps of our house feeling like a bride should, happy. I took it for granted when I saw a long black limousine waiting outside, and all the neighbors were trying to catch a glimpse of me, the bride. I felt very special as I got in the shiny limousine with Aunt Nelly and Papa. Mama told me she was going with someone else in the car behind us. Probably with José, I guessed.

On the way to the temple, I got lots of kisses from Nelly and a few hand squeezes from Papa. I believe they were as nervous as I was. I held Papa's arm as I entered the temple's courtyard. Mama was already there. Her car must have sped up ahead. Inside the courtyard, I recognized most of the faces of the people who had been waiting for us. Everything had been very well organized. All we had to do was follow directions.

Papa and I finally entered the temple with my two little cousins Palomita and Haim behind me holding the wedding gown's train. There were lots of flowers everywhere, and the candles and lights made the inside of the temple look

The Journey of Innocence

like Aladdin's Palace.

Al was waiting for me under a white cloth tent in the center of the temple. He had a very serious look about him and didn't smile back at me. He simply took my hand and squeezed it. He looked nervous, and he was very pale. He was probably wishing his father could be there to see him getting married, as Mama said afterward. The rabbi spoke in Hebrew and everybody prayed along out loud. I mumbled, making believe that I knew exactly what I was saying, and wondered how many people were doing the same.

The wine glass got broken as tradition required. Al and I kissed each other as the rabbi instructed us. And then we walked out slowly to the sound of organ music as man and wife.

In the courtyard, everybody screamed in unison, "Hurray for the bride and groom!"

Lots of rice came down upon us. Encarnação was there, too, holding a little basket with rose petals. She threw the petals at us like a prophecy of good wishes coming our way. It felt good to be surrounded by smiles, good wishes, and kisses and hugs from everyone. Papa hugged me, and Mama did, too. Then she stepped back, grabbed Aunt Nelly, and pushed her toward me. And then she walked away, just like that. I wanted to ask her to stay close to me, but she was gone, out of sight. She must be glad to see me go. It's okay. I won't miss her either.

Al and I were guided back to the limousine. This time, it was just the two of us. Mama told us, "Wait for everybody to get into their cars, so we can make a wedding procession."

But Al was impatient. After waiting a few minutes, he asked the chauffeur, "What's taking them so long? Let's just leave them behind."

I didn't have the courage to disagree. After all, he is the husband, and what a husband says, that's what it is.

The chauffeur was laughing and answered him in broken English, "Usually the bride and groom travel with the guests. Are you sure you want to break the tradition?"

Al laughed back at him saying, "Yes, I am sure. Let's get out of here."

The chauffeur started the engine saying, "If that's what you want, it's fine with me. I guess I'll be going home earlier."

I was looking forward to the procession, but, since there was nothing I could say or do, I accepted Al's decision.

When we got home, there was nobody there except the two maids hired for the occasion. They gave us both a big hug. Then we sat down in the living room and waited for everyone to arrive. Al kept asking, "What's taking everybody so long?" Mama and Nelly arrived very upset, but for different reasons. Mama was upset because she wanted the wedding procession, and of course, she blamed me. When I told her that Al was in a hurry, she said, "Yeah, Nelly already told me that Al is a very nervous type of guy, but you are the woman and you must tell him what you want."

In *The Bride's Book*, it says very clearly that the wife respects the husband's wishes, and that is what I did. Besides, I was too embarrassed to say anything.

Nelly was upset because José had lost her movie camera. She asked him to hold on to it because she needed to have her hands free to help me with the wedding gown as I entered the limousine. José got out of the taxi and left the camera behind. There was no way to recover it. No one had informed her that José was irresponsible.

The party was set up in the largest room of the house, which used to be my bedroom, facing the street. I couldn't eat anything except for a spoonful of wedding cake. My stomach was twisted inside out, and the sight of food made me nauseous. Not being hungry made me happy. It meant that soon I would be very skinny like the American girls I

The Journey of Innocence

had seen in movies and magazines.

Al got into a dispute with Cousin Rafael, who was adamant about Americans being stubborn, capitalist pigs. I had to navigate Al away from Rafael, whom I never liked anyway. I was proud of myself for being able to do that without hurting anybody's feelings. Encarnação wanted to know our honeymoon plans, and I told her Al had already set up reservations from North America for us to get the honeymoon suite for two nights at the most modern and tallest hotel in Estoril. After that, we had no other plans. Encarnação encouraged us to take the train north to Coimbra and, no matter what, go out at night and see the town's once-a-year special festivity called the *Students Festival*. She said it was the best street party anyone could imagine.

Al said that was fine with him. He loves me. He is the perfect husband. I cannot ask for more.

About three in the afternoon, I changed into my favorite green dress that Al had sent me from America, and we both said goodbye to all our guests. On the way out of the door, Mama handed me a box of pastries and said, "You both will need something to eat while on your honeymoon—it can be very debilitating. I bought them downtown at the most refined bakery. They should last for about three days. Enjoy them with Al." And she gave me that woman-to-woman understanding look that said, *Oh my goodness. You may not survive after a whole night of sex and starvation.*

A taxi had been called ahead and was already waiting to take us to the train station. We couldn't sit next to each other in the train. It was very crowded at that time of the day. I looked at Al, and he had fallen asleep. His head was bobbing around with each bump and sway of the train—*choo-choo-choooo*. I love trains, the way they move like snakes of steel steadily down the tracks. I wondered, how could Al be sleeping on our honeymoon? Aren't we supposed to be looking into each other's eyes instead?

Maybe I am not sexy enough. I know I am not, and will never be like Brigitte Bardot, his favorite actress. He had good reason to be exhausted. He had a long trip all the way from North America, and there had been a lot of running around and stress. I wondered if he was going to sleep through our honeymoon. I would have to accept that.

When we got to Estoril, Al told me that traveling by train relaxes him, and besides, he was tired. I told him that I understood. And we kissed. I like kissing him.

There it was, the *Hotel Estoril*, one of the biggest, most modern hotels in Estoril. The bellboy took our luggage with him, but I insisted on carrying my own eight-by-ten-inch matching blue overnight bag to our room. It was full of essential and personal items. It had my eyeglasses to use in case I had to see something from far away and Al was not around to see me wearing them, some money in case Al and I get separated during the trip so I could make a phone call or get a taxi, a map of Portugal in case we took the train to Coimbra so I would know when to get out of the train, and one extra pair of earrings in case I wanted to change my look. I had everything that was personal to a newly married woman inside this overnight bag, even a little sewing kit in case something got torn. Tucked away in the very bottom were the unmentionable menstruation towels, four of them, in case Uncle Augusto's shot failed to work. I also had a small perfume bottle, lipstick, and the red handkerchief Encarnação gave me, which I had not shown to Al. I would feel embarrassed if he read the imprinted English words: "Oh, please don't kiss me." The next line is, "Oh, please don't." The next line, "Oh, please." And the last line reads, "Oh." The innuendo is very clear: sex!

As soon as we got inside the room, Al said, "I am hungry. How about you?"

I nodded my head and said, "Me, too. Very hungry."

We went to the hotel's restaurant.

The Journey of Innocence

This time I did well. We had a regular Portuguese menu, and we both had steak and fries, and for dessert our waiter recommended *Crêpe Suzette*. I told Al that I had learned at the school for brides how to make them, and they are delicious. It's a French dessert and very festive with sparkling flames. The waiter had the dessert chef come to our table and prepare the *Crêpe Suzette* right in front of us. I politely waited to take the first bite until they put Al's crepe in front of him and then we both took a bite. It was delicious!

Al spit the food out of his mouth and into his plate saying, "This is horrible. It tastes like alcohol. Have you ever eaten anything more disgusting?"

"No," I said to him, lying through my teeth as I gladly swallowed my mouth full of crepe. Then, to make him happy, I added a facial look of disgust concerning the *Crêpe* dessert. "Waiter," Al called him over. "We don't like the dessert, please take it away."

"Sir," said the chef. "This is a delicious dessert. How can you not like it, and—what am I going to do with it?"

Al laughed, saying to him, "Take it back into the kitchen and make soup with it."

I thought I was going to die of embarrassment from his comment. I didn't think it was in good taste to offend the proud chef.

Then Al held my hand and kissed it as he said, "Let's go to our room."

I got scared with the idea, so I used my feminine charm. "How about a little walk to the beach first?"

I figured, the longer we stayed away from *the room*, the better.

On the way to the beach, we put our arms around each other's waist, and when I hopped up and down like a bunny, he imitated me. Acting silly made him laugh, so I took that as a signal to be myself. He hopped along with me as we walked back to the hotel. I also felt comfortable enough to sing one of my favorite American songs by Doris Day, "Que sera, sera, whatever will be, will be."

Since the first time I heard this song and saw the movie, these carefree words have given me emotional strength to accept my destiny day by day, because life is what it is and that is all there is to it. I was feeling gay, singing, hopping up and down like a bunny, and kissing Al until we entered the hotel lobby, and then *the room.*

I went into the bathroom to shower and put on my lacy, white, bridal nightgown and the matching white lacy robe, a present from Nelly. I stayed there, waiting to get the courage to come out, hoping and praying that I would find Al asleep. I was thinking about Nelly on her wedding night. She told us that she went into the bathroom of the hotel where they were staying, and when she tried opening the door to come out, the door jammed and her husband had to call the main desk clerk to open it. Poor Nelly. How she must have felt having the hotel crew opening the bathroom door on her wedding night. Nothing can be worse than that on your wedding night. I got nervous thinking it could happen to me. I turned the knob, and the door opened.

Al said, "I was starting to get worried about you in there. Are you okay?"

I nodded "yes" and noticed that he was already in his pajamas.

"We better get into bed. It's late," he said.

I felt relieved when he said that. To me it meant *I am tired, I am going to sleep. See you in the morning.* Still, I wasn't going to take any chances. I figured, if I kissed him and said good night before getting into bed, it would be reinforced that we were going to sleep. I stood next to my side of the bed and said, "We didn't kiss goodnight yet."

He replied, "Well, get into bed, and we will kiss goodnight in bed."

Due to instant panic, I became assertive, "No, we should kiss goodnight before we get into bed. That's the way it's done."

He patiently walked over to my side and gave me a kiss. I quickly said, "Goodnight. I hope you sleep well."

After that, I felt safe and secure that nothing was going to happen after all. He went back to his side and got in bed. I took the robe off and carefully laid it down on the chair next to me—in case I had to get up during the night. I got into bed and covered myself rapidly with the covers.

He started to kiss me, and I stiffened up like an ironing board when he tried to remove my gown. I was very scared. He kept saying, "Relax, I am not going to hurt you."

His hands were all over me. Every time he tried to take my gown off, I pulled it back on. Then I heard in back of my head Mama saying, "What are you doing, Verónica? You are married now. You belong to your husband. You must help him. Don't lay there like a stone turtle."

So, I stopped fighting, and when the gown finally came off, he looked at me and said, "You sure have a beautiful body."

I was glad he found my body attractive. I believed he was being truthful.

"We will keep trying each night until it doesn't hurt anymore," he said. "There's no rush."

Still, it wasn't a very good night for me. He went to sleep, and I stayed awake, looking at the ceiling. He was a stranger in many aspects because we had been together only four days, but he was a very kind husband and I felt obliged to stay awake in case he woke up and wanted to try again.

We tried again in the morning, and I was bleeding a little afterward. Maria Elena had told me that it was normal to bleed in the beginning. I wondered if it was that or my menstruation trying to make up its mind to start or not to start.

Al was not interested in having breakfast, and on the

way out, I grabbed the box of pastries Mama had given us the day before. I couldn't wait to eat them.

We walked to the beach where he rented a paddleboat. We paddled into the ocean and around the seacoast we went. After paddling for a while, we stopped to take in the sunshine, blue skies, and beauty of the Portuguese coast.

I started to open the pastry box. "Let's have a picnic in the ocean," I suggested to Al.

"We shouldn't," said Al. "Most likely, they are spoiled from the heat." He grabbed the box from my hands and threw it into the water before I could stop him. He didn't even look inside the box to see if they were spoiled. I was horrified. All those tasty morsels Mama had gone to the trouble of getting for us had been thrown out like garbage into the ocean. I was sad, but I didn't say anything.

When we got back to the shore, we had lunch at the hotel and then we went shopping. He bought me almond oil for my skin and perfume, and the day was a good one. The night was better, too, but still it wasn't easy. I love the kisses and the hugs, but I don't like sex. He laughed when he sang, "It only hurts for the first time, and then it doesn't hurt at all…" It must be an American song about losing one's virginity.

We took the train back to Lisboa this morning. Trains sure make Al sleepy. We could only stay for an hour visiting the family since Al agreed to take the next train to Coimbra, where we will spend the night. Everybody wanted to know how the honeymoon was going. Al must have said something to Nelly, because Mama came to me and said, "Your husband is having a lot of trouble consummating the marriage because you complain that it hurts. Well, you have to help and get it over with. I understand that what you are going through is not pleasant, but it is very important that you please him by having intercourse. Now, this is between us. Never, under any circumstances, give

The Journey of Innocence

him oral sex. For once you do that, you will be deprived of intercourse, and it will be your loss." I couldn't believe my ears. Mama had gone from "ground-zero" sex to "let me tell you everything about it, even if you don't want to hear it."

I made believe I was not shocked by what she was saying. After all, I was not about to share these things with anyone, most of all not my own mother. I was afraid she could read my thoughts so I kept quiet, staring and nodding.

I was glad when Al and I finally left, and soon we were on the train to Coimbra. Thank God that I am hardheaded like my father and don't give up easily. Being half German gives me an advantage over being half Portuguese. I decided, *I am not going to allow my husband to think I am a scared little girl in bed anymore. I am going to overcome my shyness and fears and bite the bullet tonight.* Once I make up my mind to do something, it's considered done.

It was a long train ride to Coimbra, and it was very hot. We were both thirsty. Al asked the conductor going by, "Excuse me, both my wife and I are thirsty. Is there any way that we can get two glasses of water?"

"Sure," was the conductor's answer as he walked away. We waited and waited, and then suddenly the train stopped at a station. A group of Portuguese soldiers traveling with us got crabby about it. "What the hell is this? Why are we stopping? This train is supposed to be a direct line. What the hell is going on?"

Everybody was wondering why the train was stopping, including myself. Perhaps we were being stopped by a band of robbers out on the track. My mind was racing at 100 kilometers an hour. From outside, someone knocked at our window.

"Open the window!" screamed the man holding a silver tray with two glasses of water.

I was surprised, and Al couldn't believe it either. "What

a service," he said. "This would never happen in America! Stopping the train just to give us water! Incredible!"

This was my first trip to Coimbra, and I was really looking forward to it. After all, the farthest I had ever been from Lisboa in all my life was to the fishing village of Nazaré. I was curious to see Portugal's oldest University, famous for its romantic students who wear black capes as they roam the city playing their guitars and looking for someone to fall in love with.

After renting a room at a hotel, we spent the day visiting the University and its old library, which is kept as an architectural masterpiece of times gone by. A security guard followed us around to make sure we didn't touch the books. Then we took a walk through the *Portugal dos Pequenitos* where the miniature buildings were built like replicas of some of the important buildings in Coimbra. This miniature city was built specifically for children, and unless we are midgets, we can't do much but stand by and admire a city that was not built for adults to use.

Al fell in love with the *Quinta das Lágrimas*, where Inez de Castro was murdered because she was Spanish and consequently not allowed to love the king's son. Al said this was his favorite place. To me it looked like any other country farm, but I told him I felt the same way. What a day. We had a great time!

After dinner I was all excited, looking forward to being part of the street party about to start, the famous Students Festival. Al lay down in bed while I was getting dressed in the bathroom. Then I heard someone snoring. I couldn't believe it. Al had fallen asleep at the wrong time. I pulled a chair next to the bed and waited for him to wake up. About an hour later, it was eleven o'clock. I looked out the window, and in the distance I could see the fireworks. I finally got the nerve to wake him, "Come on, Al. Let's go, or we will miss all the fun."

"We'll go later," he said. "Let's take a nap. I am tired." I

The Journey of Innocence

lay down next to him. An hour went by.

"C'mon, Al," I implored. "We should go now."

He put his arm around me and went back to sleep.

I was thinking, *Here I am in Coimbra and I finally have a chance to see the famous Student's Festival—a once-a-year event that people travel from all over the country to be part of—and I am in bed. I guess when a man is twenty-nine years old, is old and gets tired easier. I did marry an older man, so I will have to learn to live with it.* I played with the idea of sneaking out. He wouldn't even miss me if I went out for one or two hours. I stood by the window for a while and listened to the sounds of people going by and the festivities in the distance. Then, resigned, I put on my nightgown and lay down next to Al, who was still snoring.

I have to accept that I will never be free to do the things I enjoy. I am half happy for being married and going away from here and half sad for feeling deprived of being free, more like a prisoner.

We got up early to take the train back to Lisboa. After having lunch with the family, we spent the afternoon walking around the city going from shop to shop and doing the tourist stuff. When it started to rain, we took refuge inside the lobby of one of the houses along the *Avenida da Liberdade*. While there, we decided to kiss as we waited for the rain to stop. A woman came out of her apartment and screamed that I was a whore and should take my man to my own place.

I showed her my left hand with the wedding ring, saying, "Look, we are married, and we are only kissing."

She said, "Yeah, yeah. Go home to kiss. My lobby is not a hotel room. If you remain there kissing, I will call the police."

Al was laughing and told me he'd never heard of anything so silly. In America, you can kiss anywhere in public.

I can't wait to be in America. Al bought a few pottery kitchen items and a huge soup bowl with a cover in the shape of a lobster. Al said it was quite unique, and he had never seen anything like it before. I couldn't agree more. I could even add that it was an ugly, grotesque piece of pottery, too big and clumsy, but he liked it, so I didn't say anything contrary.

All of the packing is done. Two super-large, wooden trunks will be going by boat, one for the wedding gown and a few other clothes, and the other mostly for wedding gifts, which I am embarrassed to say, were given to us by I have no idea whom. My head has been in the clouds since Al came to Portugal. Everything is moving very fast, and the only thing that seems to have balance in my life is being with him. He asked me if I mind that we live with Nelly for a little while until we buy our own home. I thought that was a silly question. Of course I don't mind. I think it's wonderful that we will all be living together. I can't wait. I never dreamed that I could be this happy.

Nelly is not going back to America with us. She is staying in Lisboa with the family for a few more weeks. Everyone was in agreement that, in the beginning of our marriage, Al and I should spend some time alone and get to know each other better. Saying goodbye was easy. I was extremely happy to leave Portugal and no longer have to worry about earthquakes. My wish has come true, and I thank God for his kindness.

As the airplane took off, my ears felt like they were going to explode. The pain was so bad that I started to cry. Al held my hands saying, "I know you miss your family already, but I promise we will come back soon to visit them."

I was too ashamed to say that I was crying only because my ears were hurting really bad. When the stewardess came by to ask us if we wanted a drink, I told her my problem.

The Journey of Innocence

She brought me some chewing gum and that helped a little until the airplane landed at the island of Açores. I didn't cry. I was screaming. The high pressure didn't bother Al's ears. I was amazed.

While we were waiting in the Açores airport to take the next flight to America, Al bought me a gold necklace and earrings made by the island people. When I saw him pay a fortune for them, I quivered. I didn't even care for the jewelry. I thought it was too gaudy, but I didn't say anything. Mama told me many times, "When your husband buys you something, accept it with a smile. Never say anything stupid like you don't like it because, after that remark, he will never buy you anything again." So, I didn't say anything except *thank you*, and I smiled.

It was a long flight to America, and I believe I fell asleep. I woke up with sharp needle pain in both my ears, and Al nudged me to look out of the window. I could barely see the Statue of Liberty in the distance. I had to close my eyes as everything was spinning around me. I tried to look out the window again, and this time we were much closer to the ground. I saw rows and rows of brick houses with ugly brown roofs covered with TV antennas. I felt as if we were landing on another planet.

I tried to smile to Al, but it was more like an odd, painful-looking grin. I wanted to throw up, and my ears were killing me. I held on to my ears as we landed. I cried without shame. It was the most painful experience of my life, besides taking my tonsils out when I was a kid. I will never take another airplane, ever! Al was talking to me, but I couldn't hear anything he was saying. I had lost my hearing. Flying is a horrible experience. Besides, I have no reason to fly because I have no desire to see my family again. Since Mama made me swear on her head that I will write to her every week, I will keep my promise. That is enough sacrifice on my part.

I am standing on America's soil. My wishes have come true. I am looking forward to my life with Al and Nelly, to meeting cousins Ruth and Gabriel, and to seeing the movie stars living in New York City and Hollywood. Even if I don't ever recover my hearing, thank you God for everything.